LIVING ABROAD IN

Japan

FIRST EDITION

Ruthy Kanagy

© Ruthy Kanagy

AVALON
TRAVEL

C O N T E N T S

PRIME LIVING LOCATIONS 199

RESOURCES 281

About the Author

Ruthy Kanagy was born in Tōkyō and grew up on both sides of the Pacific Ocean, spending her childhood in Japan and pursuing higher education in the U.S. She has fond memories of traveling by steam locomotive and family car, camping, and visiting hot springs all over Hokkaidō. She grew up naturally bilingual, speaking English at home and Japanese everywhere else.

When she attended school in the U.S. for the first time, the language was familiar, but the cultural rules were different. She was embarrassed about not knowing any four-letter words in English. Classmates asked exotic questions, such as, "Are there chickens in Japan?" and "Are there still ninjas in Japan?" In Japan, she was frequently asked questions like, "You don't have four seasons in America, right?"

After graduating from Christian Academy in Tōkyō, Ruthy studied in the United States, earning an M.A. in Asian studies (University of Michigan) and a Ph.D. in educational linguistics (University of Pennsylvania). She taught Japanese in the U.S. and English in Japan for 22 years, and translated a Japanese children's book, *The Park Bench.*

Ruthy's passion is pedaling her Sat R Day recumbent bicycle (see her photos at http://oregonjapanlink.com). The sight of a middle-aged *gaijin* (foreigner) on a reclining two-wheeler, cycling Mt. Fuji's five lakes and touring Hokkaidō, prompted interesting reactions. Kids shouted, *"Nanda korya?"* ("What the heck is that?"); a woman working in a field said, *"Tanoshisō!"* ("That looks like fun!"). In addition to freelance translating, editing, and writing, Ruthy works part-time at Bike Friday, marketing high-performance folding bicycles to Japan.

After moving at least 30 times, Ruthy now claims Oregon as her U.S. base. She lives in Eugene and has two daughters, Erin and Elena. She also flies to Japan as often as she can get hold of a ticket.

Dedication
To Lee and Adella, who started it all.

Introduction

© Ruthy Kanagy

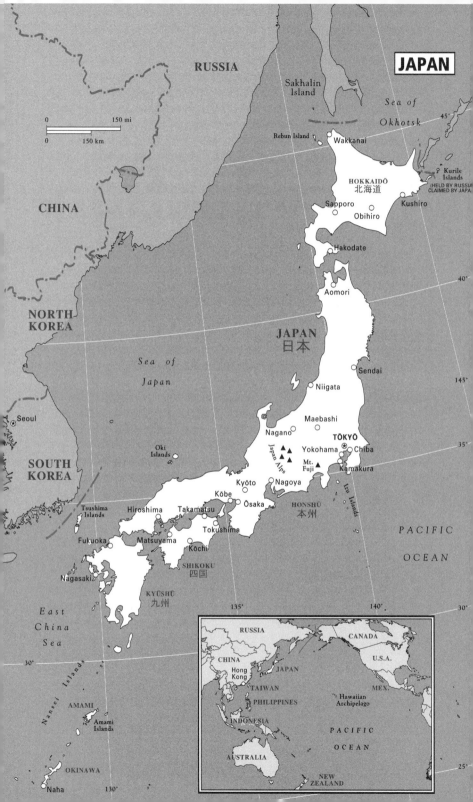

Welcome to Japan

apan in the 21st century is a fully modern consumer society with every convenience and indulgence that yen can buy. On the surface, Japan may appear completely westernized, judging by the fashions, food, and fads you see on the street. As a first-time visitor, you might wonder, "Where are the kimonos, the samurai with their swords, the geisha, and Mt. Fuji?" On the subways and streets, everyone seems busy, urgently tapping their cell phone keys with their left thumbs. The fact is, contemporary Japanese culture is a comfortable, seamless blend of *wa* (Japanese) and *yō* (western), plus many other elements. *Wa* and *yō* alternatives are available in every facet of life: housing, food, clothes, work, travel, entertainment, religion, and language. This is not surprising if you consider that people in Japan have been eating *pan* (bread) and *castella* (sponge cake) since Portuguese ships showed up in 1543, and they've been playing baseball with a passion since 1871, when the game was introduced by an American teacher. Even the nation's writing system comes from three different cultures—Chinese *kanji* characters, Japanese *kana* symbols, and the Latin alphabet.

In contemporary Japan, you can wear your hair black or bleach it blond, slip on a pair of jeans or a *yukata* (cotton kimono), sip *matcha* (powdered green tea) or a latte, and order French, Chinese, sushi, or pizza. You can play golf or practice *kendō* (fencing), go to the opera or *kabuki* (traditional theater), and cheer for the Giants or *sumō* wrestlers from the sofa or *tatami* (woven mats). After a day of hiking or snowboarding, you can soak in a *rotenburo* (outdoor spa), relax with yoga or tai chi, and collapse onto your futon or bed. In Japan, the choice is yours.

IS JAPAN RIGHT FOR YOU?

The appeal of living in a different country goes beyond fascination with cultural differences and perceived mystique—the long-term rewards come from making connections with people and encountering new ways of thinking and sharing space.

Japan offers many attractive alternatives for work, living, travel, and relationships. In terms of employment, teaching English or other skills to someone who is eager to communicate can be rewarding if you have some control over your work environment. There are also opportunities to freelance or start a bilingual online business (see Chapter 8, Employment, for examples). If you find work in a Japanese company, you will gain insight into Japanese and U.S. business cultures. As for living space, you may discover the convenience of smaller apartments with multipurpose rooms, and come to replace the concept of "more" with "less." You can enter into the life of your community and participate in local festivals and annual events. Traveling by train, plane, or ferry can be a pleasurable adventure (as long as you avoid the holiday periods; see Chapter 5, Making the Move). Exploring the scenic beauty of Japan—volcanoes, hot springs, lakes, and the sea—may encourage you to stay for a while.

Forming friendships can be one of the most satisfying outcomes of spending time in Japan. Although some Japanese may befriend you only because of your exotic allure or to practice English, many have traveled or lived abroad and are internationally-minded. Hopefully, you will meet some Japanese from your neighborhood or work environment—or perhaps through lessons in the traditional arts—who wish to form a lasting relationship. If you have something genuine to offer and are observant, patient, persistent, comfortable working with a group, and appreciative of silence, the attraction between you and Japan may be mutual and deeply satisfying.

Living in Japan over a period of time gives you the opportunity to see the world from an Asian perspective—one in which traditions and history are reflected in daily life, where family and respect for others hold great value, where working cooperatively in a group is just as important in the adult workplace as in preschool, and where persistence and personal effort are emphasized over innate ability. Viewed from the western edge of the Pacific, events unfolding in the world take on a different significance than they do in North America. You will discover all of this from your new vantage point in Japan.

The Lay of the Land

According to legend, the islands of Japan were created by the Sun goddess many millennia ago—a string of volcanoes rising from the sea like jewels, ringed by myriad droplets. Perched at the western edge of the Pacific Ocean, Japan looks east to the Americas and west to Korea and China. Four main islands—Hokkaidō, Honshū, Shikoku, and Kyūshū, plus Okinawa—curve gently from northeast to southwest, spanning the same latitudes as Maine to Florida. Slightly larger than California, this land is home to 127 million people, including 1.8 million citizens from other places. Almost 80 percent of the land is mountainous, dotted with hot springs, rivers, and lakes.

© Ruthy Kanagy

Three symbols of Tōkyō—*sakura* (cherry trees), bicycles, and Makudonarudo (McDonald's)

It's easy to fall in love with the sheer beauty of Japan, both natural and cultivated: rugged mountains and coastline, the subtle changing of the seasons, the carefully practiced ancient arts, the intriguing culture, the cuisine, and, of course, the people. Wherever you live in Japan, you're never far from mountains, rivers, hot springs, and the sea. There are endless recreational opportunities, such as climbing 3,776 meters (12,388 feet) up Mount Fuji, sleeping on the summit in a mountain hut, and watching the sunrise over the Pacific; staying at a temple in Kyōto, awakened by a 4 A.M. bell for Zen meditation; skiing the Japan Alps and picking *sansai* (mountain vegetables) in early spring; cycling Hokkaidō's green plains and rocky coast and watching salmon spawn in rushing rivers; photographing rare wildflowers on Rebun Island, off Hokkaidō, within sight of Russian Sakhalin Island; hiking the circuit of 88 Buddhist temples in Shikoku with white-clad pilgrims; visiting pottery villages in Kyūshū; and swimming the coral seas of Okinawa.

You can do all this and more if you stay long enough to explore Japan. The country's proximity to the rest of Asia means you can fly to Seoul, Hong Kong, or Taiwan in two hours or less (and just 10,000 frequent flyer miles!). Singapore, Thailand, the Philippines, and Indonesia are equally accessible, and flying down under is a breeze—with no jet lag, since Australia and New Zealand are only a time zone or two away from Japan.

REGIONS

Japan is divided into eight regions and 47 prefectures. The regions, representing both historical boundaries and present administrative divisions, are Hokkaidō, five areas of Honshū—Tōhoku (Northeast), Kantō (East), Chūbu (Central), Kinki (West Central), and Chūgoku (West)—and Shikoku and Kyūshū. There are several categories of prefectures: one metropolitan district (Tōkyō-to), a circuit (Hokkaidō), two urban prefectures (Ōsaka-fu and Kyōto-fu), and 43 *ken* (rural prefectures). What is it like to live in Japan? Your experience will differ depending on which region you choose.

Hokkaidō, the frontier island to the north, is strikingly similar to the U.S. Pacific Northwest in geography and climate, with cool summers, snowy winters, open spaces, and unspoiled nature. The Pacific seaboard of Honshū, from Tōkyō to Ōsaka and Kōbe, has the highest concentration of population and industry in all Japan. Nearly one out of four Japanese lives in the area surrounding Tōkyō, the "Eastern Capital," a megalopolis with the same latitude as Atlanta (and equal heat and humidity). Going north and west from Tōkyō through the central mountains and to the coast of the Japan Sea, you reach the Snow Country, a more traditional area less touched by urbanization. Shikoku and Kyūshū, the islands southwest of Honshū, have major cities and industries, but still maintain an agricultural base. Okinawa is semitropical and has a distinct culture and language; it is also the site of the largest U.S. military installations in Japan.

I have fond memories of growing up in Hokkaidō, in a town where my missionary parents were the only Americans; the environment was entirely Japanese, including school. High school took me to the big city of Tōkyō, where I attended an international university. As a young adult, I was drawn back to Hokkaidō to teach at a university. In midlife, I had the opportunity to go back to Tōkyō and work for three years as a language researcher and translator. The best place to live in Japan is wherever your heart takes you.

NEIGHBORHOOD LIVING

In a metropolis such as Tōkyō, it sometimes seems like we're confined to vertical slots, watching the last vestiges of green disappear under vast slabs of concrete and asphalt. But you'll find a more human scale if you observe daily life in urban neighborhoods in Japan. From my apartment, it was just a five-minute walk to the supermarket, florist, rice store, liquor store, 7-11, dentist, butcher, post office, coin laundry/public bath, daycare center, coffee shop, carry-out pizza place, junior high school, police box, sushi shop, pet store, bookstore, hospital, bus stop, subway station, and multiple high-rise apartments; not to mention several welding shops, a dozen printers, and a body shop, nursing school, funeral hall, yeast factory, brass instrument factory, and pharmaceutical plant (many small industries occupy the first floor of residential buildings). This neighborhood was just like scores of neighborhoods in other parts of the city. All you need to get around are a pair of good walking shoes, a sturdy bicycle (preferably quick-folding), and the train and bus lines. Your bicycle and a good helmet will take you to market, work, and many parks and rivers; it's also a good way to explore other regions of Japan.

GEOGRAPHY

When Japanese schoolchildren look at a map of the world in geography class, they see an island nation situated in the middle of the globe. To the east are a vast sea called Taiheiyō (the Pacific Ocean) and the American continents; to the west are the rest of Asia, Africa, and Europe. They learn

Mt. Fuji and crescent moon

that Nihon (or Nippon; another name for Japan), meaning "source of the sun," is slightly larger than Italy, Finland, and Malaysia. Japan's land area of 378,000 square kilometers (146,000 square miles) is roughly the size of the state of Montana, or one twenty-fifth the land area of the U.S., with 127 million people—half the U.S. population.

Japan has four main islands and 4,000 smaller islands, stretching 3,000 kilometers (1,864 miles) from diamond-shaped Hokkaidō in the north to the main island of Honshū, the smaller islands of Shikoku and Kyūshū, and the islands of Okinawa further south, halfway to Taiwan. Almost 80 percent of the land is mountainous, with 15 percent agricultural land, 3 percent residential, and 0.4 percent industrial. Hokkaidō has 68 people living in each square kilometer (5.6 million people total) while 5,514 Tōkyōites squeeze into each square kilometer (12 million people total).

Tōkyō, the country's capital, is located at 36 degrees north latitude, the same as the Grand Canyon and Atlanta. From Tōkyō, it is 8,740 kilometers (5,431 miles) to Los Angeles, 9,560 kilometers (5,941 miles) to London, and 1,770 kilometers (1,100 miles) to Shanghai. Korea is less than an hour away by plane (or an overnight ferry ride from northern Kyūshū to Pusan), Beijing is only two hours by plane, and the city of Vladivostok, at the far eastern edge of Russia, is just a ferry ride from Niigata on the Japan Seacoast.

EARTHQUAKES AND VOLCANOES

There's a Japanese expression about the four most fearful things in life: *"jishin, kaminari, kaji, oyaji"*—meaning earthquakes, thunder, fire, and "my old man." Earthquakes are ranked number one. Situated along the Pacific Ring of Fire from Mexico, the U.S., and Canada, across the Pacific and down the Japanese archipelago, earthquakes, tsunami, and volcanic eruptions are regular occurrences. The Greater Kantō Earthquake of 1923 and its fiery aftermath left 100,000 people dead. In 1995, the Great Hanshin-Awaji Earthquake devastated the cities of Kōbe and Ōsaka, along with the islands of the Inland Sea. There is always a danger of tsunami after a major earthquake. However, the rare dire tale aside, most earthquakes are imperceptible, and modern buildings are constructed to resist major tremors.

Japan has 60 active volcanoes. The tallest, at 3,776 meters (12,388 feet), is Mount Fuji. It last erupted in 1707 and is constantly monitored, as are all active mountains. On the plus side, all this seismic activity results in abundant natural hot springs. Anywhere you travel in Japan, you aren't far from *onsen* (hot spring) resorts and inns, where you can soak in rejuvenating minerals. Japan's rivers are short and fast-flowing, and they form deep gorges in the mountains; most have been dammed for hydroelectric power. The longest river, Shinano-gawa, is 367 kilometers (228 miles) long; the largest lake, Biwa-ko, is 674 square kilometers (260 square miles); and the deepest lake, Tazawa-ko, is 423 meters (1,388 feet) deep. When you arrive in Japan, you will be struck by the scenic beauty of the mountains, rivers, and sea.

CLIMATE

Japan's climate ranges from subarctic to subtropical. Hokkaidō has cool summers and very cold winters, similar to Alaska. Honshū, Shikoku, and Kyūshū have relatively cold winters and hot, muggy summers. Okinawa is subtropical, with an aqua sea, flowers, palm trees, and sugar cane year-round. Japan has four distinct seasons—a fact pointed out to me by many Japanese as being "unique." (In reply, I mention the changing seasons and fall colors enjoyed in many parts of the U.S. and in other countries.)

Most regions of Japan below Hokkaidō have a *tsuyu* (rainy season) lasting about six weeks. The rains begin in Okinawa and reach Tōkyō in mid-June. In summer and fall, typhoons form in the Pacific and often cause extensive flooding, landslides, and wind damage to ripening rice crops. The *taifū*, as they're called in Japanese, are numbered, rather than personified as in the U.S.—the damage from Typhoon 10 in 2003 was no less severe than what Hurricane Isabel unleashed in the U.S. in September of that same year.

Temperature and Precipitation

City	Avg. Temp.	Jan. Avg.	Aug. Avg.	Annual Rainfall (in mm/in)
Sapporo	8.2°C / 46.8°F	-6°C / 21.2°F	22°C / 71.6°F	1,130/44.5
Tōkyō	15.6°C / 60.1°F	5°C / 41°F	30°C / 86°F	1,490/58.7
Niigata	13.2°C / 55.8°F	2°C / 35.6°F	28°C / 82.4°F	1,778/70
Naha	22.3°C / 72.1°F	14°C / 57.2°F	30°C / 86°F	2,037/80.2

(Source: Tōkyō Meteorological Agency)

The mountains forming the backbone of Japan divide precipitation levels into east and west zones. In winter, prefectures on the Japan Sea side to the west are blanketed with deep snow, dumped by the northwesterly winds off the Asian continent. Niigata prefecture has an annual snowfall of 4 to 5 meters (13–16 feet), and is consequently known as *yukiguni* (snow country, celebrated in Nobel Prize–winner Kawabata Yasunari's novel of the same name). In the east, the Pacific side receives relatively less precipitation in the winter months and has hot, humid summers due to seasonal Pacific winds. In Tōkyō, the driest month is December, but one to three light snowfalls are not unusual in winter. (My parents recall a January blizzard in which my father rushed my mother to the hospital—an hour later, I was born.) Winter is also when the skies are clearest, so there's a good chance that Mount Fuji will be visible from Tōkyō high-rises.

FLORA AND FAUNA

The wide range of temperatures and plentiful rain in Japan create a rich environment for abundant flora. There are 4,500 native plant species. A variety of subtropical plants grow in Okinawa and the Ogasawara islands below Tōkyō; broadleaf evergreen forests and oak thrive in warm, temperate regions (Honshū, Shikoku, and Kyūshū); broadleaf deciduous forests and beech are found in cool, temperate areas of northern Honshū and southern Hokkaidō; and subalpine Sakhalin fir and Ezo spruce, as well as alpine plants like *komakusa* (scientific name *Dicentra peregrina*) flourish in central Honshū and Hokkaidō.

Diverse climactic conditions also foster a variety of fauna, such as

Ume (plum) blossoms bring spring in February. The petals are round, while cherry petals are notched.

Southeast Asiatic tropical animals (coral fish, turtles, sea snakes, eagles, flying foxes, and lizards), and, in the temperate zone, sea lions, fur seals, and beaked whales off central Honshū. *Tanuki* (raccoon dog), *shika* (deer), and mandarin foxes also inhabit this zone. Hokkaidō is home to subarctic Siberian animals, such as the brown bear, grouse, lizard, and sometimes the walrus. There are many types of Asian land salamanders, cicadas, dragonflies, and swallowtail butterflies. Though sensitivity to the environment is gradually increasing in Japan, many species have become extinct, endangered, or vulnerable—but take heart in knowing that on Yakushima island (south of Kyūshū), there lives a 7,200-year-old Jomon cedar with a circumference of 16 meters (52.5 feet) that has been designated a World Heritage tree.

Social Climate

SHARED VALUES

Every culture transmits values to its youth, first in the context of family, and then through the educational process. In Japan, some of the core values are thinking of others, doing your best, not giving up, respecting your elders, knowing your role, and working in a group. These concepts are taught explicitly and implicitly from nursery school into the working world. From a very young age, Japanese children are taught *omoiyari* (to notice and think of others). Students must pass difficult entrance examinations to move to the next level of education, and in the process, they learn that *ganbaru* (effort) and *gaman* (bearing it) are more crucial in reaching their goal than innate ability. In every social situation, identity is largely determined by age, gender, sibling rank, and year of entry to the group—and these are also cues for the appropriate thing to say (or not) to each other. On the one hand, these clear social roles provide a sense of security and comfort, but they can also feel binding. For those coming from a western culture with a strong sense of independence, a work situation where interactions are based on age or seniority—rather than talent or ability—may feel confining and frustrating. Greater awareness of cultural differences and values is helpful in understanding such situations.

Japanese people remember favors they have received, and they are conscientious about returning them, even after a period of time. Family ties are greatly valued, going beyond the nuclear family to their ancestors. These values are observed in the home, and, at certain times of the year, through religious rituals. The Japanese are not physically demonstrative in public, but families share warmth and affection in the *kotatsu* (family hearth), family futon for parents and young children, and in the family bath, where they scrub each other's backs. Most people are very honest—I have recovered, for example, a silver tray and a camera, both left on the subway. I feel safe riding the subway at midnight. If you get lost, there is no need to panic; people are genuinely helpful. Don't be surprised if they even lead you to your final destination. And there's always a police station nearby with detailed maps.

Japanese values are reflected in the phrases they use in daily interactions, which smooth relationships and acknowledge the presence of others. Wherever you live in Japan, everyone knows the proper words to use before and after work, before and after meals, when you part with someone and when you meet them again, and so on. If you enter a store, restaurant, bank, or post office, the entire staff will welcome you in chorus, then shower their thanks on you as you leave. You soon absorb the rhythm of these phrases so thoroughly that you will miss them when you leave Japan. If you learn just one phrase in Japanese, make it this one: *Onegai shimasu* (literally, "I request of you"). It's the perfect thing to say when you introduce yourself, when you want to buy something, when you order in a restaurant, when you try to get someone's attention, when you ask for help or a favor, and when you meet a new dance partner.

THE ISLAND MENTALITY

Before going to Japan, you may expect everyone to look the same, dress the same, live the same, and talk the same. To a certain extent, this is true. Japanese people may appear to be more or less uniform in dress or behavior. There is an underlying value of not calling attention to oneself in public, especially among the older generation. However, Japan is neither monocultural nor monolingual. In addition to the Ainu, the native people of Japan, a flow of people and ideas have entered the country from China, Korea, Portugal, Spain, Germany, France, the Netherlands, England, North America, Brazil, and more over the last 2,000 years. The religions of Buddhism and Christianity, the writing system, medicine, the models for government, business, and education, as well as sports and cuisine have—in part—come from the outside and become a part of Japanese culture. In turn, Japan has exerted an influence on many other cultures.

In the 25 years I lived in Japan, I heard many people tell me apologetically that their country was "just a small island nation." No one refers to the fact that there are plenty of other island nations, such as England, New Zealand, and Madagascar, that don't apologize. This notion of being small and isolated is balanced by another expression, *shima-guni konjō* (island fighting spirit), which reveals a more positive view. Since Japan has no land borders, children are naturally curious about what's on the other side of the vast sea. The lyrics to a popular children's song go: "The ocean is so wide and big, I wish I could go and see other lands." For Japanese people who love to travel, going abroad equals going overseas. And fly they do, by the thousands—despite the sluggish economy—to Guam, Hawaii, China, and elsewhere during three extended national holidays when everyone is trying to get somewhere: Golden Week (April 29–May 5), the Buddhist holiday of Obon (August 14–17), and New Year's (December 28 to around January 5). Needless to say, this is a good time to avoid traveling around Japan.

THE CHALLENGES

Is there a downside to living in Japan? Certainly, this is probably true in every culture. If you've never known what it's like to be a minority, you may go through a transitional period, even culture shock. You will become a foreigner, one of 1.8 million in Japan who come from Korea, China, Brazil, the Philippines, Peru, North America, and elsewhere. Like it or not, your face will lead the way when you go out. It will frequently draw the *gaijin* (outsider) stare. This is not so overt in the big cities, but in outlying regions, you may end up playing Pied Piper to a parade of giggling children. Learn to laugh at yourself and laugh with others. If you have any

Common Japanese Signs

When you go to the post office, bank, and neighborhood shops, you may notice signs in Japanese characters. (For instance, there is probably a sign on the door of each establishment, reading "pull" in one direction and "push" in the other.) Here are some common signs in Japanese characters with their pronunciations and meanings.

入り口

iriguchi | entrance

出口

deguchi | exit

押す

osu | push

引く

hiku | pull

〒

yūbin bangō | postal code (also post offices and mail boxes)

郵便局

yūbinkyoku | post office

銀行

ginkō | bank

交番

kōban | police box (on major street corners in every neighborhood)

寺

tera | temple (Buddhist)

神社

jinja | shrine (Shintō)

大人

otona | adult (wherever tickets are sold for trains, museums, etc.)

小人 ／ 子供

kodomo | child

学生

gakusei | student

Asian heritage, people will generally assume you are Japanese, although possibly with some kind of speech defect. (Unless you're fluent in the language, in which case, you will be invisible!)

Your job and apartment search will take a bit of patience. Unfortunately, there are landlords who specify "no foreigners." Help Wanted ads frequently specify age, gender, nationality, and language ability, and all require a photo. If you encounter roadblocks, think of minorities in U.S. culture, imagine what they must encounter, and move on. This may sound like a cop-out, but it rarely does any good to fight in such situations.

There are some benefits to being from another planet—or rather, country. Depending on the situation, you may be excused for not knowing Japanese and not knowing the proper customs. And one of the challenges you *can* overcome is the literacy barrier. Thankfully, some Japanese signs—such as most train station signs—have alphabetic transcriptions underneath, called *rōmaji* (Roman letters). Some also include Chinese and Korean scripts to assist tourists from those countries. But, of course, most signs are in Japanese only. When faced with an unfamiliar sign, you have two options: Ask someone for help (*"Sumimasen"* means "Excuse me"), or just point. Try to make it your goal to recognize a certain number of Japanese signs per day on your daily route. Eventually, you will memorize the shape of the characters for the places you need to go, and you can always find someone to assist you (rush hour may not be the best time to stop a stranger, but train officials will help). In sum, the best preparation for becoming a visible minority in another culture is to understand how it feels to be a minority in your own country.

History, Government, and Economy

History

The question of exactly where the people of Japan originated is still under debate. Physically, they are related to people in other Asian countries. For example, most Japanese babies are born with a bluish mark at the base of the spine, a trait common to Asians. (Pediatricians in the West, who are unfamiliar with this birthmark, sometimes wrongly suspect that something is amiss.) Historically, the truth is that large numbers of Chinese, Koreans, and Southeast Asians—including the Ainu, an indigenous people who came to the islands earlier—migrated to Japan, resulting in a blend of facial and physical features in the country's present-day people.

EARLY HISTORY

Jōmon Period

The exact origin of Nihon (Japan) and its inhabitants is shrouded in mystery, but archeological evidence shows that human inhabitants were living on the land at least 30,000 years ago. The people of this Paleolithic period were hunters and gatherers who used stone blades. At that time, the islands were not separated, but were attached to the Chinese continent. Gradually, a shift in the earth's plates and the changing climate caused sea levels to rise until they became islands. Parallel to these scientific findings is the Japanese legend about the sun goddess, Amaterasu Ōmikami, who created the islands of Japan; and her descendent, Jimmu Tennō (Emperor Jimmu), who founded an empire in 660 B.C. Each year on February 11, this mythical event from several thousand years back is marked by 127 million Japanese people as national Foundation Day—a welcome day off to go skiing, shop, or relax at home.

The prehistoric stretch from approximately 10,000–300 B.C. is known as the Jōmon period, named for the "rope marks" decorating the pottery of that era. People were organized into clans and tribes that cultivated plants. It was during this time that rice cultivation was introduced to Japan from the Chinese continent. While the Jōmon people were building simple houses with thatched roofs, the Egyptians (or rather, their slaves) were constructing pyramids on the other side of the globe.

Yayoi Period

Gradually, from around 300 B.C., a different kind of culture emerged—people with bronze and iron techniques, weapons, and less decorative ceramics. Known as the Yayoi period, this era saw the irrigated cultivation of rice and other grains spread widely. The agricultural base established more than 2,300 years ago continues to influence Japanese society today. By A.D. 300, the influence of the Yayoi culture extended over Honshū, Shikoku, and Kyūshū, the main islands (excluding Hokkaidō).

Yamato Period

Over time, the organization of tribes and clans became more hierarchical, with the *uji* (local clans) ruling over *be* (peasants) and slaves. The powerful clans of the Yamato region (present Kyōto and Nara) built huge *kofun* (mounded tombs) in the shape of keyholes to bury their rulers, and surrounded them with *haniwa* (life-sized clay sculptures). The years from 300–645 are called the Yamato period. This was the beginning of the first unified state. During the same period, statues of the Roman emperor were erected throughout the Roman Empire. This was also a time when Japan established closer contact with China and Korea. Many of the items excavated by archeologists from large *kofun* have been shown to be nearly identical to pottery and other items from the same period found in Korea. Thus, based on evidence from the burial mounds, it is thought that the ruling classes of Yamato—who came to power during the imperial dynasty and have lasted through the present Japanese emperor—must have come from Korea centuries ago. The *kofun* were built until the 7th century, and some still remain intact for you to see. Gradually, due to influence from China, the clan-based Japanese society gave way to a centralized administration centered on the emperor.

Asuka and Nara Periods

At the start of the Asuka period (593–710), Empress Suiko held court in the Asuka region of Yamato, just south of the city of Nara. Her regent was Shōtoku Taishi (Prince Shōtoku, 574–622), who played an important role in shaping Japanese society and government on the Chinese model, with a centralized government, a bureaucracy based on merit, and a 17-article constitution. Buddhism had been brought into the region in the mid-6th century, also via China. Through Prince Shōtoku's influence, the court sponsored Buddhist teachings and Confucian virtues and built Korean- (and later Chinese-) style temples and palaces. Up to this time, the language spoken in Japan had no written form. Chinese characters were slowly adopted to write Japanese. (If the American continents had been lined up next to China, we might write English in Chinese characters today.) In 645, a series of reforms—the Taika no Kaishin (Taika Reforms)—were enacted to strengthen imperial power.

> The native Japanese religion had been Shintō, worshipping kami *(the sacred in nature)* and venerating the virtues of loyalty and wisdom. The emperors were also considered divine, having descended from the sun goddess in an unbroken chain.

In 710, the imperial court built a splendid new capital patterned after the Chinese capital city of Ch'ang-an, in Nara. The native Japanese religion up to this point had been Shintō, worshipping *kami* (the sacred in nature) and venerating the virtues of loyalty and wisdom. The emperors were also considered divine, having descended from the sun goddess in an unbroken chain. However, during the Nara period (710–794), they patronized Buddhism and its teachings as a means of protecting the state and fostering a peaceful society. During this period, the ancient tales passed down orally regarding the founding of Japan were written down for the first time as the *Kojiki* (Record of Ancient

Matters) and *Nihon Shoki* (Chronicles of Japan). With the adoption of Buddhism, numerous temples were constructed in the capital and provinces, and Buddhist priests gradually gained political power and wealth. In Nara, a giant statue of Buddha was built inside Tōdai-ji temple, which is still the largest in the world and can be seen today. Around the same time on the other side of the globe, Catholic monks were gaining influence in Europe.

Heian Period

In 784, Emperor Kanmu moved the capital to Heiankyō (Heian court), where Kyōto is now, to get away from rivalries among the nobles and Buddhist clerics. This was the start of the Heian period (794–1185), when imperial culture flourished in a city that remained the capital for the next 1,000 years. Chinese characters borrowed earlier were used by the elite to write Chinese-style texts. During the Heian period, the characters were modified, and a set of syllabic letters called *kana* were invented that better represented the syllable structure of Japanese. *Kanji* (Chinese characters) are composed of many strokes and stand for whole words, but the new *kana* represented Japanese sounds and were used to write Japanese literature and other texts. Both scripts are still used today.

Many women of the imperial court produced literature and wrote diaries in the new *kana*. The most famous of these writers was Murasaki Shikibu, a woman who wrote the world's first novel (the classic *Tale of Genji*, about the amorous adventures of Prince Genji) around 1002. Politically, the imperial court came under the domination of the Fujiwara nobles, who used the strategy of marrying into the emperor's family to gain control. The court gradually lost hold of the provinces where bands of *bushi* (warriors) were in ascendancy. One of these warrior groups was the Taira family, who took over power of the court and capital in the middle of the 12th century, but they did not last for long. In Europe, Romanesque cathedrals were being built, and the Crusaders began to flex their military might.

FEUDAL PERIOD

The First Shōgun

Five years of fierce battles between the Taira clan and the rival warrior band of Minamoto no Yoritomo followed. In the famous battle of Dannoura at Ichi no Tani, on the western tip of Honshū, Minamoto (also called Genji) defeated Taira (also called Heike) and set up a military government in Kamakura, eastern Honshū, south of present-day Tōkyō. The years 1185 to

1333 are known as the Kamakura period. The emperor, far away in Kyōto, was little more than a figurehead surrounded by the court aristocracy. In 1192, the emperor granted Yoritomo the title of shōgun (generalissimo), and the *bushi* emerged as the new ruling class. In the late 13th century, the Mongols, led by Kublai Khan, twice attempted to invade Japan, but were pushed back with the help of *kamikaze* (divine winds).

A Century of Wars

The military government in Kamakura was overthrown in 1333. A new shōgun, Ashikaga Takauji, moved his military government to a part of Kyōto known as Muromachi. Thus, the period between 1333 and 1568 came to be called the Muromachi period. Takauji and his successors become patrons of the Zen sect of Buddhism. *Chanoyu* (tea ceremony), Zen-style gardens of raked stones, and brush painting developed from Zen philosophy. From 1467 to 1568, rival imperial courts in Kyōto battled for legitimacy. This was followed by almost a century of wars (Sengoku Jidai) between *daimyō* (feudal lords) battling for control of their domains. It was also during this time, in 1543, that shipwrecked Portuguese soldiers brought firearms into Japan; and in 1549, missionary Francis Xavier was the first to introduce Christianity to the country.

REUNIFICATION

From the warring feudal lords emerged two powerful military leaders—Oda Nobunaga and Toyotomi Hideyoshi—who began to reunify the country and reform its feudal institutions. This Azuchimomoya Momoyama era (1568–1600) saw the construction of splendid castles, gold, and glitter, and open contact with the outside world. Painting, decorative designs on screens, and the tea ceremony also flourished. Hideyoshi had visions of conquering Korea and China, but his invasions ended in failure, and he died in 1598.

Shōgun of Edo

In 1600, after winning the Battle of Sekigahara, Tokugawa Ieyasu took the title of shōgun and established his rule over the country from the city of Edo (now Tōkyō). The two and a half centuries from 1600 to 1868 are called the Edo, or Tokugawa, period. The shōgun controlled Edo, the core of Japan, and assigned the *daimyō* to *han* (domains) based on depth of loyalty. (The English expression "head honcho" is derived from "*han.*") Status distinctions were strictly enforced through a four-class system of *shi* (samurai), *nō* (peasants), *kō* (artisans), and *shō* (merchants). Swords were

Usui checkpoint, where pre-1868 travelers leaving or entering Nagano were stopped and searched

confiscated from everyone but the samurai, whose power depended on the peasants, who produced rice for the nation. Each peasant family was granted about a half acre of land and required to pay heavy taxes in the form of bales of rice.

Left out of the four official classes was a group treated as outcasts. They were despised for handling animal carcasses and leather, which made them unclean, according to Buddhism. Sadly, their contemporary descendants—known as burakumin—though legally in possession of every right of Japanese citizens, still face discrimination in education, jobs, and marriage.

The shōgun kept tight control over the 250 or so regional *daimyō*, decreeing that they be in attendance in Edo every other year, leaving their wives and children behind as hostages. Christianity had spread rapidly in Japan 50 years after its introduction by European missionaries. Fearing cultural and political influence from the West, Tokugawa banned Christianity, severely persecuted Japanese Christians, and banned trade with the outside world; except for the Dutch, who were corralled on an island in the port of Nagasaki. The isolation would last 250 years.

Urban Culture

During a long isolation from the outside world, things were not static inside Japan. The cities of Ōsaka, Kyōto, Himeji, and other castle towns became commercial centers where citizens enjoyed urban cultural events, such as Kabuki and Bunraku (puppet) theater. Books were published and widely disseminated; colorful *ukiyo-e* (wood-block prints; literally, "pictures of a floating world") of courtesans in kimonos, Kabuki actors, and 47 views of Mount Fuji were widely circulated. In the 19th century, British, Russian, and American ships began to approach Japan and other parts of Asia seeking trade. The shōgun failed to expel the "barbarians," and in 1853, after Commodore Perry's ships arrived in Japan, he relented. Around the same time, several powerful *daimyō* from Kyūshū fought to restore the emperor to power, then challenged and overthrew the shōgun's authority in 1868.

> *During a long isolation from the outside world, things were not static inside Japan.*

MODERN HISTORY

Meiji Era

The centuries of relative peace under samurai control gave way to a larger world, with new rulers and new rules. In an event known as the Meiji Restoration, the new Meiji Emperor was transferred from the imperial court of Kyōto in the west to Edo, which was renamed Tōkyō (Eastern Capital). The goal of the former samurai, now political leaders, was to reform the social, economic, and political institutions following Western models in order to shore up the country and the military. During this Meiji period (1868–1912), a constitution was adopted in 1889, and a parliamentary government developed. Observing the colonial practices of Western nations, the Japanese military fought wars with China (1894–1895) and Russia (1905) to assert their imperialistic aspirations. Japan colonized Korea in 1910, imposing Japanese names on Koreans and the adoption of Japanese language in schools; in addition, thousands of Koreans were forcibly brought to Japan as cheap labor in mining, construction, and shipping. This continued until the end of World War II. Today, third and fourth generation descendents of these Koreans immigrants, born and raised in Japan, are still denied citizenship.

Taishō Era

The Meiji Emperor died in 1912, and his son became the Taishō Emperor. The Taishō period (1912–1926), ruled by a Liberal party government supported by wealthy businessmen, saw increased international diplomacy

The Flag and the Anthem

Several years ago, the Ministry of Education made it a requirement that public elementary and junior high schools display the Japanese national flag and sing the Japanese national anthem at school entrance and graduation ceremonies (before the pronouncement, the matter was left up to each school). To Americans, this may not seem like a problem—most public schools in the U.S. display the Stars and Stripes daily and sing the anthem on special occasions; and in many classrooms, pupils are required to rise for the pledge of allegiance (legally, children are free not to join in the pledge, but there is pressure to do so). Many citizens voluntarily display the flag on their cars, outside their homes, and even on their clothing. Many sporting events begin with the national anthem. So, what's the problem in Japan?

More than 2,000 years of tradition and history, for one. The Japanese anthem, called "Kimi ga Yo," was composed during the Meiji Era (late 19th century), shortly after the emperor was "restored" to power, revered as the chief Shintō "kami," and believed to be divine. The lyrics of the anthem focus entirely on the emperor. Translated from Japanese, they read: "May my Lord's reign continue for a thousand, eight thousand generations, until pebbles grow into boulders covered with moss."

The issue lies in the fact that the emperor, flag, and anthem were used by the Japanese military during their imperialistic expansion into other Asian nations. These three symbols were also used against ordinary citizens as a test of their loyalty to the emperor and country. Those who refused to bow or pray to these symbols were severely punished. When World War II ended, the Allied Occupation Forces (namely, the United States) made sure that the Japanese public would never bow down to the emperor again. The Shōwa Emperor spoke publicly for the first time on the radio to renounce his divinity and proclaim his mortality. The U.S. also gave Japan a new constitution guaranteeing freedom of religion and abandonment of military force.

As a result, the forced display of these old symbols in contemporary school ceremonies troubles many Japanese—including the powerful Japan Teachers' Union—who disagree with the practice because of its association with both the emperor and Japan's militaristic past.

and Japan's economic expansion in Asia and the Pacific. Universal suffrage for men was instituted in 1925. (Women did not get the right to vote until two decades later.)

Shōwa Era

The beginning decades of Shōwa (1926–1989) were all about nationalism and military expansion. Japan dropped out of the League of Nations, and liberal politicians were replaced with ultranationalistic politicians. Spurred by the euphemistic slogan, "The Greater East Asia Co-Prosperity Sphere," Japan invaded and occupied Manchuria in

1931. This was followed by war in China and the invasion of all of Southeast Asia. The years 1937–1938 saw the Rape of Nanking, in which the Japanese military used civilians for scientific experiments, raping and slaughtering more than 300,000 Chinese—another holocaust, but this one mostly unknown to the world. The military also forced thousands of Korean, Filipino, and other Asian women into sexual slavery in the name of "serving" Japanese soldiers. (The stories of these "comfort women," now elderly or deceased, have only begun to emerge in recent years.)

In 1941, Japan attacked Pearl Harbor and brought the U.S. into battle in the Pacific. From 1937 to 1945, almost every Japanese citizen suffered hunger and severe deprivation. Children and their teachers were sent to safety in the countryside, where there was some food. Household items, such as pots and pans, and anything else made of metal were sacrificed for the military cause. At this time, the Shōwa Emperor was believed to be *kami* (divine), descended from Amaterasu Ōmikami. Any word of doubt or resistance to the national agenda could land a person in prison. Millions of young men were drafted into the war, ordered to fight to the death—

© Ruthy Kanagy

A 100-year-old tree disfigured by the atomic bombing on August 6, 1945

and even to take their own lives, for capture was considered worse humiliation than death. Intense firebombing by the U.S. military day after day brought terror to cities all over Japan. In the spring of 1945, 100,000 Okinawans (one-third of the country's population) were killed in battles between Japanese and U.S. forces for control of the islands.

On August 6, 1945, the United States dropped the world's first atomic bomb on the citizens of Hiroshima. 80,000 people died instantaneously from the searing heat, fire, and radiation, and 60,000 more perished by the end of 1945 from related ailments. Many more people died from radiation sickness, the effects of which still exist today. Three days later, on August 9, Nagasaki—the cradle of Christianity—in Kyūshū was bombed, with casualties estimated at more than 100,000. Those who were able to get some kind of medical care from the government were fortunate; Korean *hibakusha* (atomic bomb victims) in Hiroshima and Nagasaki were not. All would surely testify to their conviction that nuclear weapons must never again be used against humankind.

On August 15, 1945, another shock wave spread throughout Japan. For the first time, the Emperor's voice was broadcast on the radio to announce Japan's unconditional surrender and the fact that he was no longer *kami* (divine). From the nineteenth century to the end of World War II, Shintō had been the national religion of Japan. The emperor was worshiped as the chief *kami*. Schools and workplaces were required to display the Japanese flag—*hi no maru* (round sun)—and sing the national anthem, whose lyrics praised the emperor and were associated with the militaristic state. Trained to believe in victory and to pray to the Tennō (Emperor), the whole nation was stunned. After the war, religion was officially separated from the state by law, but controversy still remains.

From 1945 to 1952, the Allied forces occupied Japan. The United States was in charge and gave Japan a new Constitution (written in English, then translated into Japanese), restored a democratic form of government, and passed laws giving women and men equal rights and women the right to vote. At this time, Japan's per capita consumption of goods was less than one-fifth that of the United States. Over the next 20 years, the economy grew at an average rate of 8 percent per year (10 percent during the 1960s). One factor contributing to economic growth was the high personal savings rate by citizens—much higher than in the U.S.

By signing a peace treaty with the U.S. in 1951, Japan regained its independence from direct American control, but Okinawa did not. Japan's U.S.-penned Constitution contains a Peace Clause in Article 9, which states: "Aspiring sincerely to an international peace based on justice and order, the Japanese people forever renounce war as a sovereign right of the nation and the threat or use of force as means of settling international disputes." Thus, Japan is constitutionally forbidden to have or use military force.

In 1960, a security treaty was signed with the U.S. This agreement stated that the U.S. would "protect" Japan from other countries in exchange for economic, political, and logistical support for maintaining U.S. military bases in Japan. During the negotiations over the treaty (which has been renewed every 10 years since its creation), I was in eastern Hokkaidō chanting "*Anpo hantai!*" (Down with the Security Treaty!) with my grade-school chums, vaguely aware I was protesting against the U.S.

Today, 75 percent of U.S. forces in Japan remain on the islands of Okinawa. Since 1945, the U.S. has built 39 military bases on 40 percent of the arable land in Okinawa. Opposition by citizens and politicians alike is strong, and the physical and emotional ramifications of crimes by GIs against Okinawan people have been enormous and costly (U.S. soldiers cannot be arrested or tried in Japanese courts). Perhaps because Okinawa is on the margin geographically and culturally, the Japanese government has not stepped in to deal with these issues.

In 1964, international recognition came to Japan with the Tōkyō Olympic Games, and a World Exposition followed in Ōsaka in 1970. In 1972, Japan normalized diplomatic relationships with China. Although the nations are diplomatically and economically connected, memories of wartime atrocities committed by the Japanese military remain in the minds of the people of China and other Asian countries. And, almost 60 years after World War II, Japan and Russia have yet to sign a formal peace treaty because of an ongoing dispute over control of four of the Kurile Islands off eastern Hokkaidō. (The blue islands are so close to the shores of eastern Hokkaidō that I grew up thinking Russia was located east of Japan.)

1973 is remembered as the year of the "oil shock," when the Middle Eastern oil sheikhs raised the price of oil. Japan imports almost all its fuel, so heavy industries were greatly affected. As a result, there was a trend to develop more high-tech industries less reliant on imported oil.

THE PRESENT

Heisei Era

In 1989, the Shōwa Emperor passed away after being a symbol of Japan for 63 years (1926–1989). His son became emperor and took the new era name of Heisei ("Peaceful Rule"). As under previous emperors, the Japanese people continue to use a national calendar system counted from year 1, the first year of a new emperor (1989 became Heisei 1); the western calendar

© Ruthy Kanagy

Residents of Chiba near political campaign posters

may also be used, depending on the situation. In Heisei 13 (2001), a crisis of sorts arose when the Crown Prince and Princess had their first child—a daughter. While everyone in Japan was happy for the new royal baby, only a boy may become emperor. True, there are several well-known empresses in Japanese history, but current law allows only males to succeed. Royal babies born in the last 35 years have all been female; thus, the emperor system may face a turning point in the near future. Sentiment is divided on having a Japanese empress again—some want females to be allowed to succeed, while others say only males should continue to rule.

In Japan, the government and the Shintō religion were made separate at the end of World War II, but controversy remains over its practice. For example, the Japanese prime minister visits Yasukuni Shrine (the unofficial national shrine) every year to pray for the nation's war dead. In 2002, Prime Minister Koizumi, under pressure from Asian neighbors, declared his visit to be personal, not official. This statement did not appease China, Korea, and other Asian nations to whom the annual visit seems like justification of the atrocities committed against them during the war.

The year 1991 saw the outbreak of the Gulf War, initiated by the

U.S., which put pressure on the Japanese government to send the Jieitai (Japanese Self-Defense Force) and support the war. Japan declined. Two years later, Japanese troops joined a United Nations operation in Cambodia, but soon pulled out. In 1993, the Liberal Democratic Party, which had controlled the Japanese government for 38 years, was ousted by a coalition of opposition parties. In 1995, a large earthquake struck Kōbe and the Inland Sea. In that same year, a terrorist attack on the Tōkyō subway system using deadly sarin gas was carried out by the doomsday cult Aum Shinrikyō.

Also in 2003, the U.S. again tried to force the Japanese government to send Japanese soldiers to war—in this case, to Iraq. The prime minister agreed to do so in 2004. In view of the Japanese Constitution, which forbids waging war, the average citizen is against the prime minister's position.

Government

Japan, like England, has a parliamentary form of government with an appointed prime minister. The prime minister is not elected directly by the citizens, but selected by the national assembly, which has been dominated by the conservative Liberal Democratic Party (LDP) almost continuously since the end of World War II. Junichiro Koizumi was prime minister during 2003. He appoints a cabinet whose members head various government ministries. Japanese citizens elect representatives to serve in the upper or lower house of the *kokkai* (national assembly), known as the "Diet" in English.

The Japanese Constitution was adopted after World War II. It may seem curious that this Constitution was written in English by Americans and "given" to Japan. It contains several concepts not found in the U.S. Constitution, such as a peace clause (Article 9) and an equal rights clause for men and women. No matter how loudly leaders in the U.S. clamor for Japan to support and participate in war, their predecessors chose the words forbidding Japan from maintaining forces on land, sea, or air. The average Japanese I've spoken to would prefer not to be "protected" by U.S. military bases all over their country, particularly in Okinawa. U.S. military planes flying above residential areas at night disturb sleep; it is against Japanese law for the U.S. to bring nuclear-powered ships into Japanese waters; and U.S. soldiers are seemingly immune from prosecution by Japanese courts, despite repeated incidents of assaults on Okinawan schoolgirls.

In reality, Japan does maintain a voluntary self-defense force that holds frequent joint military exercises with U.S. forces in various parts of Japan. This *jieitai* functions as a sort of response team during natural disasters. On a lighter note, they also play a key role in the International Snow Festival, held every February in Sapporo, the capital of Hokkaidō, when they bring hundreds of truckloads of snow into Ōdōri Park for sculptors to carve bigger-than-life characters and monuments for millions of visitors to enjoy.

Economy

Japan enjoyed a period of rapid economic growth after the devastation of World War II. Japanese products—from automobiles to cameras to ship-building materials—became known for their quality, and Honda, Toyota, Sony, and Mitsubishi became household words in many countries. This boom period led to the establishment of a Japanese consumer society. Everyone aspired to acquire the three Cs: a car, a cooler (air-conditioning), and a color TV. (Camcorders, computers, and cell phones have now been added to the list.) Economic growth was not without problems: air pollution from exhaust and power plants, acid rain, and the degrading water quality of lakes and reservoirs threatening aquatic life. Because Japan has few natural resources other than a few minerals, it has become one of the largest consumers of fish and tropical timber, thus depleting Asia and other countries of these resources.

Japan's high growth rate and economic boom continued into the late 1980s. Then the economic bubble burst. During the 1990s, the Japanese economy suffered the worst recession since World War II, and it is just beginning to recover. As a result of prolonged recession, the traditional practice of guaranteeing lifetime employment (at least for male employees in large companies) and basing promotions on seniority broke down. Widespread layoffs affected even the most prominent companies, such as Toyota. Losing their jobs hit men in midlife particularly hard—they were too old to start fresh, but too young to retire. Some turned to opening restaurants, retraining, or driving taxis. The rate of unemployment in Japan rose above 5 percent in 2003, an all-time high. Companies that used to recruit new employees on college campuses cut back on numbers, or stopped taking women with degrees, or cancelled interviewing altogether. At present, there are increasing numbers of women who, discouraged by the lack of opportunity to join or advance in Japanese firms, seek work in foreign companies, go abroad to seek an advanced degree, or start their own companies.

However, on a more positive note, Japan had a GDP of $3.15 million in 2003, with an annual growth rate of 1.3 percent. Major industries are high-tech electronic products, chemicals, office machinery, and automobiles. Primary trading partners include the U.S., Hong Kong, Taiwan, South Korea, China, and Germany. A majority of Japanese manufacturers—led by Toyota, Matsushita, and Hitachi—expressed a positive view of the economic environment, according to a survey by the Bank of Japan. Current consumer wish lists are headed by DVD players, digital cameras, and flat-panel TVs. The cautious economic recovery at the beginning of 2004 was a turnaround from March 2003, when Tōkyō stocks sank to a 20-year low.

People and Culture

When you first come to Japan, you may observe things that look like cultural contradictions, a clash of East and West. For example, while waiting on a train platform, you might see a woman in a traditional kimono whip out her cell phone; or two businesspeople shaking hands and bowing at the same time; or a blonde Japanese with a Mohican hairdo (called a Mohawk in the U.S.). Newcomers to Japan often perceive such phenomena as contradictions, because they've never imagined these particular cultural elements in comfortable juxtaposition. They seem just as surprising as meeting an Amish farmer in Pennsylvania with a gas-generated computer in his barn. These things may never have entered your realm of possibilities before. In my experience of observing two cultures, it's no more incongruous for a kimono-clad woman to take out her *keitai* (cell phone) than for a Western man in a tuxedo to talk on one. Though we may regard modern accoutrements as belonging to the West, they are just as intrinsic a part of Japanese culture and daily life.

After all, Japan has been blending foreign elements into its culture for several thousand years (and that culture has many different facets): Buddhist thought and arts from India, China, and Korea; Christianity from the Middle East via Europe; literature and a writing system from China and Europe; medicine from Germany; parliamentary government from Europe; modern business and manufacturing practices from the U.S.; public school education from Europe and the U.S.; school uniforms from Prussia; sports from the U.S. (baseball and football) and Europe (the "other" kind of football and rugby); and, more recently, hamburgers, Starbucks, and KFC, also from the U.S.

These various social components have continually merged into the Japanese way of life, resulting in the country's diverse contemporary culture. Which things are "western," and which are "Japanese"? For children growing up among all these resources, none of this seems foreign at all—just Japanese. After all, they've met Mickey Mouse at Tōkyō Disneyland, and he was Japanese. Contradictions only appear when viewed from the outside. Though you may initially experience many unexpected or even curious events when you arrive in Japan, don't worry. Soon, eating curried rice with a soup spoon and ice cream with chopsticks (just kidding!) and bowing while talking on the phone will become second nature to you, too.

Ethnicity

JAPANESE OR *GAIJIN?*

My Japanese acquaintances often ask me, "Can you tell the difference between Koreans, Chinese, and Japanese?" Well, yes, sometimes, but I base it more on clothing, shoes, and hairstyle than facial features. I always suspect this question to be a sort of litmus test of *gaijin*-ness (outsider status), which only serves to reaffirm the gulf separating Japanese from Other. Can you tell Germans, French, and Americans apart? I wonder if the first Europeans to arrive in Japan some 450 years ago were also confronted with such questions. Every culture carries stereotypes of others based on noses, eyes, hair, and supposed national traits, but if you go back far enough, we all have a common ancestry.

Whenever I am in Japan and speak on the phone in Japanese, the person at the other end assumes I'm just your average Hanako (Jane). That is, until I tell them how to spell my name in *katakana* (script used for foreign words)—a dead giveaway. Or I meet them at the train station, and suddenly they switch to hand gestures and talking too loudly. They're convinced a person with a face like mine can't possibly understand Japanese. Since

At Hiroshige's

A three-story building of white mortar and brick stands at a busy intersection in Shimura Sakaue. Its southern face is the final resting ground for strings of baked ivy. Morning and evening commuters propel past this corner in four directions in cars, on motorcycles, on bicycles, and on foot. A faded awning above the doorway says "Coffeeshop Hiroshige" in *katakana* script. Potted palms and geraniums line the narrow curb under the bay window—a tiny green oasis amid the grim concrete and asphalt. A lopsided blue and red sign says, "Pizza & Spaghetti, Gold Coffee" in English letters. I step inside. A businessman is immersed in a comic book, weaving a trail of cigarette smoke with a raised hand. A jumble of newspapers and ashtrays covers a long counter, where the master stands ready to serve in a gray apron and gold-rimmed glasses topped by salt-and-pepper hair.

"Irasshaimase" ("Welcome"), he says. I sit by the window. Suddenly, music from another era catches my ears. "Lemon tree, very pretty, and the lemon flower is sweet, but the fruit of the poor lemon is impossible to eat." The vinyl record sends me back 30 years to my high school years in Tōkyō, craving the music from across the Pacific.

The Master appears at my table. *"Nani ni nasaimasu ka?"* ("What will it be?")

"Mooningu setto onegai shimasu." I order the standard morning set, then add, *"Burazaazu Foaa desu ka?"* ("Is this the Brothers Four?") *"Hai, Bura Foa"* ("Yes, the Brothers Four"), he replies, then goes to fill the order and chat with the regulars. Soon, he returns with a tray of fat buttered toast and fresh-brewed coffee. Cream from the small white pitcher swirls into the sea of black. I spread orange marmalade on the Texas-sized toast, accompanied by a voice crooning, "I . . . can't . . . help . . . falling in love . . . with . . . you. . . ."

At 8:30, two laborers shuffle through the door wearing crumpled gray uniforms, their reddish-brown hair shooting sideways. They look half asleep as they mumble their order of iced coffee and ham sandwiches.

And then, "Put your head on my shoulder. . . ." Sweet male voices sing in tight harmony. I choke on my toast and dab my eyes with a napkin, hoping no one's staring at the lone *gaijin* (foreigner), overcome at Hiroshige's. I'm back in Tōkyō and can't escape the longing the past brings up. The Master refills my water glass silently.

I stare out the window at the throng of people and traffic. A mom walks by with her baby strapped to her back. People headed east to the subway and west to work and school clash with each other, the concrete telephone poles, and the cars. Suddenly, a taxi jumps out from a side street and almost knocks a youth off his bicycle. Both heads tip in acknowledgment or apology, and they continue on their way.

"Last night, I said these words to my girl . . . please, please me, oh yeah, like I please you," the Beatles plead. Outside, a truck driver with a towel around his head pulls up, waiting for a break in traffic. I get up to leave while the Beach Boys remind us of the fun in the surf we are missing. I pay the Master, step out on the street, and am nearly flattened by a speeding bicyclist.

Japanese aren't used to seeing non-Asians on a daily basis, an unexpected encounter with a sharply carved face, high-bridged nose, and sunken eyes can detract from normal communication. From the Asian viewpoint, what stands out in a European American visage is not the eyes, but the high bridge of the nose. On the flip side, imagine living in Japan and being surrounded by Asian people all day; then coming home and catching a glimpse of your own face in the mirror. Does it stand out? You betcha! (Unless, of course, you are of Asian heritage and fit right in.)

Ironically, foreign models appear everywhere in advertising, and American movies and TV programs are daily fare; but to actually encounter such a face on the train or street is something else. Locals may ask for your autograph or photo, as if you were a movie star. This can feel flattering at first, but after the novelty wears off, you may wish you could blend in or be ignored. These are all normal stages while adjusting to your identity and role in a new culture.

In general, visual signals (size, appearance, clothing, hair color, piercings) seem to overwhelm the human auditory system during cross-cultural encounters. Japanese are just as startled seeing a "high-nose person" with blue eyes eating sushi with chopsticks as Americans are seeing Japanese people eat Continental-style (fork in the left hand, tines-down). My happiest encounter with a stranger was when a four-foot, nine-inch *obāchan* (granny) stopped me on the street to ask directions. I waved my hand in the general direction, and she bowed, turned, and walked away. I was so happy being treated like an ordinary person that I wanted to run after her and give her a big hug (except then I might have scared her off by acting like a *gaijin*). For me, the ultimate insult in Japanese is being called *"gaijin-san,"* which means Ms. Outsider (or Mr. Outsider). Never mind that the *-san* title, when added to others' family or personal names, is a sign of politeness— it's never pleasant to be lumped into a category you didn't choose.

Overcoming stereotypes is a mutual process that happens as you build a relationship and get to know each other. You can't prevent anyone from having preconceptions about you, but over time, through shared activities, you can reveal who you are and invite others to do the same. In Japan, people who have had experiences in which they were the minority are most likely to understand other internationals.

If you want to get beyond the initial exchange of names and pleasantries, here are some things you can do in advance of meeting people in Japan: Keep up with the daily news online—read about what's happening in Japanese politics, economy, and society. Think about what you will say when asked about the U.S. and its foreign policies. When traveling around the country, learn something about the history, products, and sights of the region and inquire about them. Try to find out who's hot in Japanese music, TV, and sports, and mention them during conversations. Of course, learning to converse in Japanese will allow you to meet and interact with a much wider range of people, and most Japanese will appreciate your efforts to communicate in their language.

MULTIETHNIC SOCIETY

Despite initial appearances, Japan is neither culturally nor ethnically homogenous. The number of people in each category may be few, but nonetheless, there is much diversity in the country. Minorities living in Japan include the Ainu, Okinawans, Koreans, Chinese, descendants of the former outcast class (burakumin), Japanese children left behind in China after World War II, Japanese children who grew up overseas, dual citizens, naturalized citizens, noncitizens born and raised in Japan, and descendents of Japanese immigrants who have returned to Japan. Societies with relatively few visible minorities can more easily downplay or ignore diversity and promote the notion of sameness (one of the underlying themes of Japanese public education).

Foremost among these minority ethnic groups are the Ainu, the native people of Japan whose history reads like that of the Native Americans—they were pushed north into Hokkaidō by the encroaching Japanese from the south in the 19th century. Many discriminatory laws were passed in the 19th and 20th centuries that destroyed the Ainu way of life and most of the language. (For example, private salmon fishing—their main source of food—was banned, as was use of the Ainu language in school.) Today, about 15,000 Utari (an Ainu term meaning "human") live mostly in Hokkaidō, trying to revive and teach their language and culture. Okinawans (called Uchinanchū in their language) to the south have a distinctive linguistic and cultural heritage that evolved from the Kingdom of Ryūkyū in the 16th century. Although its people have faced discrimination from both the Japanese government and the U.S., contemporary Okinawa has a rich heritage of music, dance, religion, and way of life.

More than a million Koreans moved to Japan by force or voluntarily between 1910 and 1945 (the period of Japan's colonization of Korea). Descendants of these Koreans are now youth of the third and fourth generation, permanent residents but noncitizens, many of whom speak only Japanese and have never been to Korea. Some have taken Japanese citizenship, but others haven't, because it means adopting a Japanese name and giving up Korean citizenship. The descendants of former outcasts from the Edo era, called burakumin (literally, hamlet-dwellers), still suffer discrimination in education, marriage, and jobs. Ethnically, they look no different than other Japanese, but their origins can still be traced because of the Japanese *koseki* (family register system), in which each Japanese individual's family origin and permanent address are recorded in a document containing every birth, marriage, death, and other personal information (such as mental illness). A copy of this family register must be presented when entering school (from kindergarten to university), applying for a job, or evaluating marriage prospects—many people hire private detectives to check out the family background of potential suitors.

More visible minorities in Japan include naturalized citizens from other parts of the globe outside Asia: immigrant workers from Southeast Asia and South America, children of international marriages (called "half" in Japan, and considered exotic if one parent is Caucasian), and residents with European, American, or African parentage who were raised in Japan. Several more invisible minorities are descendants of Japanese immigrants to the U.S. and other countries—such as Japanese Americans and Japanese Brazilians who've come to Japan to seek work or education; Japanese children born in China during the colonial years, who were abandoned in 1945 during the mass exodus of Japanese, but have returned to Japan as adults to look for their kin; and Japanese children of business families who lived overseas but then returned to Japan. Called "returnees," these latter individuals are often pressured by peers and teachers to give up (or at least hide) their foreign language skills and dual identity because these characteristics make you less Japanese.

Religion

CUSTOMS

In Japan, religious freedom is guaranteed by law—each individual is free to follow his faith or not, without fear of persecution. Interestingly, if you ask the average person in Japan about religion, she will likely reply, "I have no religion." Out of 127 million people, those who espouse formal affiliation with Shintō, Buddhism, or Christianity—the three main religions—are surprisingly few. But when you move to Japan, you will notice that there are numerous religious events at temples and shrines, and even religious parades in the street, depending on the time of year. And if you visit any of the famous temples and shrines in Kyōto, Nara, Kamakura, and elsewhere, you will see busloads of Japanese tourists with cameras who are just as interested in the sites as you are. How is it possible to profess no religion, yet participate in religious events? While growing up in Japan, I observed that in this society, religious practices and social customs are woven seamlessly through

© Ruthy Kanagy

At a Buddhist temple in the mountains, the bell is rung at 5 A.M. and 6 P.M. daily.

the yearly calendar and each individual's life cycle. In other words, people don't worry so much about whether something is religious or traditional—you do it because you've always done it that way, and your parents and grandparents did it that way, and because it makes you Japanese.

For example, what do most people in Japan do on the biggest holiday of the year—New Year's? They go to the temple or shrine (perhaps analogous to people who go to church only on Christmas). Each year, around 87 million Japanese people go to a shrine or temple on New Year's Eve or during the first three days of January. (The remainder of the population goes to Europe, Hawaii, or Las Vegas.) Those who remain in Japan go to a Buddhist temple just before midnight on December 31 to hear the *joya no kane* (temple bell) ring 108 times to atone for an equal number of sins of the past year. The solemn sound is televised nationally and internationally. As soon as New Year's Day breaks, millions elbow their way to Shintō shrines to offer money and prayers, and to buy good-luck charms (promising health, wealth, exam success, marriage, pregnancy, and protection from accidents). Shrines and temples with the largest crowds from January 1–3, 2002, were Meiji Shrine in Tōkyō with 3.1 million visitors; Naritasan in the Chiba prefecture with 2.8 million; and Kawasaki

Taishi in the Kanagawa prefecture with 2.8 million. That's almost one million people per day going to each of these sites. On January 15, everyone again goes to the local shrine for ceremonial burning of the good-luck charms and arrows from the previous year, now rendered ineffectual.

All three religions come into play at different points in Japanese people's lives—Shintō for blessings, Christianity for weddings (increasingly), and Buddhism for funerals. Shintō is a celebration of life and reverence for the sacred. Buddhism takes care of sins, ancestors, and the afterlife. And Christianity, though claiming only one half of 1 percent of the Japanese population as members, still has wide influence on Japanese society, particularly in education, social welfare, weddings, and of course, Christmas Eve. Shintō and Buddhism, as practiced in Japan, are not exclusive—members of other religions are welcome. Christianity, when strictly observed, is exclusive; but in Japan, it is not necessarily so. Almost every Japanese person makes at least one pilgrimage to Kyōto and Nara to see the famous religious and historical sites they have studied during history classes. Usually, they go as part of a three- or four-day class trip during junior high or high school, similar to U.S. students' visits to Washington, D.C. to see historical monuments and museums. How did these religions become a part of Japanese life?

SHINTŌ

Shintō is the native Japanese religion, rooted in the mythological past and the origins of the imperial line. Shintō focuses on reverence toward *kami* (the divine), which is everywhere in nature, and emphasizes purification. Though there is no identified leader or scripture, the Shintō priest in traditional garb performs purification rites where needed—such as blessing the construction site of a new house or skyscraper. How can you tell if you're entering a shrine? If you pass through a *torii* (gate with two vertical posts topped by two horizontal posts), it's a Shintō shrine. Usually, these buildings are made of unpainted wood or concrete, and some famous shrines are painted red.

The most well-known Shintō rite is probably the wedding ceremony. The bride and groom exchange sips of sake from lacquered cups nine times, in a ritual called *san-san-kudo*. The bride wears an elaborate kimono (rented for the occasion), along with a traditional Japanese hairdo, covered with a white cloth to hide her figurative "horns of jealousy."

After a baby is born, a naming ceremony is traditionally held on the seventh day. On the 31st day, baby girls are taken to the shrine to receive the priests' blessing; boys are taken on the 30th day. If you are visiting a shrine and happen to see a young woman in a kimono with a baby, accompanied by her parents, chances are they've come to dedicate their child. Another colorful event at the shrine is November 15, called *shichi-go-san* (seven-five-three). Children aged three, five, or seven go to the shrine dressed in kimonos, or fancy clothes for the festival.

In addition to their New Year's trip, many people go to shrines to pray for health, good luck in exams, finding a good marriage partner, becoming pregnant, and traveling safely. At a shrine, you first ring a bell by shaking the long rope hanging in front, then clap your hands twice and hold them together briefly while you say a prayer. You can throw some coins into the offering box. There are places to buy slips of paper telling your fortune, and charms to ward off worries. You can also purchase a wooden plaque called *ema* and write your wish on it, then tie it to the rack where other *ema* are hanging. If you travel in the countryside, you will often see statues by the side of the road or in a field—especially statues of Jizō, the guardian deity of children (usually seen wearing a red apron).

Every community in Japan has a yearly Shintō festival. Usually during the summer months, a *mikoshi* (portable shrine) is jostled on the shoulders of young men and women through the streets to bring blessings to each home. Some festivals are quite elaborate and go on for several days, such as the Sanja Matsuri (Three Shrine Festival) in Tōkyō in mid-May. Further evidence of Shintō influence in the community appears at the end of the year, when people set up *kadomatsu* (pine branches) at the gates of their homes and businesses, and car grills are decorated with charms to start the new year auspiciously.

A final manifestation of Shintō can be found in Japanese traditional wrestling, called *sumō*. The referee is dressed as a Shintō priest and stands under a suspended roof of a Shintō shrine to preside over each match. To warm up, the *rikishi* (wrestlers) first rinse their mouths ceremonially with water, then throw handfuls of salt on the earthen *sumō* ring for purification before beginning the match. In the past decade or so, many *rikishi* of foreign nationalities have joined the *sumō* world. Some, including several Americans, have done quite well, rising to the highest rank of *yokozuna* (grand champion)—Akebono and Musashimaru from Hawaii (both recently retired), and Asashōryū from Mongolia. Of late, so many non-Japanese wrestlers have joined that concerns have come up about the "*gaijin*ization" (too many foreigners) of this most traditional of Japanese sports.

BUDDHISM

Bukkyō (Buddhism) came to Japan from India, via China and Korea, in the 6th century. It was adopted by the imperial court and spread by Prince Shōtoku among the aristocrats. From the 13th century on, it

Cultural Events

January

1 *(national holiday):* Ganjitsu (New Year's Day) and Hatsumōde (first visit to shrines, such as Meiji Shrine and Narita Shrine in Tōkyō)

2: Ippan Sanga—The public offers New Year's greetings to the Imperial family inside the grounds of the Imperial Palace in Tōkyō

6: Shōbō Dezome Shiki—Fire departments perform drills, traditional ladder climbing, and demonstrations

7: Nanakusa-gayu (seven-herb risotto)—People eat a special rice gruel cooked with the seven herbs of spring, which is said to prevent illness

11: Kagami-biraki—People take down the rice cakes they offered to the family shrine at New Year's and put them in soup or mix them with sweet red beans

Second Monday *(national holiday):* Seijin no Hi (Coming-of-Age Day)

February

2: Setsubun—Bean-throwing ceremonies take place to mark the coming of spring; men who are celebrating their year of the lunar calendar conduct the ceremony (popular spots include Sensōji in Asakusa, Zōjōji in Shiba Park, Ikegami Honmonji in Ikegami, Hie Jinja in Akasaka, and Kanda Myōjin Shrine in Kanda)

11 *(national holiday):* Kenkoku Kinenbi (National Founding Day)

Mid-February: Yushima Tenjin Ume Matsuri (Yushima Tenjin Shrine plum festival)

March

3: Momo no Sekku (Peach Festival) and Hina Matsuri Doll Festival

3–4: Daruma Ichi Jindaiji Temple in Chōfu holds a daruma doll fair

20 (or thereabouts; *national holiday):* Shunbun no Hi (Vernal Equinox)

Second Sunday: Hiwatari (fire-walking ceremony) at Takaosan

April

Late March to early April: Sakura Matsuri (Cherry-Blossom Viewing)—Famous viewing areas in Tōkyō include Ueno Park, Yasukuni Jinja, Shinjuku Gyoen, Chidorigafuchi, Inokashira Park, and Koganei Park

Sunday in early April: Hana Matsuri—Flower festival at temples to celebrate Buddha's birthday; held at Gokukuji in Bunkyo-ku and Ikegami Honmonji in Ōta-ku

29 *(national holiday):* Midori no Hi (Greenery Day)

May

1: May Day, International Workers' Day

3 *(national holiday):* Kempō Kinenbi (Constitution Day)

5 *(national holiday):* Kodomo no Hi (Children's Day)

Mid-May: Sanja Matsuri—One of the largest festivals in Tōkyō, held at Asakusa Jinja in Taitō-ku

Late May: Minato Matsuri (Port Festival) on Tōkyō Bay

July
7: Tanabata Matsuri (Star Festival)
9–10: Hozuki Ichi—Ground cherry fair held at Sensōji Temple in Taitō-ku
20 *(national holiday):* Umi no Hi (Ocean Day) and Sumomo Matsuri (plum festival, held at Okunitama Jinja in Fuchū City)
Late July: Sumidagawa Hanabi Taikai—On the Sumida River in Sumida-ku and Taitō-ku

August
26–28: Tōkyō Kōenji Awa Odori—Public dance in front of Kōenji Station in Suginami-ku

September
15 *(national holiday):* Keirō no Hi (Respect for the Elderly Day)
23 *(national holiday):* Shūbun no Hi (Autumnal Equinox)
25: Ningyō Kuyō—A memorial service for old dolls is held at Kiyomizu Kannon Temple in Ueno Park of Taitō-ku

October
1 (public school holiday in Tōkyō): Tomin no Hi (Tōkyō Citizens' Day)
19–20: Bettara Ichi—Pickled radish fair at Takarada Ebisu Jinja in Chūō-ku
Second Monday *(national holiday):* Taiiku no Hi (Sports Day)

November
1–23: Tōkyō-to Kiku Matsuri—Tōkyō Metropolitan Chrysanthemum Festival at Hibiya Park in Chiyoda-ku
3 *(national holiday):* Bunka no Hi (Culture Day)

15: Shichi-go-san—Ceremony to pray for the continued growth of boys aged three and five years, and girls aged three and seven years
23 *(national holiday):* Kinrō Kansha no Hi (Labor Thanksgiving Day)
Throughout: Tori no Ichi—People buy lucky bamboo rakes to "rake in" silver and gold (good fortune); depending on the lunar calendar, there are one–three days of the cockerel during the month (there are supposedly many fires in years with three cockerel days)

December
6: Ōji Kumade Ichi—Rake fair at Ōji Jinja in Kita-ku
14: Gishisai Festival—In memory of the 47 samurai from the Edo Period; held at Sengakuji in Minato-ku
15–16: Setagaya Boro Ichi (Setagaya Flea Market)
17–19: Hagoita Ichi (Battledore Fair)—Held at Sensōji in Taito-ku
21: Osame no Daishi (Year-End Fair)—Held at Nishiarai Daishi in Adachi-ku
23 *(national holiday):* Tennō Tanjōbi (Emperor's Birthday)
28: Osame no Fudō—Year-end fairs at Fukagawa Fudō in Kōtō-ku, Meguro Fudōson in Meguro-ku, and Takahata Fudōson in Hino City
31: Ōmisoka (New Year's Eve); Misoka Ichi (Year-End Fair)—Held at Okunitama Jinja in Fuchū

Asakusa temple and shrine are always crowded with locals and visitors seeking a religious or cultural experience.

was popularized throughout Japan and developed into numerous sects. Zen Buddhism was widely practiced by the samurai class, and other sects, such as Jōdoshinshū (Pure Land), still exist today. Buddhism teaches that the ultimate state of self-enlightenment is attained by encountering truth; that life is transitory; all is insubstantial; and one should attain tolerance. Buddhism has influenced Japanese art, literature, and architecture, as well as the fundamental morals of society. Whether believers or not, most people have Buddhist funerals and are given Buddhist posthumous names.

How is Buddhism practiced in daily life? Many Japanese families have Buddhist altars in their homes—usually passed down to the eldest son in each generation—where they offer food and prayers to their relatives who have passed, to speed them on their journey to paradise. When someone dies, relatives gather and a Buddhist priest is called to the home to recite the sutra after the prescribed number of days or years (49th day, one year, and so on). On Buddhist holidays, families go to their affiliated temple to clean the family gravesite and offer incense, flowers, and prayers. The family name is carved into the gravestone, and each member that passes becomes a part of the family grave. Cremation is customary, and after the urn of ashes has rested in the home for a set number of days, it is placed in the family grave with the others.

My friend, whom I'll call Masuda-san, married late in life to a widower war veteran ten years older than herself. They purchased a comfortable condominium in Tōkyō and enjoyed traveling, photography, and their pet cat; he died 10 years later. When I first visited her home, Masuda-san was in the kitchen whipping up a sweet red bean soup. In one corner of her dining room, I noticed a polished table holding a vertical tablet with Japanese characters. In front were a plate of individually wrapped *nashi* (Asian pears) and a box of rice crackers. On the wall was a black-and-white photo of her husband in uniform. Seeing my interest, she remarked how she still talked to her husband every day—about her newfound hobby taking flower pictures, about her volunteer work at a children's science museum, about her cat. Having an altar in the home seems to tie the living closer to their kin who have gone ahead.

CHRISTIANITY

Kirisutokyō (Christianity) originated in the Middle East, moved into Europe, and was introduced to Japan by missionary Francis Xavier in 1549. For several decades, it enjoyed the blessing of the shōgun and spread rapidly; then the guillotine dropped, Japanese Christians were hunted down and killed, and the religion of the "barbarians" was banned for 250 years.

Christianity often enters daily life when parents choose what kindergarten their child will attend. Both Protestant and Catholic churches in Japan operate kindergartens for youth aged three to five and are regarded by parents as a good place for their children to begin their education. My parents started a church and a kindergarten in eastern Hokkaidō as a way of reaching out to the community and providing a service. I started my education at Aikō Yōchien (Love-Light Kindergarten), which is still going strong after 50 years. Similarly, some parents decide on Catholic school for their children—even if they are not members of the church, they still have a respect for Christian teachings. (I've met many adult Japanese who fondly recall their Christian kindergarten or Sunday school experience and the songs they sang). Some Japanese go to church to learn English, especially if the pastor is an English-speaking missionary.

In recent years, Christian weddings have become popular in Japan. Many couples opt for the fantasy wedding with a white gown, a tux, and a "wedding chapel" in a five-star hotel. Often, neither the foreign "minister" conducting the package wedding nor anyone involved in the planning or executing is actually Christian, but it pays well. It's customary for guests at the wedding reception to pay a specified fee, which helps out with the large expense borne by the couples' families. A Japanese reception is a veritable fashion show, with the bride disappearing and reappearing in different evening gowns, while pictures of the couples' individual childhoods are projected on a screen, along with predictions of their future together.

Officially, the number of Christians in Japan is small, about one half of 1 percent. However, the influence of Christianity is disproportionate to that statistic—there have been numerous Christian politicians, such as the founding members of the Social Democratic Party, Nitobe Inazō, social activist Uchimura Kanzō, Kagawa Toyohiko, and Yoshino Sakuzō; the founders of the Japan Farmers' Union and the predecessor to the Japan Federation of Labor; the founders of Christian schools, including Doshisha University, Aoyama Gakuen University, Sophia University, and Ōbirin University; and the founder of YMCA Japan (Kozaki Hiromichi). Christian writers (Endō Shūsaku, Miura Ayako, and many more) have also earned great respect in Japanese society. (See the Resources section for some reading recommendations.)

The Arts

LITERATURE

The earliest Japanese written works appeared in the 8th century, one a record of *Kojiki* (ancient myths passed down orally), and the other a *Nihonshoki* (chronological history of Japan). Both were written in *kanji* (Chinese characters) and adapted to the Japanese language. *Manyōshū*, the oldest anthology of poetry, appeared in the same century, containing 4,500 poems. Many of the poems are *tanka* (short poems) consisting of 31 syllables in 5-7-5-7-7-syllable lines. The beauty of nature and life, and, in particular, a deep sense of yearning, are important elements in *tanka*. Their words evoke a wealth of associations.

Perhaps most well known volume in the *bungaku* (literature) of the early period is *Genji Monogatari (The Tale of Genji)*, written in the 11th century by court lady Murasaki Shikibu. The novel focuses on Prince Genji and the women around him.

Heike Monogatari (The Tale of the Heike), an epic tale written in the 13th century, is about the fierce battles between the Genji and Heike clans, ending in defeat for the ruling Heike in 1185. This narrative masterpiece depicting the proud coming to ruin was chanted to the accompaniment of a four-stringed Japanese instrument called the

© Ruthy Kanagy

Making *mochi* (sticky rice cakes) on New Year's Eve at a neighborhood shrine in Tōkyō

biwa. The Heike story is part of the repertoire of Noh, Bunraku, and Kabuki theaters.

In the late 17th century (the middle of the Edo period), Matsuo Bashō developed an art form, taking the opening verse of a longer linked verse *(haikai renga)* and expressing nature, life, and the esthetic values of austere elegance *(sabi)* and delicate beauty *(shiori)*. Later, this new form came to be known as haiku, the fixed verse form consisting of 17 syllables in a 5-7-5 pattern. In the United States, students are often introduced to haiku in elementary school and encouraged to compose haiku in English. Perhaps the brevity of haiku suggests simplicity. However, in Japan, haiku are considered far too subtle and complex for children, and are often taken up as an avocation by the older generation. Winners of haiku and fixed-verse competitions often have their work published in the newspaper.

In the late 19th century, a new kind of literature influenced by the West emerged, written by authors who became well known abroad. Natsume Sōseki, one of the most popular among modern writers, published the novel *Wagahai wa Neko de Aru (I Am a Cat)* in 1905. Written from the perspective of a cat belonging to an English teacher, the piece

The beauty of nature and life, and, in particular, a deep sense of yearning, are important elements in tanka (short poems). Their words evoke a wealth of associations.

uses satirical humor to convey the author's own social views. Jun'ichirō Tanizaki wrote *Sasame Yuki (The Makioka Sisters)*, about the lives of four sisters from an Ōsaka merchant family during the late 1930s. The novel became popular for its dreamlike depiction of a happier, more affluent life than the stark reality and suffering of postwar Japan. The Japanese title means "lightly falling snow," and the book was later adapted as a motion picture containing lush outdoor scenes of Arashiyama area of Kyōto in each of four seasons.

Yasunari Kawabata is a modern writer who received the Nobel Prize in Literature in 1968 in recognition of such works as *Izu no Odoriko (Izu Dancer)*, *Yukiguni (Snow Country)*, and *Koto (Ancient City)*. His work carries one of the underlying themes of classical Japanese literature—the transitory nature of life. Numerous other Japanese authors, including Yukio Mishima, have also become well-known abroad.

THEATER

Japanese music, art, cinema, and *engeki* (theater) are inseparable from literary tradition and often deal with the same stories and themes through different media.

Noh

Japan's oldest theater, *noh*, dates back to ancient times and developed into its present form in the 14th century. It is a very formal, stylized dance-drama accompanied by song, narration, three types of drums, and a wooden flute. The masked main character performs slow dance movements enacting tales of god, man, woman, madness, and demons. The concepts are derived from Buddhist influences. ("There's no music like *noh* music," as foremost Japanese musicologist William P. Malm used to say.) Most Japanese people have never seen *noh* live. For better appreciation by the uninitiated, it's helpful to do some background reading or attend a performance with a knowledgeable person. *Takigi noh* (bonfire *noh*), performed outdoors in the summer at night—in a forest illuminated by fire from torches—is an unforgettable experience.

Kabuki

Kabuki originated in 1603, when Izu no Okuni, a former shrine maiden, arrived in Kyōto with a group of dancing girls and caused a stir. Their unorthodox dancing was banned, and some time later, *kabuki* was limited to male actors performing male and female roles in plays and dances of the 17th and 18th centuries. During the Edo period, *kabuki* became popular among the merchant class. The term *kabuki* consists of three *kanji* characters meaning "song-dance-skill." *Kabuki* is the most popular of the traditional Japanese theater types for its flamboyant colors and costumes, exaggerated gestures and *kata* (form), and revolving stages, trap doors, and even flying lions. The stories center on domestic (love triangles, love suicides) or historical (samurai battles) themes.

Bunraku

Bunraku is the traditional Japanese puppet theater that developed in the Ōsaka area. The puppets are not suspended by string; rather, each one is manipulated by three puppeteers wearing black face-covers and costumes (except the head puppeteer). The puppets are large, about two-thirds life-size, with mechanical arms and legs and moving eyes, eyebrows, and mouths, resulting in amazingly lifelike expressions. The repertoire is similar to *kabuki,* covering domestic tales and historical tales, accompanied by a *shamisen* (three-stringed lute played with a large triangular plectrum) and an extremely expressive singer/narrator who is the voice for all the characters. The term *bunraku* comes from the name of the man who built the Bunraku-za theater in Ōsaka in 1872.

MUSIC

Traditional Music

The numerous *hōgaku* (traditional music) genres and instruments are mostly unknown to those outside Japan, and even to many within. *Gagaku* is court music. Played on several distinctive reed instruments that produce an unforgettable sound, this musical style came from ancient China and was preserved for centuries. Performances take place mostly at the Imperial Palace on formal occasions. A four-stringed, pear-shaped lute called a *biwa* was played by itinerant Buddhist monks in the feudal age to narrate epic tales of battles (such as the *Tale of the Heike* from the 12th century) as they traveled from Kamakura, seat of the shōgun, to the Imperial capital of Kyōto. Another kind of lute is the three-stringed *shamisen* (one of the instruments that accompanies *kabuki* and *bunraku* theater). It has a square body and long neck and is played by plucking the strings with a triangular plectrum. *Shamisen* accompanies numerous traditional dance types, as well as *minyō* (folk music). Each region of Japan has its own folk music, handed down through the generations. At Obon (Buddhist All Soul's Day) festivals in mid-August, local communities dance to the folk songs of their region.

> *The numerous hōgaku (traditional music) genres and instruments are mostly unknown to those outside Japan, and even to many within.*

Another type of music that accompanies *kabuki* theater is called *Nagauta* (literally, "long song"), played by an orchestra of *shamisen*, three kinds of *taiko* (drums), and flutes. The *koto* is a 13-stringed chamber instrument made of hollowed-out paulownia wood. The sound board is six feet long and a foot wide, and it has movable bridges to hold up the silk or nylon strings. The performer kneels facing the *koto* and uses three finger picks to pluck the strings. Similar instruments found in China and Korea suggest that the *koto* may have come from the Continent many years ago. The five-holed *shakuhachi* is a bamboo flute with a beautiful haunting tone. *Koto, shamisen,* and *shakuhachi* are frequently performed together as a trio. Japanese children are introduced to Japanese traditional music in middle school, but unless they take a personal interest and study an instrument, traditional music is mostly passed up in favor of more accessible contemporary sounds.

© Ruthy Kanagy

Kaminari-mon (Thunder Gate) is the entrance to Asakusa temple.

Nontraditional Music

You will hear music everywhere you go in Japan—most of it loud, and almost none of it traditional. Japanese youth listen to the same kind of *ongaku* (nontraditional music) as their contemporaries across the Pacific. Their parents grew up listening to Bob Dylan, the Beatles, and other '60s and '70s rock. There are dozens of music shows on TV, with scores of live singing and dancing pop idols who participate in interview and game shows. Likewise, on the radio, J-Pop (Japanese pop music) is everywhere, with songs introduced by a hip English-speaking DJ. In addition to pop, there's also gangsta rap in Japanese and heavy metal groups such as Yellow Machine Gun (a three-woman band), Shonen Knife, and many more. Live clubs are everywhere, and often very crowded (clustered around big train stations like Shinjuku, Shibuya, or Kichijōji in Tōkyō). These clubs play all genres of rock, blues, jazz, and country—yes, you can dance the two-step with Japanese cowboys. Music is something you take with you in Japan, but not on portable CD players. Why not? Because everyone listens to MD (mini-disc) players and MP3 players. And, of course, now you can download music and listen to it on your *keitai* (cell phone).

Classical music also has a huge following in Japan. There are fine symphony orchestras in all the major cities, and educational TV broadcasts live performances. Many children start taking piano or violin lessons before kindergarten (you may hear them practicing in the adjacent apartment), then enter competitions and travel to New York or Europe for advanced study. Coffee shops catering to lovers of *kurashikku* (classical) play nothing but that. One classical music event draws a large percentage of listeners to concert halls across the countries every December. No, it's not Handel's *Messiah;* it's the well-known *Daiku,* or Beethoven's Ninth. Amateur and professional performances of the famous choral symphony continue through the month of December. Some choruses number as many as 10,000 singers, according to the *Asahi* newspaper. This all started because a German POW, confined to the island of Shikoku during the Pacific War, taught the music to his captors. The Japanese love music . . . and they have long memories. All of the old Stephen Foster songs are taught in school music curricula, and students still march to the tune of "Turkey in the Straw" for the annual all-school *undōkai* (sports day).

ART

Many countries outside Japan have museums with fine collections of Japanese *geijutsu* (art), including paintings, calligraphy, ceramics, lacquer, cloisonné, swords, wood carvings, and Japanese gardens. These art forms are more accessible to people outside Japan than are traditional theater and music. The greatest concentration of museums in Japan is the National Museum at Ueno in Tōkyō.

Shodō (Japanese calligraphy) is taught from elementary school to instill depth and beauty in writing *kanji* and *kana* characters. Calligraphy, created using brushes of different thickness dipped in *sumi* (ink) and applied to fine paper, expresses the artist's sense of beauty and personality. Calligraphy is traditionally displayed in the *tokonoma* (alcove) of a Japanese-style room in the home. Every year on January 2, students gather to write auspicious sayings for the new year, a practice known as *kakizome* (first writing), and the best receive awards.

Oil and water painting are the most widespread forms among Japanese artists. Traditional Japanese painting on silk or Japanese paper using *sumi* and mineral colors is also taught. Early Japanese painting was influenced by Buddhist art from China. During the Edo period, *ukiyo-e* (wood-block prints) became the first mass-produced art. Subjects included portraits of famous *kabuki* actors, beauties, and *sumō* wrestlers, as well as landscapes, historical themes, and nature.

Ceramics also play an important role in Japan. The earliest prehistoric period (called Jōmon; see Chapter 2, History, Government, and Economy, for details) is named for the type of pottery produced, namely earthenware with a cord design. Up to the 6th century, Japanese ceramics were influenced by Korean and Chinese craftsmen bringing in new techniques. Seto City in the Chūbu region of Honshū became so famous for fine ceramics that ceramic wares are now called *setomono* (Seto objects) in Japanese. Each region of Japan has at least one or two towns famous for the type of pottery they make, and for techniques such as *rakuyaki* (Raku firing). Lacquer is a product of many countries in Asia. It uses a liquid from under the bark of a lacquer tree, which is then mixed with pigment. Applied and dried in the right kind of air, the layers of coating take on a high sheen. Lacquer was used on Buddhist images and buildings, as well as tableware and *hashi* (chopsticks).

Japanese sword-making came to Japan from China and Korea and has a long history. During the Edo period, swords were very important to the samurai class for protection (they could carry two), and they were considered the soul of a warrior. Now they are largely decorative, acquired either as heirlooms or by collectors. Traditional wood-carving of various types also developed over a long period of time. For household furniture such as *tansu* (dressers to store kimonos), it was crucial that the wood be resistant to the hot and humid climate.

Japanese gardens are known the world over for their careful simplicity and asymmetry, belying close attention to detail. They require intensive manual labor to maintain. There are many famous gardens throughout the country, including Kenrokuen in Kanazawa, Suizenji in Kumamoto, and Katsura Rikyū (Katsura Imperial Garden) and Ryōanji (Zen Garden) in Kyōto.

Planning Your Fact-Finding Trip

Many people are attracted to one or more features of Japan's culture, such as karate, *sumō,* Zen Buddhism, anime, high-tech gadgetry, or even another recent invention—endlessly revolving plates of sushi on a conveyor belt. Wouldn't it be a dream come true to savor sushi every day, see *sumō* live, trek to famous temples, and have 50 channels of anime at your fingertips?

If you've ever traveled overseas, you know how exhilarating it is to experience first-hand all the things you've only heard or read about. At the same time, even the most perfect trip includes frustrations—in addition to the normal delays and changes you face when traveling, you are also an outsider. These pluses and minuses multiply when you consider a longer-term move to your dream culture.

A fact-finding trip is an important step to take before deciding on a permanent move. Unlike the casual tourist, you are on a mission to discover whether or not you can be fulfilled living in a foreign environment for an extended period. You must think about how you will feel as a minority member of society, particularly if you have never experienced that status before. Lack of fluency in the language will limit you until you gain more skills (although people will sometimes make more of a fuss over you if you *don't* speak Japanese, because they want to sharpen their English skills). It's always advisable to take a preliminary trip, talk to people who have moved there, and gather as much information as you can about your potential home.

A fact-finding trip entails goal-directed travel to specific areas of the country in order to observe and learn as much as possible about a city or prefecture. Other main reasons for a preliminary trip include surveying job possibilities and looking at housing options. The more background reading and research you do before you go, and the more contacts you make by email or letter, the more you stand to gain from the trip.

Preparing to Leave

THE LANGUAGE BARRIER

If it's your first time traveling to an unfamiliar country, you may arrive in Japan, look around, and realize with a start that you can't read any of the signs. You may feel a bit disoriented or even culture-shocked. Yesterday, you were a fully competent and literate human being, and today you're reduced to a dependent without even a basic education. This happened to me some years back, when I traveled to Korea, Japan's closest neighbor. I couldn't read the menus in restaurants and couldn't find the schedule and fare for the bus to Seoul. I didn't know Korean and couldn't decipher Hangul (Korean letters). Had I been with someone who could speak Korean, it would have been easier—but even so, I'm glad I went. Your first visit to Japan will present some challenges. But rest assured that Japan is a safe place, and most people will go out of their way to be helpful.

If you have already studied Nihon-go, the Japanese language, make use of this knowledge, gather up a few guidebooks, and you're ready to pack. If you don't know Japanese but have a good ear, a sense of humor, and a skill for drawing and pantomime, pick up a good phrasebook (try starting with the basic one in the Resources chapter of this book) and try to learn as much as you can during the trip. Take along a chart of the two phonetic syllabaries. The 46 square-shaped letters (each letter represents a syllable) are called *katakana,* and the 46 rounded letters are *hiragana.* The corresponding letters of the syllabaries are pronounced the same, even though they look slightly different (just like the printed American alphabet versus one written in cursive). If you master *katakana,* you will be able to read the menus in coffee shops and western-style restaurants. *Katakana* is also the script used to write foreign names and places.

CURRENCY

Japanese currency is called *en* in Japanese and "yen" in English. The most common bills in circulation are *sen-en* (¥1,000), *gosen-en* (¥5,000) and *ichi-man-en* (¥10,000); *nisen-en* (¥2,000) bills exist, but they're infrequently used. Unlike the greenback, *en* denominations are issued in various colors and sizes, which will help you tell them apart. Coins come in *ichi-en* (¥1), *go-en* (¥5), *jū-en* (¥10), *gojū-en* (¥50), *hyaku-en* (¥100), and *gohyaku-en* (¥500) units, also in different sizes and colors. Five- and 50-yen coins have a hole in the middle (*go-en* is a pun on the words "good luck").

The international symbol for *en* is ¥, as in ¥1,000. The foreign exchange rate for Japanese yen to the U.S. dollar fluctuates daily and ranged from ¥106 to ¥130 to the dollar in 2003. (Gone are the days of the fixed rate ¥360 to the dollar.) For convenience, we will use the rate of ¥110 to calculate U.S. dollar equivalency throughout this book.

Shopkeepers rarely object if you proffer a ¥10,000 note (nearly $100) to purchase a pack of gum. Vending machines accept ¥1,000 notes (almost $10) and dispense everything from hot and cold drinks, cigarettes, and liquor to magazines, film, batteries, and rice. Most train ticket machines take 10,000 bills. You will no doubt become accustomed to carrying a greater amount of cash for your daily needs than you did back home.

For your fact-finding trip to Japan, it is best—and safest—to carry funds in U.S. travelers checks in $100 denominations. Smaller denominations and yen travelers checks are more trouble than they're worth. Plan to convert a substantial sum of dollars ($500 or more) into yen cash upon arrival at the airport. This is crucial if you're arriving on a Friday through Sunday, or on a national holiday. (Remember, you lose a day when traveling from North America.) You will need funds immediately: The two- to three-hour bus or train ride from Narita International Airport to Tōkyō will put you back ¥3,500 ($30), and a taxi ride can cost the equivalent of several hundred dollars. The foreign exchange counters at major airports like Narita and Ōsaka are reputable and offer competitive rates.

Traveler's checks can be cashed at banks displaying a "Foreign Exchange" sign. However, bank hours are limited to 9 A.M.–3 P.M. on business days. Note that travelers checks cannot be used in place of cash, except at a few large department stores and shops that cater to foreign tourists. Personal checks are not accepted, since personal checking accounts do not exist in Japan. (Some banks will process a U.S.-drawn personal check, but it will take up to six weeks and involves a substantial fee.)

A bank card is an alternative to travelers checks. You will be able to withdraw yen directly from your account at most ATMs in major airports and larger cities. Be sure to get a list of your bank's branch locations in Japan before leaving home.

Taxes and Tipping

In Japan, where the customer is king, shopping is a pleasure and the service is excellent. Major credit cards such as Visa, MasterCard, and Diners Club are accepted by hotels, larger shops, restaurants, and taxis, but many smaller shops, eateries, and inns take only cash. A 5-percent consumption tax will be added to your bill. Tipping is not practiced in

Japan in restaurants, taxis, hotels, or anywhere else, and will likely be re-fused if you try.

DRESSING FOR THE WEATHER

Keep in mind that Japanese people dress up when going out—whether it's shopping, riding the train, or taking an outing. Only joggers wear sweat suits, and women dress conservatively in nice two-piece ensembles and shoes. (I recommend avoiding revealing clothing, tube tops, and miniskirts unless you enjoy lots of stares—even more than the usual *gaijin* stare.) If you're arriving in the summer and traveling anywhere south of Hokkaidō, be prepared for hot, sweaty weather. Light wash-and-wear clothing is best (avoid cotton if you want it to hang-dry overnight). For women, moisture wicking tops, skirts, dresses, culottes, hats, a folding umbrella, and a light jacket are sufficient. Japanese men always wear long pants unless taking part in sports. In Hokkaidō, you'll be thankful on summer evenings for a warm sweater and jacket. In fall and spring, add some long-sleeve tops and long pants. In winter, it's a good idea to have a warm jacket or coat, gloves, a scarf, and a hat. Trains and stores are too warm sometimes, but you'll be glad for the layers when you step outside. Southern Kyūshū and Okinawa are a bit warmer.

TIME ZONES AND ELECTRICITY

Japan is in one time zone, although it's wide enough for two. To calculate the time in Japan from the United States, note that it changes depending on daylight saving time. Japan time is the same year-round. When the U.S. is in daylight saving time, Japan is 13 hours ahead of Eastern Time and 16 hours ahead of Pacific Time. During U.S. standard time, Japan is 14 hours ahead of Eastern Time and 17 hours ahead of Pacific Time. The easiest way to calculate the hour in Japan is to go forward 12 hours, then add one to five more hours depending where you live.

If you're taking a hair dryer or other electrical items on your trip, note that Japan is 100V, as opposed to 120V in the U.S. This means that your appliances will work—they'll just have a little less power. (But don't go to Hong Kong and plug your hair dryer in, like I did—it promptly blew up from the 240V current.) Also, note that eastern Japan (Tōkyō and northeast) is on 50Hz, while western Japan (Ōsaka and west) is 60Hz.

WHEN TO GO

Avoid traveling to Japan during the following peak times: December 26–January 4 (New Year's), April 28–May 6 (Golden Week), and August

14–17 (Obon). Everyone in Japan is either headed home to their folks' or going abroad. It's like the Thanksgiving travel crush multiplied tenfold. Not only airplanes, but also trains, highways, theme parks, hiking areas, and hot springs—in short, all popular destinations—are extremely crowded. There are also many people traveling around the following 14 national holidays: New Year's Day (January 1), Coming of Age Day (second Monday in January), Foundation Day (February 11), Spring Equinox (March 20 or 21), Green Day (April 29), Constitution Day (May 3), Children's Day (May 5), Ocean Day (third Monday in July), Respect the Aged Day (third Monday in September), Fall Equinox (September 23 or 24), Sports Day (second Monday in October), Culture Day (November 3), Labor Thanksgiving Day (November 23), and the Emperor's Birthday (December 23). In addition, governments and most offices are generally closed December 29 through January 3. Christmas is not a national holiday—it's celebrated Christmas Eve, and then everyone goes back to work and school.

Spring and fall are generally the most pleasant seasons to visit Japan. In the spring, cherry blossoms bloom in sequence from south to north (opening in late March in Tōkyō, earlier southwest). April and May temperatures are moderate and comfortable. If you don't mind the rain, June to mid-July is not too bad, but then Tōkyō and southwest Japan turn extremely humid and hot. Unless you enjoy Washington, D.C. in August, it's unpleasant weather for travel. If you want to come in July or August, the choice destination is Hokkaidō, with wonderfully cool summers and no concentrated rainy season. In the fall, red Japanese maples and other colors are breathtaking beginning in September in the north through November in the south, including Kyōto.

In most areas of Japan, except for southern Kyūshū and subtropical Okinawa, winter is brisk. Some accommodations are drafty and not well-heated, so unless you thrive in the snow, it may not be the most comfortable season. However, if you're curious about Japanese New Year's festivities—special decorations, foods, mass pilgrimages to shrines and temples, special television shows—by all means, come! Just be sure to book your hot springs inn early (prices are higher during holidays). In Hokkaidō, the snowy mountains and caldera lakes are beautiful, although walking on snow and ice is tricky. Attracting several million visitors, Sapporo hosts the International Snow Festival during the first week of February. If you want to see the rare *tanchō-tsuru* (red-crested cranes) dancing in eastern Hokkaidō, winter is the best time, though frigid (and you will be joined by scores of other photographers).

Arriving in Japan

TRANSPORTATION

Whether you're riding long-distance trains, buses, or ferries, public transportation is an easy, safe, fast way of getting around Japan from north to south. The *shinkansen* (nicknamed the "bullet train" in English) speeds along elevated rails. It's speedy and comfortable, but sometimes costs more than flying. This is where the Japan Rail Pass can save you a great deal of yen, and it's available in one- to three-week versions. With this pass, you can travel freely on any public JR (Japan Railway)-operated train, bus, or ferry (except Nozomi, the fastest *shinkansen,* which costs extra). However, note that the Rail Pass is only valid for temporary visitors, i.e., tourists staying 90 days or less. And the pass must be purchased *outside* Japan from your travel agent, then exchanged for the actual pass after you arrive in Japan. (See Chapter 11, Travel and Transportation, for further information.)

© Ruthy Kanagy

Local Japan Rail (JR) train

Sample Itineraries

If this is your first trip to a non-English-speaking country and you are concerned about communicating, taking an organized tour might be the best option. You can join a tour originating in the United States, or fly to Japan and join a tour of several days in a region that interests you. The Japan Travel Bureau (JTB) offers Sunrise Tours in varying lengths from three to 14 days, and Japan Holiday Tours offers one- to five-day tours of Tōkyō, Nikkō (north of Tōkyō), Mount Fuji, Kyōto, and Nara. The longer tours start the moment you arrive at Narita Airport near Tōkyō or Kansai Airport in Ōsaka. Whether you're traveling solo or with a group, the Japan National Tourist Organization (www.jnto.go.jp) is a good source of information.

Another option is to make use of the volunteer guides in many cities throughout Japan—Hiroshima, Ōsaka, Kyōto, Nara, and more. The guides are local residents interested in speaking English and showing their city to visitors from abroad. Make a reservation by phone or email one to two weeks in advance. See the Japan National Tourist Organization's website for a list of cities and regions with volunteer guides, as well as contact information.

The following sample eight-day itineraries are only suggestions. If you have two weeks, try combining two itineraries or spending some extra time in one or two regions. (See the Practicalities section, below, for additional information on places to visit and hotel recommendations.)

HOKKAIDŌ AND TŌKYŌ

Days 1–3: Arrive in Sapporo, explore Ōdōri Park and Ainu Museum, and visit Sapporo International Plaza Foundation for living information; take a day trip by train to Otaru or by bus to Shikotsu-Tōya National Park.

Days 4–5: Take a train to Obihiro, visit city hall for information, and check out Obihiro University, Joy English Academy, and El Paso Restaurant; stay at Tokachigawa Onsen (hot springs).

Days 6–7: Fly to Tōkyō, take a bus tour (Asakusa Temple, Shinjuku Gardens, Meiji Shrine, Ginza, etc.), visit Kinokuniya Bookstore in Shinjuku for books and maps, and walk around areas that interest you.

Day 8: Depart from Narita Airport in the afternoon.

If you have more time: Add two days to visit Kushiro and eastern Hokkaidō, and one to two days for Hakodate in southwest Hokkaidō.

TŌKYŌ AND THE CENTRAL MOUNTAINS

Days 1–4: Arrive in Tōkyō at Narita Airport, take a half-day or full-day bus tour (Asakusa Temple, Shinjuku Gardens, Meiji Shrine, Ginza, etc.), visit Kinokuniya Bookstore in Shinjuku for books and maps, walk around the areas near different train stations, and visit businesses and universities that interest you.

Days 5–7: Take the train to Minakami in Gunma prefecture, stay at a traditional hot springs hotel, visit Café Manna and its American owner, then take a train to Karuizawa resort and/or Matsumoto city (see the Japan Alps and Matsumoto Castle).

Day 8: Take the train back to Narita Airport and depart.

If you have more time: Add two to four days in Tōkyō to scout out housing and work possibilities; and take a day trip to Mount Fuji by bus.

KANSAI, HIROSHIMA, AND SHIKOKU

Days 1–3: Arrive at Kansai International Airport, explore Ōsaka (Dōtonbori, Ōsaka Castle, shopping arcades), and take a day trip by bus to Kyōto.

Days 4–6: Take a train to Hiroshima, stopping at the tourist information center at the station; see Peace Memorial Park, Hiroshima Castle, and Miyajima Island; also visit Hiroshima University and any businesses that interest you.

Day 7: Go on a day trip by ferry to Matsuyama in Shikoku Island, visit Dōgo Onsen and Matsuyama Castle.

Day 8: Depart from Hiroshima Airport.

If you have more time: Spend two to three days in Kyōto and Nara, or add two to three more days to travel around Shikoku by train—visit Kōchi, Tokushima, and Takamatsu cities to get a feel for the different regions.

Practicalities

Most people arrive at Narita Airport near Tōkyō to launch their adventure in Japan, but there's no reason why you have to start there. To see most of the last frontier, Hokkaidō, the speediest route is to transfer from Narita Airport to Haneda Airport (Tōkyō's domestic airport) and catch a domestic flight to the capital city of Sapporo (New Chitose Airport), Obihiro, Kushiro, or Hakodate.

SAPPORO

There are numerous direct flights from Tōkyō and other cities to Sapporo. The airport for Sapporo is called the New Chitose Airport. The train ride from the airport to Sapporo takes around 35 minutes.

If you come to Japan in spring, you can follow the plum and cherry blossoms from south to north.

You can also travel to Hokkaidō by train. From Tōkyō, you can take the Tōhoku (Northeast) *shinkansen* to the city of Hachinohe, then transfer to the Hakuchō special express and go through an hour-long undersea tunnel to Hakodate, the southern point of Hokkaidō. Finally, take the Hokuto special express train to Sapporo, a trip of just under four hours (11 hours total for the journey). If you want to be more adventurous, sleep your way to Hokkaidō on an overnight train leaving Tōkyō's Ueno station each day.

Sapporo has many areas to explore. Ōdōri (Main Street) Park is a wide expanse of green many blocks long. In February, it is the stage for the Yuki-Matsuri (Snow Festival) with giant snow and ice sculptures. Susukino is filled with restaurants, bars, and nightspots. Other places to visit are the Historic Pioneer Village, Ainu Museum (Utari Center near Ōdōri), Hokkaidō University, and Makomanai (site of the 1972 Winter Olympics). The Sapporo International Plaza Foundation next to Ōdōri is a place to go for information on living in Sapporo (see the Resources section for contact information).

In addition to staying at hotels, Japanese-style inns, and youth hostels, there is another lodging option in Hokkaidō. Toho Yado (www.toho .net/yado.html) are a series of family-run bed-and-breakfasts throughout Hokkaidō with shared rooms (separated by gender) and meals by request. You can learn a lot about the region or town, and they may offer tours for a fee. This is a great way to meet Japanese travelers.

Hotels

Hotel Sapporo Met's
Kita 17-jō Nishi 5-chōme 20
Kita-ku, Sapporo-shi, Hokkaidō
tel. 011/726-5511
www.hotelmets.co.jp/english

Sapporo Ōdōri Kōen Hotel
Nishi 8-chōme
Chūō-ku, Sapporo-shi, Hokkaidō
tel. 011/261-0123

OBIHIRO

Obihiro is two hours east from Sapporo on the *Tokkyū Ōzora* (special express "Big Sky"), tunneling through the Hidaka Mountains and across the broad Tokachi plain. Obihiro is a midsized city with all the modern conveniences, but surrounded by crop farms, sheep, and the Daisetsuzan Mountains in the distance. There are also parks, the Tokachi river (where salmon return to spawn), and a hot springs resort called Tokachigawa Onsen. Many young Japanese entrepreneurs return to Tokachi after living in the big city of Tōkyō down south, then realizing what they were missing. Some have started restaurants and English schools. There is also an agricultural university.

Hotels

Tōkyū Inn
Minami 11-2 Nishi 1-jō
Obihiro-shi, Hokkaidō
tel. 0155/27-0109

Kokumin Shukusha Hotel Tokachigawa
2 Minami 6-chome
Tokachigawa Onsen
Otofuke-chō, Katō-gun, Hokkaidō
tel. 0155/46-2555

KUSHIRO

From Obihiro, travel another two hours east on the *tokkyū* along the coast to Kushiro, the fishing capital and major port of eastern Hokkaidō. It is also the gateway to Kushiro Wetlands National Park and Akan National Park, which can be reached via the Kushiro or Akan bus lines. During the winter, you can see the rare *tanchō-tsuru* (red-crested crane) in the wetlands when they come for feeding. Akan has a caldera lake with unusual round moss balls *(marimo)* that grow only here. There are volcanoes and bubbling hot springs, as well as numerous hotels and inns, alongside

A Stay at a Japanese Inn

Kampo no Yado (National Health Insurance Lodge) charges members ¥6,700 ($61) for one night and two meals (it's ¥1,500/$14 extra if you're not a member). I pay the higher rate and consider it quite reasonable for Japanese-style lodging at Ōnuma National Park in southern Hokkaidō during the peak of the fall colors. The hotel is set in a forest on a high bluff, away from the tourist shops. A large stuffed deer greets me in the entrance. As I fill out a registration form at the front desk, 25 older women march single-file toward the exit. Each carries a towel and a handbag under her arm, and each has white steam rising from her wet hair. As they pass the counter, they nod their thanks to the man behind the desk. The hotel is popular with day visitors, who come to soak in the mineral baths for ¥700 ($6) or pay ¥3,000 ($28) to include a full-course meal afterward.

I open the door to my room. A low rectangular table sits in the middle, with a tray of utensils for making green tea. Next to the window, with its view of multicolored leaves, sit a coffee table and two chairs. Against the wall, where the traditional *tokonoma* (art corner) should be, I find a metal safe, a telephone, a night lamp, and a television. In the closet, there's a pink bath towel and a white *yukata* (light cotton robe) with red polka dots. Dinner is served in your room at whatever time you request; breakfast is served in the dining room from 7 to 9 A.M.

There's a knock on the door, and a maid enters with a large tray. She kneels on the *tatami* mat and sets the food on the low table. I kneel on the *zabuton* (square cushion) with my feet tucked under, and stare at the 12 dishes, each a different color and shape, containing an array of food. I lift the lid of a small, black, lacquered bowl carefully, and the steam rises from the *osuimono* (clear broth). A

the lake. Akan is home to many indigenous Ainu, who make a living by selling wood carvings of bears and other subjects.

From Kushiro, continue east by bus to Nakashibetsu and Shibetsu, gateway to Shiretoko Peninsula and National Park in northeast Hokkaidō. From June to October, it's possible to cross over Shiretoko Pass and continue in a circular route around Hokkaidō back to Sapporo. Alternately, take the train west from Kushiro back to Sapporo and south to Hakodate.

small crock pot sits over a burner. The maid lights the white fuel, and the blue flames heat the broth. I add clumps of minced chicken, Chinese cabbage, white squares of tofu, *enoki* (long, skinny mushrooms), carrots sliced in the shape of cherry blossoms, chrysanthemum leaves, and translucent *shirataki* noodles. The flame burns just long enough to cook the stew perfectly before going out.

Something from the sea and something from the mountain are the marks of a balanced meal. I discover a dish of boiled shiitake mushrooms and a cube of beef, with sticks of green *sansai* (wild greens) tied into a bundle. In a flat dish are three strips of raw red meat, sandwiched by two lemon wedges. I'm not going to ask what they are—it might be *basashi* (raw horse meat), a delicacy in some areas of Hokkaidō. When you find an unidentified fishy object in a Japanese meal, the trick is to take the item, put it inside your left cheek, quickly shovel in a mound of white rice, chew quickly to blend, and then swallow. The principle is "Eat now, ask later." If needed, order beer! Rice is the staple of life in Japan, and there is no charge for second, third, or even fourth helpings. (Green tea is always complimentary in any Japanese restaurant, and it also works for washing down unfamiliar foods.) I call room service and ask for a bottle of Ōnuma Beer.

I save the *chawanmushi*—a sort of creamy soufflé containing something from the sea (shrimp) and from the mountain (chestnuts and bamboo shoots), topped with *mitsuba* (a leafy green)—for last. The wrapper on my *hashi* (chopsticks) says, "Made of genuine Hokkaidō *bodaiju*."

The sound of piped muzak, a man talking on the phone, and someone brushing her teeth drift into my private room, along with the patter of rain. It's time to change into my *yukata* and explore the *ofuro* (bath).

Hotels

Akan Park Inn
2-1-1 Akan Kohan Onsen
Hokkaidō
tel. 0154/67-3211
fax 0154/67-2752
y-takuji@ivory.plala.or.jp

Kushiro Prince Hotel
7-1 Saiwai-chō
Kushiro-shi, Hokkaidō
tel. 0154/31-1111

Pension Green Park (Kushiro)
3-7-11 Tsurugadai
Kushiro-shi, Hokkaidō
tel. 0154/41-2685

HAKODATE

Hakodate is the southernmost city in Hokkaidō (on a peninsula somewhat resembling Italy) and was the first area in Hokkaidō settled by Japanese from the south. (The native Ainu people had arrived long before.) It is a major port and shows early Western influences in its cathedrals, convents, and a Catholic school. It was the northernmost outpost of the Tokugawa shōgunate until 1868, and fishing and seafood are the major industries in this city surrounded by the sea. Hakodate's night view is famous, and a cable car or city bus ride leads to the top of Hakodate-yama.

North of Hakodate is Ōnuma National Park, dominated by Mount Komagatake, an active volcano that looks down on big and small lakes. It is lovely in all seasons, especially autumn, and has a cycling course around the lakes.

Hotels

Aqua Garden Hotel Hakodate
19-13 Ōte-machi
Hakodate-shi, Hokkaidō
tel. 0138/23-2200
www.makeland.co.jp/
aquagarden/english.html

B&B Pension Hakodate-mura
16-12 Suehiro-chō
Hakodate-shi, Hokkaidō
tel. 0138/22-8105
www.jpinn.com

CENTRAL HONSHŪ

If you're continuing from Hokkaidō south to Tōkyō and have a Japan Rail Pass, take the train from Hakodate through the undersea tunnel linking Hokkaidō and Honshū, then travel south through the Tōhoku (Northeast) region of Honshū. You will pass through Aomori prefecture, known for its superb apples, then Morioka, Sendai, and eventually to Tōkyō. Transferring to a *shinkansen* in Hachinohe will speed your journey, but if you're in no hurry, you can get off the train to explore any city and sample the special *eki bentō* (boxed lunches) sold on the platform at each major station.

TŌKYŌ

If you arrive at Narita Airport, there are many ways to get to Tōkyō. The Limousine Bus goes to major hotels and train stations in Tōkyō, taking one to two hours. The JR line Narita Express takes you to Tōkyō station in 60 minutes, or to Shinjuku station in slightly longer. The Keisei Skyliner goes to Ueno station in Tōkyō in 55 minutes.

You can make a day trip from Tōkyō to Kamakura. Kamakura was the home of the shōgunate during the Kamakura period. There are many

© Ruthy Kanagy

Neon lights at Akihabara, the Electric City, in Tōkyō

historic temples and shrines, along with a giant outdoor Buddha—the largest such statue in Japan. Many craft and souvenir shops line the main street. Take a ride on the Eno-den (Enoshima street car), which has been in operation for many years.

Hotels

Asia Center of Japan
8-10-32 Akasaka
Minato-ku, Tōkyō
tel. 03/3402-6111

Sun Hotel Asakusa
1-9-2 Asakusa
Taitō-ku, Tōkyō
tel. 03/5828-3351
asakusa@sun-hotel.co.jp

GUNMA

The central mountains of Gunma and Nagano prefectures are only two hours away from Tōkyō's congestion, offering a nearby escape. At the northern end of Gunma, below the imposing Tanikawa mountain range is Minakami, a hot springs resort town. The pace of life is much slower here, as illustrated by the traditional farmhouses surrounded by rice and mulberry fields. The rushing Tone River provides exhilarating summer

Fall leaves decorate a gorge in Gunma prefecture.

rafting; mountain climbing and winter sports are also available. A *"gaijin"* (foreigner) village has built up over time, with most homeowners coming for weekend getaways from the city.

Hotels

Hotel Sannokura (Minakami)
510 Konita
Minakami-chō, Tone-gun,
Gunma-ken
tel. 0278/72-2340
www.sannokura.com (in Japanese)

Hotel Metropolitan Takasaki
222 Yashima-chō
Takasaki-shi, Gunma-ken
tel. 027/325-3311
www.jrhotelgroup.com/eng/
hotel/eng110.htm

NAGANO

Nagano, the "roof of Japan," hosted the 1998 Winter Olympics, so a *shinkansen* line was specially built to transport all the visitors to various events. Just over an hour from Tōkyō is the highland resort community of Karuizawa, where those with means have summer vacation homes. An outlet mall next to the station sells L.L. Bean and Nike products and is quite popular on weekends (expect traffic jams if you are driving). A bicycle is the best way to explore the back roads of Karuizawa, taking you to many museums, galleries, cafés, and antique shops. The hairpin curves of the old route over Usui Pass descend to the town of Yokokawa, 18 kilometers (11.2 miles) below. On the way, you pass a historic brick railroad bridge built in 1895 and now used as a hiking trail. Fall is a particularly lovely time in Karuizawa.

To see more of Nagano prefecture, take the *shinkansen* northwest from Karuizawa to Nagano, the capital city of the prefecture and site of the Olympics. From Nagano, travel south on the Shinonoi line to Matsumoto, a major castle city from the feudal period and the gateway to the Japan Alps. From Matsumoto, go south on the Chuo line all the way to Nagoya. In Nagoya, you can transfer to the Tokaido *shinkansen* traveling west to Kyōto.

Hotels

Matsumoto Tourist Hotel
2-4-24 Fukashi
Matsumoto-shi, Nagano-ken
tel. 0263/33-9000
info@trist.co.jp
www.trist.co.jp (in Japanese)

Hotel Metropolitan Nagano
1346 Minami-Ishido-chō
Nagano-ken
tel. 026/291-7000
www.jrhotelgroup.com/eng/hotel/
eng109.htm

ŌSAKA

If you land at Kansai International Airport near Ōsaka, it's 60 minutes by train or bus into the city. If you're coming from Tōkyō to Kyōto by *shinkansen*, it's about three hours to Kyōto and another 30 minutes to Ōsaka. Ōsaka is a bustling city of business and pleasure, with many areas to explore. Dōtonbori, along a canal, is filled with restaurants and people. There are shopping streets specializing in knives and other gourmet kitchen wares, several underground shopping streets, and Ōsaka Castle Park. From Ōsaka to Kyōto, it's a 30- to 40-minute trip north by Hankyū train (or by *shinkansen*, if you're using the Japan Rail Pass).

Hotels

Hotel Kitahachi
7-16 Doyama-chō
Kita-ku, Ōsaka-shi
tel. 06/6361-2078

Hotel Oaks Shin-Ōsaka
1-11-34 Nishi-Nakashima
Yodogawa-ku, Ōsaka-shi
tel. 06/6302-5141
shin-osaka@h-oaks.co.jp
www.h-oaks.co.jp/english

New Oriental Hotel
2-6-10 Nishi-Motomachi
Nishi-ku, Ōsaka-shi
tel. 06/6538-7141
noh@joytel.co.jp

KYŌTO

Kyōto was the ancient capital of Japan for 1,000 years. There are more than 1,000 temples and shrines in the city, and many famous festivals in the spring and summer. There are always school kids in uniform and Japanese tour groups exploring the city. Kyōto is fairly easy to get around by city bus, train, and subway. Spend as many days as you can here, but a minimum of two.

Kyōto is laid out like a grid, with major streets going east and west or north and south. Starting at the north, Ichi-jō (First Avenue; *jō* means "avenue") runs east and west; then Ni-jō (Second Avenue), home to the shōgun's Nijo Castle; and so on. Shi-jō (Fourth Avenue) has many department stores and restaurants. Kyōto Station is on Hachi-jō (Eighth Avenue). Karasuma-dōri (*dōri* means "street") extends north from Kyōto Station to the Imperial Palace.

Hotel

Hotel Station Kyōto
260 Ameya-chō, Shichijō-Agaru
Higashi-Notoin, Shimogyō-ku, Kyōto-shi
tel. 075/365-9000
st-kyoto@mbox.kyoto-inet.or.jp

NARA

An hour south of Kyōto or an hour east of Ōsaka is the city of Nara. If you have time to visit Nara, you'll find the oldest capital of Japan, a much smaller-scale Kyōto. Some of the best temples are Hōryūji and Tōdaiji, with its massive statue of Buddha. The deer in Nara Park will welcome you (hold on to your hat). From here, you can return by train to Ōsaka and points west.

Hotel

Hotel Asyl Nara
Aburasaka-chō
Nara-shi, Nara-ken
tel. 0742/22-2577 or 0120-200-350 (toll-free in Japan)
http://worldheritage.co.jp/topen.html

KŌBE AND HIMEJI

Kōbe is a major city set between the Rokkō Mountains and Ōsaka Bay. From Ōsaka, you can journey here on regular trains or by *shinkansen* in 30 minutes. In the Great Hanshin-Awaji Earthquake of 1995, thousands of buildings and highways were destroyed in Kōbe, and many lives were lost. Most communities have been rebuilt.

The next stop west of Kōbe on the *shinkansen* is Himeji, home of Himeji Castle. *Hime-ji* means Princess Way, and it is the most beautifully preserved feudal castle in Japan. Only a short walk from the train station, it's worth a stop, especially if you have the Japan Rail Pass with on-and-off privileges. The rapid express trains from Kōbe also stop at Himeji.

Continuing west, you will pass the town of Bizen, the center of Bizen pottery; then Okayama, the capital of Okayama prefecture. Further west is Kurashiki, a well-preserved example of a feudal town, with canals, willow trees, and old storehouses. Then you'll arrive at historic Onomichi on the Inland Sea. You can go by ferry to Shikoku, the smallest of the main Japanese islands; or go over land and sea via a series of bridges called Shimanami Kaidō (the island and wave route) that skips and hops across small islands all the way to Imabari, in Ehime prefecture on western Shikoku island. If you continue west on the main route by *shinkansen,* you will arrive in Hiroshima.

Hotels

Kōbe Tōkyū Inn
6-1-5 Kumoi-dōri
Chūō-ku, Kōbe-shi
tel. 065/6235-2498

Himeji Castle Hotel
210 Nishino-machi,
Sanzaemon-dōri
Himeji-shi
tel. 0792/84-3311

HIROSHIMA

Hiroshima is a city of seven rivers, sandwiched between the mountains to the north and facing the Inland Sea to the south, and best known for the atomic bomb dropped on it by the United States in August 1945. Peace Memorial Park documents in very real and human terms what happened that day, and its displays should be experienced by anyone who considers him or herself a world citizen. A tablet before the eternal flame states, "We will never let this mistake be repeated." Drawings and garlands of thousands of folded paper *tsuru* (cranes) are colorful and moving. Every year on August 6 (the anniversary of the Japanese date of the bombing), citizens from around the world gather to pray for peace and for no other country in the world ever to suffer a nuclear holocaust.

Hiroshima is famous for its cuisine, particularly *okonomiyaki* (literally, "grill what you like"). Think of it as a Japanese version of pizza (regular pizza is also quite popular). Pour some batter mixed with noodles on a hot grill, then add beef, scallops, or squid, chopped cabbage, and onions and fry it until done on both sides. Eat with mayonnaise or brown sauce.

Miyajima is quite famous as an island with a floating Shintō shrine. It's a short ferry ride from Hiroshima and always crowded with visitors and deer. You can see traditional houses on the hill behind the shrine. Depending on the tides, you may also see the shrine "floating" above the waves, supported by stilts—a great photo opportunity.

Hotels

**Hiroshima Ekimae
Green Hotel**
10-27 Matsubara-chō
Minami-ku, Hiroshima-shi
tel. 082/264-3939
www.ekimae-green.com/english

Hotel Silk Plaza Hiroshima
14-1 Hatchōbori
Naka-ku, Hiroshima-shi
tel. 082/227-8111

SHIKOKU

Continue by ferry to Shikoku. The Inland Sea, known for oyster cultivation, is dotted with islands that glisten in the sun. What would it be like to live on one of the islands? Amy Chavez has been doing just that for several years. Author of the JapanLite column in the *Japan Times* newspaper, she lives on Shiraishi Island, population 800. You can meet Amy and her fellow islanders at www.amychavez.addr.com, and then you'll be well equipped to explore Shikoku's four prefectures: Kagawa-ken in the northeast facing the Inland Sea, Tokushima-ken in the east, Kōchi-ken

© Ruthy Kanagy

The top of Matsuyama Castle offers a stunning view of the capital city in northwest Shikoku.

along the southern Pacific coast, and Ehime-ken at the northwest corner, opposite Hiroshima. The pace of life is slower in Shikoku, and there is more elbow room when exploring the mountains, gorges, rivers, and beaches.

Hotels

Matsuyama City Hotel
2-8 Ōte-machi
Matsuyama-shi, Ehime-ken
tel. 089/932-1121
city@mocha.ocn.ne.jp

Takamatsu Terminal Hotel
10-17 Nishinomaru-chō
Takamatsu-shi, Kagawa-ken
tel. 087/822-3731
hotel@webterminal.co.jp

OKINAWA

Okinawa, far south of Kyūshū halfway between Japan and Taiwan, is most accessible by air. If you have time to see the Hawaii of Japan, you'll find an area with its own distinct history, language, and culture. It was established as the kingdom of Ryūkyū at the beginning of the 15th century and traded with both China and Japan. Okinawa was taken in 1609 by a Japanese clan from southern Kyūshū. During the Meiji era (1868), it was made a prefecture of Japan and called Okinawan-ken. The Ryūkyū language is distinct from both Japanese and Chinese, and the cuisine, clothing, housing, and religion are unique to the islands. You can feel the splendor of the last Ryūkyūan king by visiting ornate Shuri Castle. Sadly, Okinawa was the stage for some of the most horrifying battles during World War II, victimized by Japan and the United States. The United States controlled Okinawa and took almost half the prime land for U.S. military bases. Okinawa was reverted to the Japanese government in 1972. Like the Ainu (native people) in the far north, Okinawans have faced discrimination in education and employment. Today, there is something of a revival to teach the younger Okinawan generation their cultural roots. Several singers popular in Japan, such as Amuro Namie and Natsukawa Rimi, are of Okinawan heritage.

Hotel

Hotel Emerald
1-2-25 Shuri
Naha-shi, Okinawa-ken
tel. 098/862-8001
www.hotelemerald.net (in Japanese)

Types of Accommodations

One of the delights of traveling in Japan is the variety of accommodations: There are western-style hotels, business hotels, *ryokan* (Japanese-style inns; pronounced in two quick syllables, starting with a flick of your tongue like a soft "d," then a rapid "yo" like "yogurt"), *minshuku* (family-run inns), and youth hostels. Hotels are moderate to expensive (e.g., ¥10,000/$91 per person and up); business hotels have fewer amenities, smaller rooms, and lower prices. *Ryokan* prices are a little higher, but usually include two meals and an authentic Japanese atmosphere that you can't experience at the Hilton.

If you are looking for relatively inexpensive accommodations, an organization called the Welcome Inn Reservation Center (www.itcj.or.jp) takes reservations for 276 hotels and inns accustomed to foreign guests. The maximum rate is ¥8,000 ($73) for a single and ¥13,000 ($118) for a double. Tipping is not practiced in hotels or anywhere else in Japan, but a smile or nod is appreciated. Kintetsu International (www.knt.co.jp/koku-sai/top.htm) also takes online reservations for hotels and *ryokan*.

You haven't really experienced Japan until you've spent the night in a *ryokan* (Japanese-style inn) in a scenic location with *onsen* (natural hot springs). Most *ryokan* charge ¥12,000–20,000 ($109–182) per person—not per room—but that includes two ample meals, usually served in your room. Tax and service charges are additional. When you get to the inn, take your shoes off at the entrance and change into slippers provided by the inn. At the entry to your Japanese-style room, remove your slippers to walk on the delicate *tatami* mats. There will be a low table in the middle of the room with flat cushions around it for kneeling. A thermos of hot water and a tea set are provided for making *ocha* (green tea) with a cookie or sweet. Where are the beds? Hiding in the closet. After dinner, a maid will come and lay out the futon for you.

To soak in the soothing spa, take along the folded cotton *yukata* (cotton kimono) and *obi* (sash) provided to wear afterward. The *ofuro* (baths) will be quite large, very hot, and separate for men and women. A Japanese bath is meant for soaking *after* washing and rinsing outside the tub. There may be also a *rotenburo* (outdoor spa) with shrubs or trees for privacy.

To find a *ryokan*, contact the Japanese Inn Group (www.jpinn.com), which offers rooms to international visitors for around ¥5,000 ($46), with meals extra.

Minshuku are family-run inns similar to bed-and-breakfasts, except with dinner also included in the price. Meals are served in a dining room, rather than your room as at *ryokan*. The price for two meals and lodging is typically around ¥7,000 ($64).

There are about 350 youth hostels in Japan (www.jyh.or.jp/english), scattered from Hokkaidō to Okinawa. They often mandate a curfew and rules for cleaning your room and attending meetings, but these are also opportunities to learn about Japanese culture. Hostels offer accommodations at a reasonable fee of around ¥3,000 ($27) per night.

Types of Food

TRADITIONAL

In a country surrounded by bountiful oceans, all manner of food from the sea has become part of the diet, from various kinds of seaweed to fish and whales (although there is mounting international pressure to cease and desist from killing the latter). Seafood seasoned with soy, along with rice and vegetables, are still the main ingredients for a healthy traditional meal. The idea that "sushi" refers to raw fish is a misconception common outside Japan. Sushi literally means "vinegared rice,"

> *In a country surrounded by bountiful oceans, all manner of food from the sea has become part of the diet, from various kinds of seaweed to fish and whales.*

referring to the seasoning of the rice before it is squeezed *(nigiri)*, rolled *(maki)*, or hand-rolled *(temaki)* and combined with strips of seafood (raw or not), vegetables, or eggs.

The national drink is also made from rice. Sake (pronounce the "e" as in "café"), served hot or cold, is a favorite accompaniment to traditional meals. When you arrive in Japan, you may be surprised to find vending machines everywhere supplying sake and alcoholic beverages (they shut down after 11 P.M. and display signs warning youth under age 20 not to purchase the products).

INTERNATIONAL

Meat consumption has increased dramatically in recent years, as can be witnessed at any Makudonarudo (McDonald's), Mos Burger, or Yakiniku (Korean barbecue) establishment. Don't be surprised to see new items on the menu at McDonald's, such as Teriyaki burgers and melon shakes. Mos Burger is famous for rice burgers—two grilled rice patties sandwiching strips of meat and vegetables. Eating more meat has resulted in rising cholesterol levels and higher rates of heart disease.

Although the traditional beverage, *ocha* (green tea), holds an honored place both in the tea ceremony and in everyday life (*ocha* is always free in Japanese restaurants), coffee has become extremely popular. Doutor was the first discount coffee shop to open in Japan. They revolutionized the market by selling coffee for ¥180 ($1.50) per cup, instead of the typical ¥400 ($3.80) or ¥500 ($4.75). Low prices, rapid service, and availability make it a place many commuters stop in the morning on their way to work. More recently, Starbucks landed from Seattle and has spread rapidly, as have numerous other chains. Japanese coffee is made to order, brewed by the cup, served in a fancy cup and saucer, and, many will say, is worth the price. Anywhere you find coffee, expect smokers to abound as well. If you don't smoke, try asking for *ki'n-en-seki* (a nonsmoking seat). If you're lucky, you'll be directed to two or three tables at the corner of a large room. Then enjoy the rush—no one in Japan has heard of decaffeinated.

When eating out or in, you'll have an array of choices that go beyond the traditional boundaries of Japanese cuisine, western, Korean, Indian, Nigerian, and so on. You can find pizza with sun-dried tomatoes and artichoke hearts, or *ika* (squid) and *nori* (dried seaweed); have your spaghetti in a bread bowl; and top it all off with *cream anmitsu* (sweet bean à la mode) for dessert.

Daily Life

© Kathy Kanagy

Making the Move

Visas and Immigration

A sashō (visa) is one of those necessary evils required for going international. Hopefully, in the future it will be possible to simply live as a world citizen and only need a visa for interplanetary travel. In the meantime, if you are headed to Japan and want to stay longer than 90 days, you will need some type of a visa obtained through a Japanese consulate in the United States. Your actual zairyū kikan (period of stay) in Japan and your zairyū shikaku (status of residence) will be recorded in your passport by an immigration officer at the airport where you land. A landing permit will be stamped in your passport, and your date of entry and the duration of valid stay in Japan will be written in as well. Make sure not to overstay your welcome!

One more critical point: Check that your passport is valid for at least

The Family Register System

Japan uses a family register system, in which an individual's personal details, such as birth and marriage, are officially recorded and notarized in a joint document for the whole family. Every time you want to do something official, such as register to enter each level of school, get a job, or get married, you must submit an official copy of your family's *koseki* (family register) to the appropriate place. The register contains all the births, deaths, marriages, divorces, mental illnesses, crimes, adoptions, and other events in your clan, going several generations back. When reaching adulthood (age 20), Japanese citizens can opt to establish an individual register, naming themselves as head.

Although foreigners living in Japan are not subject to the family register system (which is only for citizens), they are required to notify the government of any births, deaths, marriages, and divorces that occur in Japan, in accordance with the Family Register Law.

In order to make a report, go to the family register section of your local municipal office. The information you submit will be kept and used as evidence of your family status in Japan; you should also notify the government of your home country.

Birth Registration

Application Period: Within 14 days of birth.

Required Items: Birth registration form (available at your local ward or municipal office), birth certificate (ask the attending physician or midwife to complete the certification attached to the birth registration).

Note: Since a foreign parent must also complete the child's foreign resident registration and status of residence applications, in addition to birth registration, try to complete these forms together: 1) apply for a passport (at the appropriate foreign embassy); 2) apply for status of residence and period of stay (within 30

three months if you're arriving in Japan as a temporary visitor (90 days or less), and at least as long as the visa status and length of stay for which you're applying. You could be denied entry when you land if your passport expires sooner than your allowable period of stay.

TEMPORARY VISITORS

If you are an American entering Japan as a temporary visitor (tourist), you don't need a visa for a stay of up to 90 days. However, you must show a valid passport and a return ticket dated within 90 days. Authorized activities for temporary visitors to Japan include sightseeing, vacationing, playing sports, visiting family, going on site inspection tours, participating in lectures, and meeting business contacts.

What if you decide you want to stay longer? You will need to leave Japan, apply for a longer-term visa (such as a student visa, work visa, or cultural visa—see the next section) at a Japanese consulate outside Japan, and

days at the Tōkyō Immigration Bureau); and 3) apply for foreign resident registration (within 60 days).

Marriage Registration

Qualification: The conditions for a marriage to be considered valid differ from country to country. Foreigners in Japan should follow the laws of their own country. For Japanese citizens, legal marriage means the transfer of one person's name from their family register to the spouse's family register, and taking that family's surname. The name to be transferred can be either the wife's or the husband's. Sometimes, when a family has only daughters, one of the daughters will be matched to a man who is willing to enter her family's register and take her family name—and become a legally adopted son.

Required Items: Marriage registration form (the signatures of the man and woman to be married are required, along with the signatures or name stamps of two witnesses). Japanese nationals must also have their full or individual family register.

A foreign spouse must have the following: 1) passport; 2) foreign resident (alien) registration card; 3) birth certificate (with Japanese translation attached); and 4) a certificate affirming that he or she is legally competent to marry, issued by a diplomatic office or consulate in Japan (with Japanese translation attached). If you are unable to obtain this final document, you should include a copy of the law of the home country (with Japanese translation attached), a certificate issued by a consul office, or another such official document.

Note: A foreigner cannot obtain Japanese nationality simply by marrying a Japanese citizen and submitting a marriage registration. A foreigner's status of residence can be changed to a Spouse Visa. Contact the Immigration Bureau for details.

then reenter the country. See "Changing Your Status of Residence," later in this chapter, for more information.

VISA APPLICATIONS

If you are not a temporary visitor, but instead plan to stay for longer than 90 days and/or intend to work in Japan, you will need an appropriate visa to remain in the country. Before arriving in Japan, you must apply for a visa at a Japanese embassy or consulate in the United States. The Embassy of Japan is located in Washington, D.C., and its website (www.us.emb-japan.go.jp) gives detailed instructions on application procedures. Visit the same site (or the Resources section of this book) for locations and contact information for all consulate-generals of Japan in the U.S.

When you apply for a visa, you will need to submit the following documents in person (or possibly by mail—check with the individual consulate):

1. A valid passport

2. A Visa Application Form to Enter Japan (Form 1-C)

3. One two-inch-by-two-inch photo

4. An original *zairyū shikaku nintei shōmeisho* (certificate of eligibility) from the Immigration Bureau of Ministry of Justice in Japan (www.immi-moj.go.jp), and one photocopy. You should obtain this certificate through your sponsor in Japan. Getting a visa will go most smoothly this way, but if you have no certificate of eligibility, you will need the first three items above, plus the following documents:

5. A copy of the acceptance letter from the Japanese institution you will attend. In addition, if you are attending a vocational school, you must present evidence of your Japanese language skills (such as showing you passed Level 2 of the Japanese Language Proficiency Test—for more information, visit the Association of International Education at www.aiej.or.jp and click on English).

6. Documents certifying that you can defray all expenses incurred during your stay in Japan (such as a bank statement or official proof of receipt of scholarships or grants).

7. A photocopy of all the above documents.

The exact documents required vary depending on the particular status of residence. See the next section for more information.

TYPES OF VISAS

Student Visa

A student visa is for those entering a college or junior college in Japan for longer than 90 days. If you are going to Japan on an exchange program with your university, or have been admitted directly to a Japanese university or junior college, you need this type of visa to enter the country. Housing is often included for participants, and the host university may assist you in obtaining a student visa.

If you are already in Japan, you may be able to get a student visa if you enroll full-time in a Japanese language school or *senmon gakkō* (technical school). In this case, your school may be able to act as your sponsor or guarantor. With a student visa, you are allowed to work legally up to 20 hours per week (teaching English, working in a fast-food restaurant, etc.), but first you must apply to the immigration bureau for permission.

Cultural Activities Visa

Cultural activities include academic or artistic activities that provide no income, or activities for the purpose of pursuing specific studies on

A slice of daily life along the old Nakasendō route in Tōkyō, now truck Route 17

© Ruthy Kanagy

Japanese culture or arts, or activities for the purpose of learning about Japanese culture or arts under the guidance of experts (excluding activities allowed by a student visa). The period of stay is usually six months to a year.

Work Visas

There are 14 categories of work visas. Each type has specific parameters: professor, artist, religious activity, journalist, investor/business manager, legal/accounting service, medical service, researcher, instructor, engineer, humanities service/international services, intracompany transferee, entertainer, and skilled labor. In addition to the brief descriptions below, you'll find detailed information on the website of the Embassy of Japan (www.us.emb-japan.go.jp).

At a minimum, you should have a college degree in any field, or prove that you have significant experience (ten years is a good length—in Japan, it takes ten years to become a sushi chef or to master any art) in a certain field. Then you will need to seek out a school or business to give you a job and be your guarantor to obtain a working visa. Work visas are generally good for six months, one year, or three years. The longer you stay in Japan, the better your chance of obtaining a longer visa.

Instructor
This visa is for providers of language instruction and other education at elementary schools, junior high schools, senior high schools, schools for the blind, schools for disabled children, *kakushu gakkō* and *senshu gakkō* (miscellaneous schools), or equivalent institutions.

Artist
An artist visa is for producers of artwork that provides income, such as composers, songwriters, artists, sculptors, craftspeople, and photographers.

Humanities/International Services
This type of visa is for those who engage in service requiring knowledge pertinent to jurisprudence, economics, sociology, or other human science fields. These services must require specific ways of thought or sensitivity based on experience with foreign culture, such as interpreting, translation, copywriting, fashion design, interior design, sales, overseas business, information processing, international finance, design, or public relations and advertising based on a contract with a public or private organization in Japan.

Investor/Business Manager
An investor/business manager visa covers those involved in the operation of international trade or other businesses, investors in international trade or other businesses, and those who operate or manage international trade or other businesses on behalf of foreign nationals (including corporations) who have begun such an operation or invested in such a business. The business in question must meet certain conditions of scale. Applicants who wish to engage in business management must fulfill specific conditions concerning work status and personal history.

Professor
This visa is granted to those who perform research, research guidance, or teaching services for institutions specializing in education, such as professors and assistant professors at universities, college, or *kōtō senmon gakkō* (technical colleges).

Researcher
The Researcher visa is for research activities performed under contract with public or private institutes in Japan, excluding activities described under "Professor," above. I had this visa while I was a foreign researcher at the National Institute for Japanese Language in Tōkyō. At first, my re-

search visa was valid for one year. Then I renewed for another one-year period. The next time I went to renew my visa, they gave me a three-year research visa without my asking. Luckily, I had the proper certificate of eligibility form from my institute, and my immediate supervisor kindly agreed to act as my guarantor. (That's a big favor to ask, because if I got in trouble with the law or skipped the country with unpaid rent, my guarantor would be personally liable. Treat guarantors with care.)

REQUIRED MUNICIPAL OFFICE PROCEDURES

Alien Registration

Once settled in Japan, you must complete more official paperwork—this time at your local municipal office. Everyone who is staying in Japan more than 90 days must go through *gaikokujin tōroku* (alien registration) within the first 90 days of entry to Japan. Here's the official description: All foreigners residing in Japan (except those who have received permission to enter Japan temporarily or for transit purposes, diplomats, consular officials, their families, and persons staying in Japan under the Japan-U.S. Status-of-Forces Agreement) are obliged to register as foreign residents when they enter Japan, obtain foreign citizenship while in Japan, or are born in Japan. Foreigners should complete Alien Registration (also called Foreign Resident Registration) at their local ward or municipal (city, town, or village) office (at the Foreign Resident Registration Desk) and receive a foreign resident registration card.

Here's what you need to take when applying for initial registration:
1. Two photographs (taken within the last six months; not required for applicants under 16 years of age) 4.5 centimeters (1.8 inches) in length and up to 3.5 centimeters (1.4 inches) in width, showing a full frontal view of the face without a hat.
2. A signature is required.

When applying for initial registration, you will be informed when your foreign resident registration card will be issued. You must pick up your card within this period. However, foreigners under 16 years of age will be issued a card immediately upon application.

Foreign resident registration cards give the person's name, date of birth, sex, nationality, address, status of residence, occupation, place of work, and other details. The card for permanent residents and special permanent residents include all these items of information except occupation and place of work. Foreigners 16 years of age or over must carry this card with them at all times. Please keep in mind that police and other officials may ask to see your card whenever necessary.

Why do foreigners have to register? By registering, your identity and residence are verified, and you will have a card to keep with you at all times. This is "necessary for the administration of public programs such as education, welfare, medical fees, and immigration control," according to the Immigration Bureau. Thankfully, gone are the days when you were forcibly fingerprinted into a little brown notebook you had to carry around.

Your Alien Registration Card must be carried with you at all times, and should be turned in when you leave Japan without a reentry permit in your passport.

IMMIGRATION BUREAU RESIDENCY PROCEDURES
You will need to apply at your regional immigration bureau in Japan when temporarily leaving Japan, extending your period of stay, and for any procedure related to your status of residence (such as changing your visa category or requesting permission for any activities other than those authorized). When making such applications, you must present your passport and Alien Registration Certificate.

© Ruthy Kanagy

Tōkyō Metropolitan Government buildings in Shinjuku offer resources for residents.

Temporarily Leaving Japan

If you are leaving Japan temporarily (for a home visit, to tour another country, etc.), you must apply for a *sainyūkoku kyoka* (reentry permit) in order to come back into Japan. You can do this at the Tōkyō Regional Immigration Bureau and other branch offices. Apply for either a single reentry permit (for ¥3,000/$27) or a multiple reentry permit (for ¥6,000/$54). The latter is good for the duration of your visa (six months, one year, or three years) and handy if you expect to travel out and back several times. These procedures must be strictly followed, or you run the risk of not being allowed to enter Japan again. I learned this the hard way when, ignorant of the rule, I went on a one-week vacation to Korea from Hokkaidō, where I was teaching at a university. When I landed in Sapporo at New Chitose Airport, I was detained and questioned for several hours as to why I did not have a reentry permit. Without a permit, I had forfeited my teaching visa. I was only released after I had written a letter of apology (in Japanese) stating that I would not make the same mistake again and promised to go to the immigration bureau to sort things out. I was lucky!

Extending Your Period of Stay

Your *zairyū kikan no kōshin* (period of stay) is determined together with your status of residence at the time you land in Japan. Foreigners are only allowed to stay in Japan within a set period of time. If you would like to remain in Japan under the same status of residence beyond your authorized period of stay, you must apply for and obtain an extension. To do so, apply at your local immigration office no later than the expiration date of your authorized period of stay (applications are usually accepted up to two months in advance). Anyone who stays in Japan beyond the authorized period of stay is subject to punishment and/or deportation by law.

Changing Your Status of Residence

Foreigners who would like to stop their present activity and concentrate on an activity that is different from what is authorized under their current status of residence must apply for—and obtain—a change of *zairyū shikaku no henkō* (status of residence). The submission of such an application does not necessarily guarantee its approval. Anyone receiving income from an activity other that what is authorized under his or her status of residence, or anyone who conducts unauthorized activities with remuneration without first obtaining this permission, is subject to punishment and/or deportation by law.

Unauthorized Activities

Foreigners who would like to engage in an activity involving the management of a business or any remuneration other than what is authorized under the assigned status of residence must apply for—and obtain—permission to do so in advance. Foreigners engaging in an activity other than those authorized are subject to punishment by law.

PERMANENT RESIDENCY

The main benefit of this status is not having to apply for visas every time you want to live in Japan—but keep in mind that half the "registered foreigners" in Japan are second- or third-generation permanent residents (usually Korean or Chinese). It's not impossible to obtain *eijūken* (permanent residency), but it takes connections, money, a good guarantor, and up to about ten years. If you marry a Japanese person, the time can be as short as five years. I also know a number of internationals in Japan who got permanent residency after living in the country for five years—without being married to a Japanese. So, it's possible, albeit difficult, to move the process along more quickly.

Traditional-style house on a large lot

© Ruthy Kanagy

Naturalization

What if you want to go all the way and become a citizen of Japan? Just so you know, in most cases this means giving up your present citizenship. Children born with dual citizenship don't *legally* have to give up one or the other, although the Japanese government would like them to do so. At the Immigration Bureau, there are posters of people standing on a globe, cheerfully saying, "Let's all choose just one citizenship." If I didn't have to give up my U.S. citizenship and could just add Japanese to the list, I'd do it in a heartbeat.

If you want to pursue Japanese citizenship, naturalization is the primary way for foreigners to do so. Application for naturalization must be made at the Ministry of Justice, Nationality Division, Tōkyō Legal Affairs Bureau, Kudan Building No. 2, 1-1-15 Kudan Minami, Chiyoda-ku, Tōkyō 102-8225, tel. 03/5213-1234.

Moving with Children

DEPENDENT VISA

If you are coming to Japan with a student or work visa and have family members accompanying you, they will need to apply for a Dependent Visa at a Japanese consulate office *outside* Japan in order to enter the country. A spouse or children of someone residing in Japan with the visa status of Professor, Researcher, or Cultural Activities are eligible for dependent residence status. Normally, the period of stay for dependents is three months, six months, one year, or three years. If your dependent plans to stay in Japan for more than 90 days, he or she must also apply for alien registration.

MAKING THE ADJUSTMENT

Children face their own challenges when moving to a new country. Make sure to provide plenty of support—familiar books, toys, music, photographs of extended family and close friends, and some favorite foods. Allow them time to get adjusted to their new surroundings, and try not to push them to play with children they don't know. If your children are old enough, help them write a postcard or email to a friend back home. Above all, as a parent, give them your time and emotional support, although you may be busy with the many tasks of setting up house in a new culture. When your children are ready, plan ways to learn Japanese together, go shopping, or take outings. But I recommend starting slowly—riding a subway may be a big enough activity by itself. Don't fill up the schedule too much.

Sunday is for family recreation.

I was four years old the first time I went to a new country. My parents were going back to Indiana for a year of furlough from their missionary work, and I found myself in a strange place filled with new tastes (like Froot Loops), a new language, and relatives I'd heard about but had never met. I was too young to go to school, so I stayed home and played with buttons from my grandmother's sewing basket. The second time we moved back to the States, I was eleven and attended an English school for the first time. I could speak English, but heard a lot of words that weren't in my vocabulary, and sometimes got laughed at for not knowing common slang words. Your child may face similar challenges living in Japan or going to a Japanese school. Finding him or her a buddy to help ease the transition will make a big difference.

> *Despite some adjustments, the pluses of growing up in two cultures far outweigh the challenges.*

But despite some adjustments, the pluses of growing up in two cultures far outweigh the challenges. Learning two or more languages from infancy has been shown to stimulate and develop brain cells, since brain capacity increases through mapping multiple sets of vocabularies and grammars. On a social level, knowing more than one language and culture gives children (and adults) a broader worldview and empathy for people from other places. Home is no longer just one country—"one nation indivisible" extends to "one earth indivisible." There are practical advantages as well—being bilingual and bicultural will be an advantage when your child establishes a career. You as a parent can give your family that opportunity.

Moving with Pets

You may want to bring your favorite cat, dog, or other pet to Japan. It can be done, but there are many requirements involved. First of all, upon arrival (with the proper documents), your pet will be quarantined for two weeks or longer at the airport. During this period, you are responsible for feeding and caring for your pet, who will be housed in a kennel. (If you're landing at Narita Airport, note that Narita is located in the neighboring Chiba prefecture, not in metropolitan Tōkyō. Depending on where you are staying, it could take two or three hours to get to the airport from Tōkyō.) Also keep in mind that most apartments in Japan do not allow pets. A few do, but you will have to hunt for them; and there may be extra fees for keeping a pet, such as a deposit.

In my case, I decided not to bring my dog to Japan and left her with several trustworthy friends at home. I didn't want to subject her to the trauma of air travel, quarantine, and adjustment to an unfamiliar place. Moreover, there was no grass or dirt near my apartment, only concrete and asphalt—not much space to run around, and not much fun.

However, if you do decide to bring your pet—and you may have compelling reasons—here's how. The agency that regulates the transport of animals into Japan is the Animal Quarantine Service of the Ministry of Agriculture, Forestry, and Fisheries (www.maff-aqs.go.jp/english/index.htm). Their policy on dogs reads as follows:

If you bring a pet dog with you from abroad, it will be detained for a quarantine inspection for a fixed period of time after arrival in Japan in order to examine it for the presence of rabies and leptospirosis. Detention inspections are normally conducted at Animal Quarantine Stations and require that animals be isolated from people and other animals in order to check for the presence of illness or disease. Detention will continue for a period of 14 to 180 days, depending on the existence and the content of rabies vaccination and health certificates issued by the relevant authorities in the country of departure. However, if you bring a dog with you from one of the designated rabies-free areas (only Hawaii in the U.S.), the detention period may be as short as 12 hours.

In addition, if your dog has not had a rabies vaccination, she will be kept in detention for a period of 30 days—if you have a certificate issued by a government agency in your country of departure containing a statement to the effect that the animal was raised in isolation and that certain conditions have been satisfied. Please be aware that you will not be able to bring your dog into Japan if you do not have a health certificate issued by a government agency. There are 17 ports and airports in Japan through which you may bring your dog (visit the URL provided above for contact information).

There is no cost for the rabies and leptospirosis examination while your dog is held in detention. However, the dog's owner is responsible for the care of his or her dog during that time.

There is a requirement that you register a dog (91 days old or older) at the local municipal office and receive a dog license. In addition, the dog must have a rabies vaccination once a year at some point between April and June, and receive a Completion of Rabies Vaccination Tag. The license and tag must be attached to the dog's collar at all times.

All dogs must be leashed or caged when outdoors, except in designated dog parks (see http://living-with-dogs.com/en/dogrun/drjp-e.html

Dressed-up dog at Asakusa

© Ruthy Kanagy

for park descriptions). Some restaurants and hotels accept pets. For further information, contact your local municipal office.

See the Ministry of Agriculture website for requirements for cats and other pets. For additional information, contact your local ward or municipal office, local public health center, or the Veterinary Sanitation Section, Living Environment Division, Bureau of Public Health, Tōkyō Metropolitan Government (tel. 03/5320-4412).

What to Take

Almost everything you need to set up house in Japan can be purchased after you arrive—linens, kitchenware, furniture, television, DVD players, and so on. Many household items can be found for a reasonable price at "recycle shops" and ¥100 stores (the equivalent of a dollar store, but with many more items). In a nutshell: Take only what you can't live without.

However, do bring as much money as you can for startup costs. Getting the key to an apartment can set you back as much as $5,000. Costs are lower in smaller cities and towns away from urban centers. Any amount up to ¥1 million ($9,090) in any currency is not subject to customs declaration when you enter Japan.

Electronics and Media

As far as voltage goes, your laptop computer will operate with no problem in Japan (which uses 100V versus our 120V). You can also buy a computer in Japan—the English classifieds might be a good place to find one—although the Japanese keyboard has a slightly different configuration. Software sold in stores is, naturally, all in Japanese.

Your American cell phone, however, will not work in Japan. Phone voltage is too different—100V and 50Hz in the east (including Tōkyō), and 60Hz in the west (including Kyōto and Ōsaka). But the good news is that used electronics stores are abundant and cheap.

To protect market share, DVD software and players are regulated through region-specific codes. If the DVD and player are not from the same region, they are incompatible. For example, region 2 software (manufactured for Japan) can only be played on region 2 DVD players. The regions are designated as follows:

Region 1—United States, Canada
Region 2—Japan, Europe, Middle East, South Africa, Egypt
Region 3—East Asia, Southeast Asia, Hong Kong
Region 4—Australia, Central America, Caribbean, South America

Region 5—Former Soviet Union, North Korea, Mongolia, South Asia, Africa (other than South Africa)

Region 6—China

So, if you bring your DVD player from the U.S. to Japan, it most likely will not be able to read Japanese software. However, some software and players are region-free. So, if you purchase a region-free (or code-free) player, it will play most any DVD from any part of the world. Make sure to note whether the warranty is international or limited to the country of purchase.

Standard TV frequencies and FM radio (from 76 to 90 MHz) are different than in North America. You can get English news and other bilingual broadcasts in Tōkyō and other large cities.

Comfort Food

Most large department stores in Japan have an international foods section where you can find such exotic items as Skippy's peanut butter, taco shells, and pretzels. But if you have any favorite seasoning mixes, spices, herbal teas, microwave popcorn, macaroni and cheese, or tortilla chips, you may want to bring along a supply. Also, don't forget that decaffeinated coffee doesn't exist in Japan!

Clothing and Shoes

If you are a tall woman (over 5'7") or wear shoes larger than a size eight, it's a good idea to bring most of the clothing and shoes you will need in Japan from home. Larger sizes are available, but only in major department stores and specialty shops, and prices are quite steep. Japanese clothing and shoes tend to be well-tailored and high in quality, but shoes may cost $200 or more, and a two-piece suit for women $300 or more. Women's clothing sizes are 9, 11, 13, 15, 17 (L), 19 (2L), 3L, and 4L. However, if you're smaller in stature, you'll have no problem finding clothing to fit.

Men's shirts come in the following neck sizes, in centimeters: 36 (14 in), 37 (14.5 in), 38 (15 in), 39 (15.5 in), 40 (16 in), 41 (16.5 in), 42 (17 in), and so on. Shoe sizes for both genders are also measured in centimeters. The following sizes are approximate: 23 (women's 6.5), 24 (women's 7), 25 (women's 8.5, men's 7), 26 (women's 9.5, men's 8.5), 27 (men's 9.5), 27.5 (men's 10.5). Again, if you wear a larger size, bring your own shoes to Japan. (See sizing chart in Resources.)

SHIPPING COMPANIES

The cost of shipping to Japan may seem reasonable, but the cost of shipping goods home again is quite high. This applies to books as well. U.S. post offices have large canvas bags that hold up to 40 pounds of books, but shipping them back from Japan is the hard part. I paid about $100 for each small box of general goods, and only a little less to mail books to the U.S.—and the books had to be in small parcels of 10 pounds or less to qualify for book rate. My total cost was about $1,000 for postage.

To get an idea of shipping costs to or from Japan, contact Nippon Express or OPAS Ship to Japan (an affiliate of DHL) for free estimates. See the Resources section for complete contact information.

Other means of transporting items, such as via container ship, are available if you plan to bring a large quantity of household goods. However, packing light and buying or borrowing once you reach your destination helps to establish solidarity with your new home, and shopping for items is an excellent way to interact with your new neighborhood and introduce yourself to local shopkeepers.

Language and Education

Nihon go (Japanese language) is standard throughout Japan, taught in schools and used in public and private life. *Hōgen* (regional dialects) are spoken in many parts of the country, and Okinawa has its own language. However, the use of standard Japanese is widespread, thanks to television and a common educational curriculum. Though the writing system is complex—it combines 2,000 characters borrowed from Chinese, along with several sets of phonetic letters—Japanese people are highly literate. Nine years of schooling are devoted to learning to read and write the characters.

Spoken Japanese is not as hard as you might expect. Unlike in many European languages, you don't need to worry about gender or person agreement or plural and singular forms. The subject of most sentences is understood from context, so a few key phrases will go a long way toward communicating with Japanese acquaintances. If you learn the appropriate greetings for various times of day, when leaving and coming back, before and after eating, and when offering and receiving something, your interactions with locals will become much smoother.

Most people will appreciate your attempts to speak Japanese. Just for fun, try greeting your Japanese neighbor or shopkeeper some morning by naming the Midwestern state of "Ohio" in a cheery voice. They'll probably say *"Ohayō"* ("Good morning") back, and might even add, *"Nihon go jōzu desu ne"* ("Your Japanese is very good"). With some effort and discipline, you can learn to carry on basic conversations in a matter of months, especially if you surround yourself with Japanese language and people.

Learning the Language

Over the past 500 years of contact with the West, Japanese has absorbed thousands of words from English, German, French, Portuguese, and other languages. These words accompanied new information about government, economy, medicine, education, sports, cuisine, and clothing. Many new terms continue to arrive alongside computers and other forms of technology.

Most Japanese words are written in Japanese script, but the Latin alphabet is used extensively for special effects in advertisements and music, and as an aid for foreign visitors. Signs in train stations are generally transcribed alphabetically underneath the Japanese script for the benefit of those who cannot read the characters.

WRITTEN JAPANESE

Japanese is written in a combination of *kana* and *kanji* scripts. *Kana* are 46 phonetic syllables. *Kanji* are 2,000 characters borrowed from China in the 6th century, when the Japanese had no written form. Japanese characters took the shape and meaning of *kanji*, but incorporated Japanese pronunciations, in addition to retaining some Chinese pronunciations. *Kana* come in two versions, both with the same pronunciation (think of cursive versus printed writing). *Hiragana* are smooth and rounded in shape, while *katakana* are square and angular. Unlike the American alphabet, where a letter is either a single consonant or a vowel, each *kana* is a whole syllable, such as *ka* or *shi*.

Hiragana are used to show verb endings (past, present, polite, and so on) and appear in many native Japanese words. In contrast, *katakana* are used to write words borrowed from Western languages, as well as sound effects (for example, in anime action). They are also used for emphasis,

This sign outside a traditional house reads: "Tea ceremony and flower arranging school," with names and phone numbers.

similarly to our use of italics. If you go to any coffee shop or fast food restaurant, the menu will be written almost entirely in *katakana,* because most items originated in the West. Thus, "ko-o-hi-i" (coffee) contains four *katakana* letters, and "ha-n-ba-a-ga-a" (hamburger) has six *katakana.* Spelling is not a problem for Japanese children, because the name of each *kana* and its sound are one and the same. Once they learn the 46 *kana,* first graders can write long compositions.

Kanji are another story. The Ministry of Education, Culture, Sports, Science, and Technology (hereafter called the Ministry of Education) has designated approximately 2,000 *kanji* as official characters for use in written Japanese. Learning this many characters takes time. In school, students learn 100 to 200 *kanji* a year and have weekly *kanji* quizzes. Since it takes nine years for Japanese children to learn all the *kanji* characters, anyone new to Japan should not expect to master them in a year or two. Take your time learning *kanji*—when you are surrounded by them, you will soon learn to recognize the names of cities, your local train station, and the characters for your favorite department store. There are many good books on learning *kanji;* a few are listed in the Resources section of this book. It may take a while until you can read a

How to Read Japanese

You will see four kinds of scripts used in Japan—*hiragana, katakana, kanji,* and the alphabet. *Hiragana* are used to write verb endings (past, present, polite, etc.), grammatical markers (subject, object, topic, etc.), and many native Japanese words (as opposed to words taken from Chinese or English). *Katakana* are used when writing words from foreign languages other than Chinese, as well as for sound effects (as in animation) and italic-like emphasis.

In contrast, whole concepts and words borrowed from Chinese (they're at least 5,000 years old) are written in *kanji.* Written Chinese consists entirely of tens of thousands of *kanji,* but Japanese limits *kanji* to a select 2,000. Their forms and meaning come from China, but the pronunciation is Japanese. It's important to realize that even though the Japanese borrowed China's writing system, they applied it to their own native language. Spoken Chinese and Japanese bear no resemblance to each other; Chinese is tonal, while Japanese is not.

newspaper, but if you become familiar with the most frequently used *kanji,* you'll learn how to guess the rest. *Kanji* are your friends, once you get acquainted with their shapes, strokes, characteristics, and common traits. You have to know most of the *kanji* to be able to read a newspaper and feel comfortably literate.

SPOKEN JAPANESE

Basic Japanese conversation is not as difficult as you may think. A lot can be said in few words. Unlike in many European languages, you don't have to worry about gender markers, plurals, the future tense (it's the same as present tense), or conjugating verbs for the first person, second person, and so on. The subjects of sentences are generally understood from context and omitted when understood, just as in Spanish. The pronouns I, you, she, they, etc., are infrequently used; instead, names or titles are used when referring or talking to people.

Desu is the "to be" verb, and it doesn't change with the person. Word order in Japanese is almost a mirror image of English word order: subject, then object, then verb. So, if you want to say "I'm Tom," say *"Tomu desu";* if you want to say, "She's Mary," say, *"Merii desu";* and if you want to say, "They are my friends," say, *"Tomodachi desu"* (*tomodachi* means "friend" or "friends").

Regional Dialects

A dialect is the familiar, at-home language that stamps you as part of a particular town or region. It's the way you talk with family and neighbors, with shopkeepers, and over cups of sake. The funny thing is, your own accent and way of speaking feel so natural that you don't know it's a dialect until you meet someone with a different accent who tells you so. In Japan, depending on the social status assigned to your particular community by those of higher status, they may tell you that you talk funny, especially if you're from Aomori in northern Honshū and they're from Tōkyō. This happens over and over as young people from the outlying prefectures of Japan move to Tōkyō to go to school, find a job, or become musicians.

Japan is still rich in *hōgen* (dialects), due to extremely mountainous terrain that separates one community from the next, but in recent years they have reportedly begun to diminish. Starting in 1868, the Tōkyō dialect became viewed as standard and was adopted in schoolbooks throughout the country. Japanese dialects can broadly be divided into east and west from Nagoya, in the middle of Honshū, halfway between Tōkyō and Ōsaka. Depending on where you choose to live, there may be more or less of a local dialect, as in Tōhoku or northeast Honshū, central and western Honshū, and in the cities of Ōsaka, Kōbe, and Kyōto. Shikoku and Kyūshū have regional dialects, and Okinawa has its own language. The primary exception is Hokkaidō, where its recent history of immigration by Japanese from many different prefectures in the south has resulted in the use of standard Japanese. But no matter where you are in the country, most people speak standard Japanese, with the possible exception of the oldest generation.

WHERE TO STUDY

I highly recommend that you study Japanese before going to Japan. Most colleges in the States teach the language, and many have intensive summer programs where you can learn a year's worth of Japanese in nine weeks. If you aren't near a university, check the Resources section in this book for online Japanese learning sites. Another option is to look for a private tutor—a Japanese student or visitor living in your town. Try to memorize at least the 46 *katakana* letters before you arrive in Japan, and learn how to write your name. Many universities in the U.S. have study abroad and exchange programs with universities in Japan that include housing, language studies, and cultural activities for three months to a year. Once you arrive in Japan, you can find a language school in any sizeable city, and, most likely, a network of volunteer citizens who can teach you Japanese. Check with the *shiyakusho* (city hall)—or *kuyakusho* (ward), if you're in Tōkyō—for details.

Would you like to get paid to learn Japanese? The Japanese Ministry of

English with a Japanese Touch

If you develop an ear for English words pronounced in the Japanese style, you'll have an instant vocabulary of thousands of Japanese terms! And if you learn to pronounce English words with a slight Japanese accent, it will become much easier for Japanese speakers to understand what you say.

Vowels

The five English vowels (a, e, i, o, u) can be pronounced 14 different ways. For example, the same letter "a" in apple, ate, father, Paul, and beautiful represents five different sounds. But in Japanese, the five letters for vowels have only one possible pronunciation apiece:

Say "a" like p*a*pa
Say "i" like p*i*zza
Say "u" like p*u*t
Say "e" like pet
Say "o" like port

If there are multiple vowels in a row, as in the word *aoi* (blue), say *a-o-i* as three distinct vowels.

Consonants

If you know Spanish, you're already ahead in pronouncing Japanese, since words in both languages have mostly consonant-vowel syllables. All Japanese words end in a vowel sound, except for those ending with the letter "n." If two vowels are next to each other, pronounce each vowel separately.

A word of caution: The spoken Japanese representation of "r" bears no resemblance to the American pronunciation of "r." It is more like a soft "d" sound, very close to the Spanish "r," where your tongue flaps against your palette briefly. We use this sound frequently in English words, but it looks like a "t": karate, party, photo, butter. So, whenever you see the syllables ra, ri, ru, re, or ro written out, remember the "t" you're accustomed to making—then, without rounding your lips, make that same sound.

Japanese words follow a consonant-vowel, consonant-vowel sequence. So, if each consonant sound in a foreign term is not followed by a vowel, insert the sound "u" after it—unless the consonant is "t" or "d," in which case add the sound "o." Here are some commonly used words in Japanese. Each syllable (separated by hyphens below) has the same length, and pronunciation is somewhat monotone.

English Word	Japanese Pronunciation
bed	be-d-do
pet	pe-t-to
cheese	chi-i-zu
McDonald's	Ma-ku-do-na-ru-do
orange juice	o-re-n-ji ju-u-su
pineapple	pa-i-na-p-pu-ru
steak	su-te-e-ki
skirt	su-ka-a-to
computer	ko-n-pyu-u-ta-a
girlfriend	ga-a-ru fu-re-n-do

This process of "nativizing" foreign words is nothing new. Think of how English speakers pronounce these imported words: sake, karaoke, karate, Paris, and Renault. The way we say them wouldn't be recognized by native speakers. Just as we automatically Americanize foreign words, the Japanese unconsciously give English words a Japanese accent. If you also pronounce English words with a Japanese touch, it will ease communication with your neighbors.

Education, Culture, Sports, Science, and Technology (www.mext.go.jp/english) has scholarships for foreign students who wish to enroll in a Japanese university for a year or more. You may have to apply from overseas. These programs offer the advantages of a sponsor and a student visa; one drawback may be restrictions on working while enrolled as a full-time student.

Recently, many online Japanese language and learning sites have cropped up. One good example is a new site for mobile phones called TangoTown (http://tangotown.jp/tangotown), designed to assist English-speakers living in Japan. It includes Japanese and *kanji* dictionaries, phone listings, bilingual articles, phrasebooks, games, and daily lessons like "Word of the Day" and "*Kanji* of the Day." See the Resources section for additional information on language sites.

Education

Public school education in Japan began in the early Meiji period (1868) and was modeled on European and American systems. Until that time, education was limited to males of the upper class. Today, all Japanese children must complete ninth grade, the final year of junior high school. After age 15, school is no longer compulsory—yet more than 95 percent of students complete high school, because without a diploma, job options are severely limited. Boys and girls take all their classes together, from science and language to home economics and shop, and they learn starting in the first grade to clean their classrooms and their school every day in teams. The school year begins in April and ends the following March, with 220 school days divided into three terms. Summer vacation is the longest, lasting from July 20 (Ocean Day) to the end of August, with some variations. The national government has always been a strong presence in Japanese education, as indicated by the Ministry of Education, Sports, and Culture, which screens school textbooks and establishes a uniform curriculum. When students move to another part of Japan, they may very well continue using the same textbook on the same page where they left off.

Every culture teaches certain values to its youth at home and in school. Japanese schoolchildren learn the social rules considered essential for their educational years and for life as an adult member of society. One key notion is *minna issho* (everyone together/the same). Rather than praising a child's innate ability or I.Q., teachers repeatedly reinforce the idea of *ganbaru* (trying hard). Before high school, students are not tracked by ability level into different reading or math levels; instead, each class represents a heterogeneous mix of talent and interests. All students are expected to put great effort in their studies, as well as in the mandatory after-school clubs that commence in junior high. Students who move on to high school must call forth strenuous effort—most are coached on passing the stiff subject-based entrance exams at an after-school *juku* ("cram school") that they attend on a daily basis. Almost half of Japanese young people seek a university degree, many with the goal of interviewing for jobs with prestigious firms. Some students may choose to take a break by traveling or studying overseas before starting a career.

ELEMENTARY AND JUNIOR HIGH SCHOOLS

School organization is fairly uniform throughout Japan under the direction of the Ministry of Education. In the 6-3-3-4 system, six years of elementary school (ages 6–12) and three years of junior high school (ages 12–15) comprise nine years of compulsory education. Three years of high school and four years of university are optional, and students must pass difficult examinations to gain entrance to the school of their

Mothers walking home with new first-graders

© Ruthy Kanagy

choice. The school year is divided into three terms beginning in April and ending the following March, for a total of 220 instructional days per year (compared to 180 days or less in the U.S.). Until 2003, students attended school for a half-day on Saturdays, but this practice has been phased out. Summer vacation begins nationwide on July 20 and lasts about 40 days.

The Ministry issues curriculum guidelines and screens textbooks. There is much less autonomy at the school district, building, and teacher levels than in the more decentralized U.S. model. On the other hand, scholastic achievement is higher in Japan, according to the results of comparative studies. Also compared to the States, classroom size is large, with up to 40 students. Another difference is that the same group of classmates studies all their subjects together in the same classroom in elementary and junior high school. In junior high, teachers of different subjects rotate through the classrooms while the students stay put. Students are not tracked according to reading level, math skills, or other abilities during the first nine years of their education. Instead, they learn to study in heterogeneous groups (a wide range of abilities) and work cooperatively in *han* (teams).

Everyone in Japan studies English from grades 7–12 and in university. However, the primary goal of English class is to pass the problems on entrance exams for high school and university—and since the students are so busy, they don't have much opportunity to learn to speak English. In addition, most Japanese teachers of English rarely have the chance to speak the language. Teaching methods still involve translation and memorization of vocabulary, again in preparation for exams.

CHOOSING A SCHOOL

Japanese Schools
Although foreign residents are not obligated to attend Japanese educational institutions, children of the appropriate age may enter or transfer to local elementary and junior high schools. If you would like your child to attend a municipal school, you may inquire about elementary and junior high schools in your neighborhood at School Affairs No. 1 Subsection, School Affairs Section, City Board of Education, Tōkyō, tel. 03/3546-5514. You can also obtain information from your local city hall if you live in the 23 *ku* (wards) or the outlying cities in Tōkyō. In some cities, foreign parents whose children go to private kindergarten (ages 3–5) may be eligible for a subsidy from the city. Municipal elementary and junior high schools

Elementary-school children wear leather backpacks covered with yellow safety signs.

provide school lunches. Some financial support is also available for elementary and junior high school students.

International Schools

International schools may be a good choice if you live within reasonable commuting distance and are prepared to pay the fees. Tuition and fees can run $10,000–20,000 per year. International schools with instruction in English include Nishimachi International School (in Minato-ku), American School in Japan (near Mitaka), and Christian Academy in Japan (west of Ikebukuro).

With all these options, how do you choose between Japanese and international schools? Consider the following factors: Is the school within walking distance, or does it require a bus or train ride? (There are no public school buses.) Where do the children in your neighborhood go to school? Who will your child play with after school? If your children don't know Japanese, is there a teacher at the school who can communicate in English and coach them in Japanese? How much will it cost? Choosing a school also relates to your worldview as a parent—namely, whether you would prefer that your children find a little bit of America in Japan, or if you would rather they experience total immersion in Japanese culture.

One more point to consider—do you want to give your child the opportunity to become bilingual and bicultural? In my view, this is the most critical question. My experience of attending Japanese kindergarten, elementary, and junior high schools laid the foundation for my career and contributed to my identity. Childhood is the best time to become a natural bilingual who understands another culture through its language. Whether your stay in Japan is more or less than a year, it's a once-in-a-lifetime chance for your child to learn Japanese and make Japanese friends. English-speakers can travel the world and insist that everyone speak *our* language, but understanding the values and culture of another country comes only through learning the local language.

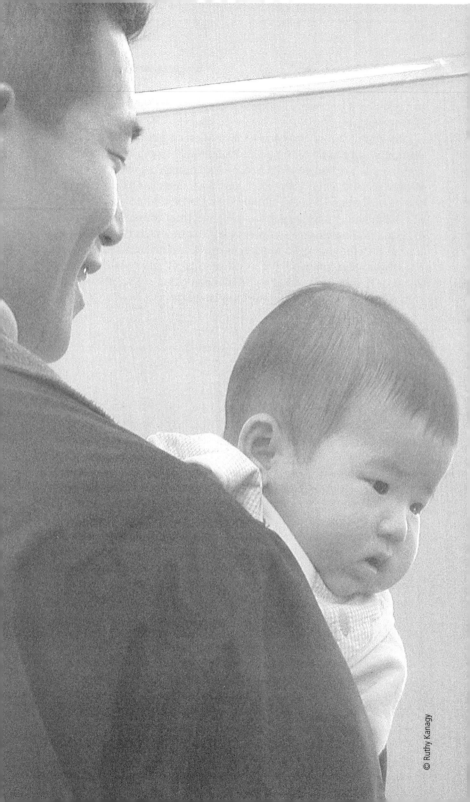

© Ruthy Kanagy

Health

People in Japan enjoy one of the longest life expectancies in the world. Japanese women live an average of 85.3 years, according to 2003 statistics, while men have an average life span of 78.4 years. These figures have been rising since World War II and suggest that Japanese society must be doing something right, healthwise. Could it be related to the fact that basic health care is guaranteed to everyone in Japan—young, old, urban, rural, rich, poor—through a system of public medical insurance? The practice of immunizing every baby at public health clinics and every school-age child at school may also contribute. Foreign residents living in Japan for longer than a year are also included in the national health insurance and public health care systems.

Types of Insurance

For those considering a move to Japan, there are a couple of options for medical insurance: private health insurance and traveler's insurance from the U.S., or public insurance in Japan. Public medical insurance in Japan comes in two varieties, Employee Health Insurance and National Health Insurance.

PRIVATE INSURANCE

If you're visiting Japan for a short time and need to see a doctor, you can go to any hospital, wait with others in the waiting room, be seen, pay, and get a receipt—which you can then submit to your own insurance company back home. They will decide how much to reimburse, and hopefully, your bill will be at least partially covered. Costs for medical treatment and hospitalization, though significant, are generally lower in Japan than in the U.S. If you're only in the country for the short term, this plan may be manageable. But for those who plan to stay in Japan longer, the following options are available:

TRAVELER'S INSURANCE

Before going to Japan, it's a good idea to obtain traveler's insurance to cover examinations, treatment for an accident, or a medical emergency. Read the terms of your traveler's insurance carefully, as some illnesses with preexisting or chronic conditions, as well as dental care, may not be covered. It's a good idea to get treatment for any medical conditions before going overseas.

PUBLIC MEDICAL INSURANCE

As a resident of Japan, you will be required to enroll in a public medical insurance plan to ensure that you are covered at all times. The following several sections are based on an official description of the plan from the Tōkyō Metropolitan Government website.

> *As a resident of Japan, you will be required to enroll in a public medical insurance plan to ensure that you are covered at all times.*

The aim of the Japanese insurance system is mutual assistance in case of illness or injury. Subscribers pay regular insurance premiums according to level of income, and medical expenses are paid from the general fund. There are two types of public medical insurance: Kokumin Kenkōhoken (National Health Insurance) and Kenkōhoken (Employee Health Insurance), both described in more detail below; the latter is organized within the workplace, and subcategories include Kyōsai Kumiai Hoken (Mutual Aid Association Insurance) and Sen'in Hoken (Seaman's Insurance).

National Health Insurance

Those not covered by Employee Health Insurance at their workplace must join Kokumin Kenkōhoken (National Health Insurance). For eligibility information, inquire at the National Health Insurance counter of your municipal office and application procedures. Foreigners who have completed foreign resident registration (alien registration) and have a status of residence of one year or longer must join.

Insurance premiums are calculated depending on municipality, and everyone aged 40–64 must pay a Long-Term Care Insurance premium as well. Premiums may be paid in installments at your local municipal office, bank, or post office, or by automatic debit from a designated bank account. For foreign residents who earned no income in Japan the previous year, the premiums for the first year (April to the following March) may run as low as ¥2,000 ($18) per month. However, if you do earn money in Japan, your premium will rise accordingly. For a family, it can go as high as ¥50,000 ($455) per month.

Each insured household is provided with one copy of an insurance card. If you present this card at the medical facility where you receive treatment, you need only pay 30 percent of the charged medical expenses. However, part of the cost of outpatient medications and meals during hospitalization must be paid separately. You will receive the benefits when you submit your insurance card at the reception desk of the hospital or other medical institution and receive medical treatment. If you receive emergency medical treatment and do not have your National Health Insurance card on hand at the time, you may initially be required to pay the full medical bill. Take the hospital bill receipt to the National Health Insurance Section of your local municipal office, which will refund 70 percent of the cost of any treatment covered by the insurance.

Some types of expenses are covered as special categories. When a child is born, a lump sum benefit of ¥300,000–350,000 ($2,727–3,182) is paid per child. If an individual pays more than a designated amount of medical expenses at one medical institution during one month, he or she can obtain a refund of the amount in excess by applying to the local ward or municipal office. When a member of the household dies, ¥30,000–70,000 ($272–636) is provided.

Promptly notify the National Health Insurance Section of your municipal office of any of the following changes: You move out of (or into) your municipality; you leave or enter Japan; a child is born in your household; a household member dies; there is a change in your address, your name, or the head of your household; you reach the age of 70 and/or become eligible for Retirees' Medical Treatment; you lose your insurance card; or you join or withdraw from another public insurance plan.

Medical Fee Subsidy System for Foreign Students

Foreign students in Japan are also obliged to join the National Health Insurance plan. In conjunction with the plan, the Association of International Education, Japan operates a subsidy system in which it pays 80 percent (of the 30 percent of medical fees) of individually borne expenses.

Employee Health Insurance

The plan for Kenkōhoken (Employee Health Insurance) is designed for full-time employees, such as salaried workers in companies, factories, stores, or offices. All employees are obliged to enroll in this plan regardless of nationality, sex, or personal preference.

The Employee Health Insurance premium is calculated by multiplying the subscriber's standard monthly income, determined on the basis of his or her salary by the insurance premium rate. A portion of the premium is paid by the subscriber and the remainder by the employer.

This insurance covers illness, injury, childbirth, and death for the insured person, as well as for his or her dependents. By presenting the insurance card when receiving treatment for illness or injury, the insured pays only 20 percent of charged medical expenses. Dependents pay 30 percent of medical expenses for outpatient care and 20 percent for inpatient care. Part of the cost of medications for outpatients, in addition meals during hospitalization, must be paid separately. (As of 2004, the deductible for employed persons was raised by the government from 20 percent to 30 percent, much to the consternation of the working world.)

TAKING YOUR CHANCES

What if you have no insurance and don't or can't enroll in National Health Insurance? If I were to remain uninsured, I'd feel safer taking my chances in Japan than the U.S. However, it's much wiser to be safe than sorry—when riding my bicycle in Tōkyō, I was hit by a motorcycle that went through a red light. I was taken to the emergency room by ambulance. The cost, including the ambulance, X-rays, and tests, came to ¥55,000 ($500).

If you need to find a hospital with an English-speaking doctor, call the Tōkyō Metropolitan Health and Medical Information Center (tel. 03/5285-8181).

Daikon radishes are dried, then pickled as a source of vitamins in winter.

Medical Services

PHARMACIES AND PRESCRIPTIONS

Previously, *yakkyoku* (pharmacies) were located inside hospitals. You picked up your prescriptions (different-colored powders) in little white unlabeled bags to take home. Today, hospitals and pharmacies operate more separately from each other, but doctors will still usually direct you to the pharmacy right next door; and most patients follow the recommendation because it's convenient.

Not all drugstores dispense prescriptions—some handle only over-the-counter drugs and cosmetics. You can find out which type of drugstore you've entered by asking, *"Shohōsen?"* ("Prescriptions?"). A prescription from your doctor in the U.S. cannot be filled in Japan, but a Japanese doctor may be able to prescribe similar medication following a consultation with you. Sometimes, the same medication will be unavailable, or it may come in a slightly different format—for example, the time-release capsule you took back home may only come as a fixed dosage tablet in Japan. If you are concerned about taking the exact same medication while overseas, you should ask your doctor at home to prescribe the maximum allowable supply (usually 3–6 months), then ask a friend or family

Medical Culture

Every culture has different notions of how to stay healthy and what to do when you get sick. In Japan, the stomach is the center of wellness, so it should always be covered. At night, kicking your futon covers off and exposing your stomach to the air is a sure way to catch a cold. Parents sometimes tease younger children by saying, "If you don't cover your stomach, the Thunder God will come and snatch your *oheso* (belly button)."

Also according to local belief, gargling with plain water as soon as you come home is a good way to prevent sickness, especially in crowded urban areas. If you do catch a cold, wear a white mask over your nose and mouth, so you don't pass it on to someone on the busy trains and streets. If your cold doesn't get better in a couple of days, go to the hospital to get checked out. Meanwhile, eat a bowl of steaming *okayu* (rice porridge) and *umeboshi* (pickled plum). It will surely make you feel better.

member to mail your prescription refills when you need more. I followed this route for several U.S. medications, and it worked out fine. Just remember that when mailing medications overseas, you should make sure they are labeled clearly as such. It's also wise to include a note from your doctor verifying their legitimacy.

If you receive a prescription from a doctor in Japan and are enrolled in National Health Insurance, up to 70 percent of the cost is covered (the remainder is your copayment). Don't be surprised when medications come in blister packs in a small white paper bag, instead of a sealed plastic bottle. Each medication is described in Japanese on a sheet of paper enclosed in the bag; ask the pharmacist for help if you can't tell which medication is which. It seems that patients are more trusting of doctors in Japan, and they don't tend to ask many questions—but that doesn't mean you shouldn't. Doctors often have some training in English and German, and they may be able to understand your questions.

HOSPITALS

About a third of the hospitals in Japan are privately owned. Many are named something like Yamada Internal Medicine Clinic or Suzuki Pediatric Hospital, from which you may assume that Yamada or Suzuki is the name of the doctor. In other words, most doctors not only have an examining office, but an entire hospital with anywhere from a few to many beds. Individual ownership seems to result in a high ratio of hospitals in every community; in general, the larger the hospital, the better its reputation. This is especially true for university research hospitals—consequently, they are always crowded, and waiting times can be long.

Drugstore advertising Chinese medicine and natural medicine

Typically, you don't need to make an appointment to see a doctor. You just show up and sit in the waiting room, and you'll be seen in order of arrival. At the Itabashi Chūō Byōin (Itabashi Central Hospital), where I went after a bicycle accident, the doors to the waiting room opened at 6:30 A.M. Each person who arrived sat in order on benches. At 7 A.M., the line shuffled toward the row of appointment machines, at which point you insert your hospital ID card into the machine, select the appropriate department for examination, and receive an appointment number (starting with the earliest person to arrive that morning). Since examining hours don't begin until 9, you could go home or run errands until just before the time you figure your turn will come. The alternative, if you didn't get arrive early enough in the morning to ensure a spot, is to sit and wait an hour or two or more, knowing you will be seen sometime that day. Every culture dispenses medicine in its own way—it's up to you to decide which method you prefer.

Examining rooms are organized differently as well. When you go to see a doctor in the U.S., a nurse guides you to a private room with a door that locks; and you wait, perhaps flipping through magazines, until the doctor comes in, shuts the door, and sits down. In Japan, the doctors all line up behind a curtain to see patients. Sometimes there's also a curtain partition between doctors. Patients sit on a bench in the hallway outside the main curtain. You can't see anything, but you can hear everything that's going on. When it's your turn, the nurse calls your number, and you draw the curtain aside, go in, and sit down. The doctor will have just finished seeing another patient and will stay put while new patients file through. I observed few doctors wearing latex gloves or washing their hands between patients, but everyone got examined eventually.

PUBLIC HEALTH CENTERS

There are public health centers in every town and city throughout Japan, offering a wide range of services, including health consultations, mental health and welfare counseling (including alcohol abuse and promotion of appropriate treatment), and guidance on specific diseases. They are staffed by physicians, public health nurses, nutritionists, and various kinds of inspectors. Different public health centers have different procedures and provide different types of services. If you can't speak Japanese, it's a good idea to have a Japanese speaker accompany you when you visit your public health center for the first time. Many centers have evening hours, and some are open on Saturdays.

At Itabashi Central Hospital, many outpatients arrive by bicycle.

In addition, local health centers provide consultations and education to encourage citizens to take care of themselves throughout their life cycle. Such services are directed at pregnant women and infants, adults, and the elderly.

Public health care covers noncitizens. If you have applied for an alien registration card at the municipal office, they will have your name and address on file and will contact you when it's time for a specific type of check-up for your age bracket. I received letters from the public health department of Itabashi city telling me which tests were due for women my age. Over several years, the tests included a vision check, a chest X-ray (called *rentogen,* from the German), a mammogram, a Pap smear, urinalysis, and a fecal exam. All you need to do is call, make an appointment, and show up on the assigned day. Everything is free!

STD Testing

Public health centers offer free anonymous consultations for AIDS. Some public health and local health centers also have checkups for other sexually transmitted diseases. If you are in Tōkyō, the Tōkyō Metropolitan Testing and Counseling Office in Minami Shinjuku also conducts AIDS tests and consultation services, and there is an AIDS Telephone Service by the Japanese Foundation for AIDS Prevention. See the Resources section for contact information.

IMMUNIZATIONS

In Japan, the government takes care of immunizations for designated diseases to prevent epidemics among children. Babies are immunized at hospitals at no or minimal cost, and each school sets aside days for the whole student body to be immunized against such diseases as polio, diphtheria, whooping cough, measles, rubella, Japanese encephalitis, and tuberculosis.

Throughout the year, specific days are also set aside for annual physicals for all students, including a heart exam, urinalysis, a fecal exam, and a dental exam (with certificates for students with no cavities). Doctors, nurses, dentists, and X-ray trucks go to each school. Students also take fitness tests, in which they perform such tasks as running, pull-ups, push-ups, and grip tests (much like presidential fitness tests in the U.S. before they were eliminated due to budget shortages in some states). Public health is carried out with little privacy—as students get older, it can be rather embarrassing for them to line up in the gym, boys in one line and girls in another, waiting to see a male doctor behind a curtain—but everyone is treated equally, and no one falls through the cracks.

PREGNANCY AND CHILDBIRTH

In Japan, when you get pregnant, you go to the municipal office to file a pregnancy notification. In exchange, you receive a Mother and Child Health Handbook. This handbook is used to keep a written record of your physical and dental health, as well as that of your child (from birth to age six). Take the handbook along when receiving various types of prenatal checkups and services. Maternity classes on health management during pregnancy, preparation for childbirth, and care for newborn babies are also offered. After the baby is born, local health centers provide health checkups for infants aged 3–4 months, 18 months, and age three. The mother's checkups after giving birth are given at the same time as the health checkups for infants between three and four months. Local health centers also offer BCG (Bacille Calmette-Guerin) vaccinations against tuberculosis.

However, please note that delivery costs are not covered by National Health Insurance, and must be paid personally. The average cost is about ¥300,000 ($2,727), including seven days of hospitalization. However, if you are enrolled in National Health Insurance, you will receive a one-time childbirth benefit of ¥300,000. For detailed information, contact your nearest local health center or other health facility.

Environmental Factors

POLLUTION

Air and water pollution certainly exist in Japan. Power plant emissions result in air pollution, acid rain, and acidification of lakes and reservoirs, degrading water quality and threatening aquatic life. Air pollution from vehicle exhaust is concentrated in urban areas. In recent years, the government has passed increasingly stringent exhaust emissions regulations, and these have improved the air quality noticeably. Still, if you suffer from asthma or allergies, you might think twice about living in Tōkyō or other large urban concentrations.

Another urban disease is caused by cedar pollen, which triggers widespread allergies from January to April each year. During this period, you will see thousands of commuters wearing surgical masks to work or school. The cause, ironically, is due to the reforestation of denuded mountains surrounding the cities. In the Kantō plain, cedar seedlings were

> *In recent years, the government has passed increasingly stringent exhaust emissions regulations, and these have improved the air quality noticeably.*

Smoker's salon for those who can't live with the on-street smoking ban

planted everywhere, creating a monoculture forest; decades later, the pollen from the flowering trees blows into the metropolis. I've been told that even if you have no allergic reactions for five or six years, you can suddenly develop a sensitivity to cedar pollen. Be sure to take precautions.

The extremely high humidity throughout most of Japan means mold, fungus, and dust mites flourish in bedding and in woven *tatami* mat floors. To combat mildew, homemakers hang futons and bedding over balcony railings in the sun to dry as often as possible. You can also purchase portable futon dryers, so you're not limited to cleanliness on sunny days.

You can feel quite safe drinking the water in Japan. Many people prefer bottled water, but unless marked otherwise, tap water is fine to drink. As for swimming in rivers and the ocean, it makes sense to stay within designated areas. Many previously polluted rivers have been cleaned up by citizen environmental groups and local governments, and as a result, fish now swim in areas where there were none for many years.

PRESERVING RESOURCES

Japan consumes a large amount of scarce resources like imported fish and tropical timber. On the other hand, the country has been active in joining with other nations to sign international agreements on environmental issues, such as banning nuclear tests; protecting the Antarctic, endangered species, the ozone layer, and wetlands; and controlling whaling (which is still controversial). Japan also hosted the United Nations Framework Convention on Climate Change-Kyōto Protocol in 1997.

Recycling has become more widespread in Japan. Glass, cans, paper, magazines and drink cartons are picked up and recycled. Some supermarkets stamp a card each time you bring your own shopping bag; after 20 stamps, you receive a ¥100 ($.90) coupon for groceries. Many communities also have ecology centers, with classes for children and adults on how to conserve, reuse, and enjoy the earth's resources.

CRIME

Japan has a relatively low crime rate compared to many countries (including the U.S.), resulting in part from social values that emphasize getting along with others, despite crowded conditions. The low rate also stems from strict laws against drugs and weapons. Although difficult to eliminate completely, illegal drugs are much less readily available, and the consequences of carrying even a small amount of a drug, such as mari-

© Ruthy Kanagy

Go to the nearest police box if you're lost or need help.

juana, are severe. Guns are illegal, and crimes committed with guns—usually carried out by the *yakuza* (similar to the Mafia)—attract national attention. Crimes such as bank robberies and hold-ups are most often committed using a knife—with a knife, there's a chance to run away.

Sadly, as in any country, violence exists within families, in schools, and on the street. But on the whole, Japan feels safe, and riding trains and subways feels fine even at midnight (although a drunk businessman may try to speak English with you). If you are young and female—and especially if you're not Japanese—it makes sense to stay in groups and know your surroundings. People of any age or gender should use common sense: Find out where the neighborhood *kōban* (police box) is located, and introduce yourself to the police officers patrolling your street on bicycles. If you ever get lost, remember that the *kōban,* with its detailed maps, is the best place to go, and the police officers on duty will do their best to help you find your way.

© Ruthy Kanagy

Employment

The employment situation in Japan has changed markedly in the past
decade. Although there is some evidence of slow economic recovery
(along with the lingering recession), guaranteed lifetime employment and advancement by seniority—the hallmark of Japanese business
health—have virtually disappeared. Male graduates from top universities
have difficulty landing jobs with prestigious firms, many of which have
dropped campus recruiting. Female graduates already had difficulty ac-
cessing corporate jobs, based on the assumption that they would get married within a couple of years and "retire" from the company. But as it turns
out, many graduates don't want to work for a big *kaisha* (company).

These days, newspapers frequently report on a growing number of
Japanese youth who choose to become *freeters* (part-time workers). They
stay up all night, sleep during the day, and live off one or more part-
time jobs—a life far removed from the overworked salarymen (white-
collar workers) in neckties and suits, crushed on commuter trains. Of
course, *freeters* also have no guaranteed paycheck. Compared to their

125

peers of the past, who went straight from university to a company job, the earning power of young people has diminished dramatically. On the other hand, many still live at home, which frees up more yen. A number of youth also choose to pursue nontraditional paths, such as going overseas to work, travel, or earn an advanced degree.

Where do foreign residents fit into the employment picture? Thousands of immigrants from Brazil, the Middle East, and other parts of Asia have flooded into Japan to take factory and other jobs that most Japanese don't want. By contrast, English-speaking foreigners have earned a living in Japan for many years by teaching their native language. If anything, interest in learning English at increasingly younger ages has intensified, so teaching is still an option—provided you come with solid training, the appropriate degree, and, preferably, an introduction. In Japan, *kone* (connections) still have influence, and an introduction from someone in a position of authority carries weight. You may not know anyone in Japan right now, but you can meet people on your fact-finding trip (see Chapter 4) and make connections in advance of your move.

Self-Employment

Some people come to Japan knowing that they want to start their own business. Others work for an employer for a few years, perhaps teaching English, then decide to branch out on their own. Whatever the path, many Americans and other internationals have found a niche doing what they like and calling all the shots. Among the self-employed people I know in Japan are Web designers, video producers, photographers, restaurant owners, translators, English-school operators, agribusiness owners, and more.

Benefits of self-employment include being your own boss, having control over the product or service you sell, setting your own hours, choosing who to hire, and possibly hand-picking your clients. On the other hand, it takes capital to start a business, and if you are not a Japanese citizen or a permanent resident, it is difficult to obtain a bank loan. You will need a Japanese sponsor in order to get a proper working visa and help secure funds. Language skills also play a pivotal role—if your business targets only English-speakers, you may be able to get by without knowing much Japanese. However, if you hope to work with Japanese customers, advanced language skills are a must. One solution may be to have a Japanese partner (or spouse) to help with the business. Finally, keep in mind that your customers will demand very high standards of quality and customer service.

OPENING A BUSINESS

You don't need to be a citizen or even a permanent resident to start your own company in Japan. In fact, a Japanese law passed in 2003 says you can incorporate for just one yen! (See the sidebar "How to Incorporate.") On the other hand, there's no law requiring you to incorporate. If you have a proper working visa, all you need is a website or another means of publicizing your existence.

Small Businesses

Support for small businesses comes from many sources. In Tōkyō, the Metropolitan Government works with the Tōkyō Metropolitan Small Business Promotion Agency to offer training, financial assistance, equipment loans, facilities, and facility management services to help small businesses get started. Under the Small and Medium Enterprises Support Law, the Small Business Promotion Agency (www.tokyo-kosha.or.jp) has been designated a support center to provide comprehensive advice services throughout Tōkyō.

If you incorporate, your company can write off many types of business expenses—check with your local municipal tax office for specifics. Another

Café Manna is owned by an American in Gunma.

How to Incorporate

There are many options for running your own business in Japan—as a freelancer, as a business owner, or as an incorporated company. It is a good idea to discuss with many people whether you need to incorporate or not, as there are advantages and disadvantages to both options. If you don't establish a company, you are free to come and go; but if you have a company, you can't just abandon it if you decide to leave Japan, and many businesses don't really require incorporation. I decided to incorporate because I needed the credibility to sell food and health products throughout Japan to individuals and businesses, work with big organizations and government bodies on some projects, and acquire solo distribution rights for some products.

If you decide to incorporate, you can do it yourself or go through a *gyōseishoshi* (scrivener). Unless you plan to incorporate for other people, it's more time- and cost-efficient and less stressful to get a scrivener to take care of the process. I interviewed five scriveners, and the one I chose charged the smallest fee (¥50,000/$455). He was also unconcerned that I am a foreigner, whereas other scriveners thought that was a big issue and asked me too many visa questions.

If you go for incorporation, you will need to have at least ¥3 million ($27,273) in the bank, or use the new law of ¥1 incorporation, which requires that you generate ¥3 million during the first five years of operation. I believe I was the first foreigner in Hokkaidō to incorporate with the ¥1 law, which was new not just to me, but also to my scrivener and everyone else. The biggest challenge lay in the fact that the new law applies only to people who start from scratch—and I had been running my business for five months, so I had to officially "stop" and "restart" again. This meant stopping all work, breaking my links, canceling my business networking membership, and even deleting my website, which could not be re-launched under the same design. (I actually forgot to delete my website, which caused no end of trouble.) In addition, not working for a month without receiving any unemployment benefits wasn't much fun.

Nobody will ask you for a special visa when you incorporate, but renewing your visa afterward may prove a little tricky. In my understanding, if you can't get an investment visa (for which you need two full-time Japanese staff and a visible profit), you can just renew your freelance visa (which requires a minimum income of ¥200,000/$1,820 from one or more places).

Everyone's situation is different. I suggest you talk to many people and consult numerous networks for advice. And just like back home, establishing or incorporating will be the least of your worries—the main one is actually making your business work. Japan has an honest but complex and frustrating business infrastructure. If you keep your cool and take care of all the paperwork, then you can overcome the hassle and incorporate.

—by Natalia Roschina, Director of For ALL Co., Ltd. (www.agribusiness-for-all.com), Sapporo, Japan

agency called JETRO (Japan External Trade Organization) helps foreign companies invest in Japan. They provide Japanese market reports with information about specific segments of the market designed to help business owners look at opportunities for investing and for exporting manufactured products to Japan.

Invest Japan! (www.jetro.go.jp) is an online journal put out by JETRO that provides comprehensive information on the investment environment in Japan, including macroeconomic data, laws and regulations, and examples of foreign companies operating in the country. JETRO also publishes books, such as *Setting Up Enterprises in Japan,* that summarize national investment laws and procedures. Visit the organization's website for a complete list of titles.

TYPES OF BUSINESSES

You can open a restaurant, online retail business, Web design business, translation company, English school, bagel bakery, or one of many other types of businesses in Japan. Bed-and-breakfasts, known as *penshon* (as in a European-style pension), are quite popular in resort destinations, and may be a viable option as well. When deciding on the type of business you'd like to run, consider the cost of property in your area, your customer base, and your Japanese language ability (there are likely to be more English-speakers in urban than rural areas). Conduct thorough market research and become familiar with consumer trends and preferences in Japan—the *Nihon Keizai Shinbun (Japan Economic Newspaper)* and additional sources listed under Small Businesses, above, may prove helpful. Observe successful American businesses in Japan and consider how they adapted to Japanese consumer preferences. For example, what changes in operation did 7-11, Kentucky Fried Chicken, McDonald's, Kinko's, and Starbucks make when they came to Japan? How did they adapt their business models to fit their new customer base? What are their most popular products? If you don't have a business background, you might consider taking business or marketing classes at Temple University in Tōkyō.

Once you decide on your product or service, talk to as many people as you can in that business. A good real estate agent will not only help you find a suitable property to rent or buy, but can also introduce you to local business owners. Consult your local municipal office for advice, and make certain that you have the right type of working visa to operate a business legally in Japan (see Chapter 5, Making the Move, for details on visas). Nonpermanent residents may incorporate in Japan, but they must produce the proper paperwork and register with the Justice Department. If you have nonpermanent status and wish to take this route, you must register a *teikan* (notarized article of incorporation), your company seal registration, and evidence that you have deposited the required amount of capital (¥3 million/$27,272) in the bank.

The following international residents of Japan operate several different kinds of online retail businesses, a translation company, and a restaurant:

Kristen McQuillin started a Web design business (www.mediatinker.com), catering to English companies. Despite her lack of Japanese literacy, she managed to learn how to navigate Tōkyō, and even produced a DVD guide for newcomers based on her experience, called *Hello Tōkyō*.

Philbert Ono is a Tōkyō-based translator, photographer, and owner of the website PhotoGuide Japan (http://photojpn.org). He sells rare Japanese photo books and offers an auction proxy service enabling customers outside the country to bid for items at Japanese auction sites, and he also offers free consultation for students and researchers on Japanese photography.

Philip Bennett and his wife Akiko own and operate Café Manna, far from the neon city lights in the mountains of northern Gunma prefecture. They serve homemade pizza and pasta alongside the rushing Tone River. According to Phil, the requirements for a foreigner operating a restaurant are no different than for Japanese citizens. You must obtain a certificate from the Hokenjo (Public Health Department), a process that entails attending a lecture, paying a fee, and submitting a stool sample. The Hokenjo must approve your plans and make sure the eatery will meet sanitary standards. Twice a year, inspectors (fellow restaurant owners approved by the Hokenjo) visit the restaurant and make a perfunctory check.

Natalia Roschina is a New Zealander living in Sapporo, Hokkaidō. In 2002, seeing a need for a practical, easy, fun, and different approach to information technology, she started IT for ALL, followed soon after by Agribusiness for ALL and Health for ALL. See the sidebar "How to Incorporate" to read Natalia's story in her own words.

Dan Kanagy of Tōkyō owns WordWise, a translation company (and he's also my brother). After working for a Japanese translation agency for several years, he decided to go freelance and incorporated as a *yūgen gaisha* (Limited Liability Company) in 1994. He comments that "I incorporated more for positioning myself in the market. Some companies will only order translations from companies and not individuals. Being incorporated indicates a level of commitment to working in Japan. You may also be perceived as being more reliable and trustworthy than an individual. There is a tax advantage, but that wasn't the main reason." Dan also explains that tax benefits vary by your level of income. Forming your own *yūgen gaisha* also depends, in part, on your visa status. His visa status, *Jinbun Chishiki Kokusai Gyōmu* (Humanities Specialist/International Services), requires an employment contract. As far as the Immigration Bureau is concerned, he is an employee of a Japanese translation agency.

English Schools

A number of people I know started their own English schools after teaching for a Japanese agency or school for several years. Considerations for this type of venture include real estate costs for renting a building. Another significant factor is competition. In larger cities, there is intense competition from the big commercial educational chains, such as NOVA and Aeon, with huge advertising budgets. In smaller towns, you might be able to spread the word about your school by word of mouth without spending a lot on advertising. Once you find a suitable building, the most difficult step is to secure a bank loan. A Japanese bank will not extend a loan any longer than the validity of your visa (maximum three years, unless you have permanent residency). You will need a guarantor who is willing to carry the financial risk. Having a Japanese spouse who can act as the guarantor can speed things up.

Once you start your school, if you decide to hire a foreign teacher, you will need to incorporate as a *yūgen gaisha* (Limited Liability Corporation) in order to sponsor your employee's visa. See the preceding section for more information.

Employers

A wide range of jobs may be found in Japan in such fields as information technology, research and development, administration, finance, sales, consulting, Web design, marketing, teaching, translating, and many others. If you have the relevant degree and sufficient experience, don't hesitate to apply for a position that interests you. At the same time, keep your competition in mind—young Japanese men and women who have returned to Japan from overseas with MAs and MBAs. They're bilingual and prepared to work hard, and they don't just apply to Japanese companies; they apply to *gaishikei* (foreign affiliate companies). Recently, many highly skilled Japanese women have begun flocking to foreign companies, where there is a greater chance of promotion based on merit.

> *If you have the relevant degree and sufficient experience, don't hesitate to apply for a position that interests you.*

LANGUAGE SKILLS

Without Japanese language skills, you will have a tough time competing

A shopkeeper takes a break from hauling pears.

with bilingual applicants. If you have studied the language, one way to demonstrate your ability is to show that you have a certificate at a certain level. Japan has standardized tests and certificates for skills in every possible field, from abacus and calligraphy to IT and foreign languages. Many people take extracurricular classes in certain skills to prepare for these tests so that they can list them on their résumés.

You can get a certificate to prove your ability in Japanese by taking the Japanese Language Proficiency Test (JLPT), which is administered every December in locations within Japan and around the globe. Level 4 is the beginning level, and Level 1 the highest. Outside Japan, contact the Japan Foundation Los Angeles Language Center (tel. 213/621-2267, fax 213/621-2590, noryoku@jflalc.org) for information. In Japan, contact the Association of International Education Japan (AIEJ), JLPT Section, Testing Division (tel. 03/5454-5577, www.aiej.or.jp). If you study Japanese before arriving in the country, you won't regret investing your time and effort.

It's true that some Help Wanted ads specify "no Japanese language required." However, you will get much more out of your experience if you understand what's going on around you.

TEACHING ENGLISH

If you're interested in teaching English in Japan, bring along your diploma, ESL certificate, transcripts, awards, birth certificate, letters of recommendation, résumé, and passport photos—you will need all these materials to apply for teaching and other jobs. You might also pick up a good book on how to teach English, along with a grammar reference book.

English teaching jobs in Japan have become more competitive, with longer hours, more duties, and less pay. At a minimum, you should have a college degree, and preferably a license in teaching English as a second language. Private English conversation schools are everywhere in Japan, or you can teach English privately, but in that case you'll need a working visa and a guarantor. The Japanese government has a program to place assistant English teachers in junior and senior high schools in Japan (www.mofa.go.jp/j_info/visit/jet), but you're not allowed to pick your own placement location. Many elementary schools have also begun offering English as part of global studies for kids; if you're interested, bring along some books and teaching materials for children.

Government-sponsored and commercial organizations recruit thousands of native English speakers from around the world annually, bring them to Japan, and assign them to elementary, junior, and senior high schools to serve as assistants to Japanese teachers of English. In this type of position, you will be expected to keep school hours (8:30 A.M.–4:00 P.M. or later) Monday through Friday, and to attend some school events on weekends. The average pay is ¥250,000 ($2,270) per month (less 7 percent in income taxes). These organizations hold interviews overseas in late fall or winter; teaching begins in April. Housing may or may not be subsidized.

Perhaps the most well-known of these programs is the Japan Exchange and Teaching Program (JET), begun in 1987 by the Ministry of Foreign Affairs, which notes in its official materials that "it is desirable that applicants are adaptable and develop a positive interest in Japan and its culture."

WORKING ON A FARM

A more casual employment option is to travel to different parts of Japan and work on organic farms and for other similar businesses in exchange for food and a place to sleep. An international organization called WWOOF Japan (www.wwoofjapan.com) has a membership program that allows people to experience Japan at little or no cost, in return for helping business proprietors with their work. Hosts include organic farms, family inns, healing centers, ski resorts, and more. A one-year membership costs ¥4,000 ($36).

The Job Hunt

Before you arrive in Japan, start perusing the job market by reading on-line newspapers and magazines from Japan; you might even subscribe to a trade magazine or journal in your field. Through professional associations and online discussion groups (such as YahooGroups), you may be able to find contacts in Japan who hold jobs that interest you. Search the websites of Japanese companies—many have overseas branches you might contact. The same technique may help if you're looking for teaching jobs at academic or commercial schools. If you decide to take a reconnaissance trip to Japan before making the big move (see Chapter 4, Planning Your Fact-Finding Trip), you might be able to write ahead and arrange to visit schools, possibly for an informational interview. Keep in touch to let them know of your interest.

JOB LISTINGS

As you might expect, Tōkyō has the most jobs, but also the greatest con-centration of people competing for them. This reason may compel you to widen your search to cities in other regions of Japan, such as the Kansai area (Ōsaka, Kōbe, and Kyōto), Shikoku, Kyūshū, or Hokkaidō. English-language newspapers in Japan (national dailies include *Japan Times, Asahi Evening News, Daily Yomiuri,* and the online *Mainichi Daily News*) have Help Wanted ads in numerous fields—but remember that many ads specify age limits, gender, Japanese language ability, and other restrictions. If you don't meet all the criteria, it isn't worth your time to apply, unfortunately.

If you're looking for a teaching job, remember that the Japanese school year begins in April. That means schools will recruit new staff between De-cember and January or February.

INTERVIEWS

When interviewing for jobs in Japan, remember that your attitude and per-sonality count just as much as—or more than— your background. At the entry level, companies often prefer to hire a "blank sheet," then train the employee to fit into their corporate culture. A few simple dos and don'ts can make or break your interview:

First, be on time—if you're unsure of the location, go the day before to scope out the area.

Dress is also important. The key word is conservative—look conser-vative, act conservative, be conservative. The Japanese prefer no facial hair on men, trim haircuts, no visible tattoos, no facial piercing, and no earrings on men (think 1950s America, and you can't go wrong). Suits in dark colors are the standard uniform, with polished shoes and socks with no

On escalators, stand on the left and let walkers pass on the right.

holes! (Slip-on shoes are best for removing and changing into slippers, which will happen in public schools and elsewhere).

Maintain a respectful demeanor. Bow slightly with your eyes down when you enter the room. Wait to sit until your interviewer indicates where. Be attentive, and don't talk too much. Wait to be asked questions, and don't chatter on or boast about your background and experiences. Your interviewer may want to know why you came to Japan, how tall you are (in centimeters!), if you're married, if you have kids, and how you like sushi. English-speakers tend to talk with their hands, but in Japanese settings, it's more polite to keep your hands down. You may also notice less eye contact—it's considered more respectful not to stare at elders, so try not to gaze directly for too long.

Finally, it's a good idea to carry your résumé and credentials in a folder or binder. Japanese companies typically ask for a photograph (passport-size) affixed to the résumé, as well as date of birth. Education and job experience are listed from your first/oldest position up to your most recent. Be sure to list any certificates you have earned (such as the Japanese Language Proficiency Test), licenses (include the date you acquired your driver's license), computer skills, and personal interests. Japanese university seniors practice mock interviews and read numerous interviewing advice books. Students who usually wear jeans and T-shirts suddenly show up during campus recruiting season in dark suits—their overnight initiation into the uniform of the working world. You would be wise to follow their lead.

Finance

If you've decided to live in Japan, you are probably concerned about how to make your dollars stretch. You've kept an eye on the yen-to-dollar exchange rate, which seems to fluctuate anywhere from ¥103 to around ¥130—a significant difference in the amount of funds you will need to start out. The following questions may be going through your mind: Where will I keep my money? Can a foreign resident open a savings account or checking account in a Japanese bank? How do I transfer funds to and from my U.S. bank? When I start working, how will I receive my salary—cash, check, or deposit? You may have heard that personal checks are uncommon in Japan, and wonder how to go about paying your utilities and other bills. All of these concerns and more are addressed below.

Balancing Your Budget

Tōkyō, Ōsaka, and other large cities are expensive, and the cost of owning a house is prohibitive. The average Tōkyō family can't hope to own a house, and many call a *manshon* (condominium) home. Space is at a premium. A tiny studio in Tōkyō rents for ¥68,500 ($650) per month, and prices rise as you get closer to the city center. Many families choose to live in another prefecture where housing is more affordable, leaving the breadwinner with a two-hour commute to work. Once you get away from the metropolis to outlying regions, you can expect to pay 30 percent less for housing; it may also be possible to build or buy a traditional house. As far as food is concerned, try to develop a taste for Japanese cuisine. If you shop like the locals do and eat vegetables, fish, tofu, and rice instead of steak, you can maintain a healthy diet without breaking your budget. You may even discover the secret to Japanese slimness.

The Japanese fiscal, educational, and employment year begins on April 1 and ends the following March 31. When plotting your arrival in Japan, keep in mind that the second half of March is not a good time, as much of the country's population will be balancing books, transferring from one

Local real estate agent displays ads for rentals and property for sale

© Ruthy Kanagy

job to another, or traveling on spring break. You will need a healthy supply of cash or travelers checks to convert to yen to set up house—keep in mind that it may take as much as six months' rent (in cash) to sign a two-year apartment lease. That's about ¥80,000–100,000 ($4,500–5,500) just for the key to the front door.

If you are fortunate enough to have lined up a job before coming (or soon after landing), you typically won't see a paycheck until you have worked for six weeks. (I learned the hard way that my payday was the 20th of the month *following* the month I started working. My job started on October 1, but I didn't receive my first paycheck until November 20.) It's critical that you bring sufficient funds to live for the first two months. At first, you will need to pay cash for everything, from rent to utilities to insurance, until you set up a bank account. Then everything becomes much easier: You can pay all your bills via automatic transfers from your account (personal checks are not used in Japan). Using this system, you don't need as much cash—but even so, you may find you tend to carry a fair amount. It just seems to go faster in Japan.

If at all possible, try to spend no more than one third of your monthly income on housing. Become accustomed to less space and simpler living. This will help a great deal in keeping a balanced budget.

Paying the Price: Tōkyō, New York, and London

Item	Unit	Tōkyō	New York	London
rice	10 kg	¥3,963/$36	$19	£15.83/$29.30
bread	1 kg	¥421/$3.80	$4.87	£.66/$1.22
milk	1 liter	¥203/$1.85	$2	£.44/$.81
eggs	1 kg	¥310/$2.80	$4.76	£1.97/$3.65
beer	1 can	¥204/$1.85	$.76	£.95/$1.76
regular gas	1 liter	¥106/$.95	$.39	£.60/$1.11
newspaper	1	¥133/$1.20	$.62	£.47/$.87
hamburger	1	¥110/$1	$1.59	£.78/$1.40
hotel	1 night	¥16,026/$146	$176	£141/$261
movie	1 ticket	¥1,800/$16.35	$10.77	£6.29/$11.50
round of golf	1 person	¥14,720/$134	$23	£22.20/$41.11

Source: Based on information from Toukei de Miru Nihon (Statistical View of Japan), *published by the Tōkyō Metropolitan Government Statistical Bureau, 2001*

Banking

BANK ACCOUNTS

Japanese banks keep short hours (9 A.M.–3 P.M. Monday–Friday), and I've never seen a drive-through teller. But banks are convenient in other ways. Having a Japanese *ginkō kōza* (bank account) is a convenient means of receiving your salary and paying bills. Automatic bank transfers and cash-based transactions are widespread and efficient, eliminating the need for a personal checking account (not to mention writing checks and licking envelopes).

Major Japanese banks with numerous branches include the Bank of Tōkyō-Mitsubishi, Mizuho Bank, Sumitomo Mitsui Banking Corporation, and UFJ Bank. In addition, each prefecture and city has regional banks. Tourists with temporary visitor status (staying in the country for 90 days or less) generally cannot open bank accounts; at least a six-month visa is necessary. Some banks, such as Citibank Japan, require ¥300,000 ($2,727) in cash and a visa valid for at least one year to open an account.

To open an account, you must show your foreign resident registration card, Certificate of Completion of Foreign Resident Registration (obtained at your local municipal office), passport or driver's license, and *inkan* (a name stamp or seal; also called *hanko*). In Japan, the *inkan* is the legal equivalent of signatures in the U.S. Have one carved to your specifications (such as the characters for your family name) out of plastic, wood, or ivory. The stamp is kept in a small oblong case, and some have a round built-in container of red ink called *shuniku*. When you open an account, the bank will take an imprint of your name stamp, and you will need your stamp for future transactions. Your official stamp is registered at city hall, which issues certificates of authenticity needed for many types of transactions.

If you don't have an *inkan,* you may be able to use your signature, but some banks hesitate to allow your signature in place of a name stamp. From the Japanese perspective, signatures are considered too easy to forge, as compared to a registered *inkan.* You will use your registered stamp (or signature) when making withdrawals from your account at the teller window, and when closing your account—but only your ATM card is needed for using a cash machine (no signature or stamp required).

When you go to a bank to open an account, first take a number from the machine on the counter that indicates your place in line. Then complete an application form for new accounts, also available at the counter. If you're unsure which form to complete, say, *futsū yo-kin kōza,* which means "regular savings account," and someone will help you. In Japanese banks, someone in uniform usually works in the waiting area to attend to customers. You won't see any lines of people waiting for an open teller window. Everyone takes a number, sits down, and waits until their number is displayed and called.

After you fill out the forms and present some cash to open an account, you will receive a bank account booklet and a small gift (such as a Hello Kitty towel or a toothpick holder). Once you have opened an account, you can apply to have all your utility bills paid by automatic transfer. You will need one statement from each of the utilities addressed to you to prove your residence. You may also apply for a *kyasshu kādo* (ATM card), which will be mailed to you along with your *anshō bangō* (PIN number) to use the ATM.

At the ATM, you can make withdrawals and deposits, check your balance, and print entries in your bank book (by opening and placing the book in the slot face-up). You can also transfer money from your account to other banks to make payments. Cash machines are usually located inside the bank and are not accessible 24 hours (generally 9 A.M.–7 P.M. weekdays and 9 A.M.–5 P.M. Saturdays and Sundays, but be sure to confirm ahead of time). The interest rates in Japan on savings accounts are extremely low—as low as .5 percent. So, you won't get rich on your savings. On the other hand, interest rates for borrowing money, such as educational loans or house loans, are also low.

POST OFFICE ACCOUNTS

In addition to handling mail, Japanese post offices offer savings accounts and insurance. *Yūbin cho-kin* (post office savings accounts) are extremely convenient because, unlike your local bank, which may not operate nationwide, there's bound to be a post office around the corner everywhere in the country. Post office cash machines are open 9 A.M.–5 P.M. Monday–Friday. In addition, at least one post office in each district makes its cash machines available on Saturdays, Sundays, and holidays. The machines are located inside the post office entrance.

To open a post office account, fill in the savings deposit application form available at the counter. Show some form of identification, such as a Japanese driver's license, your foreign resident registration card, a Certificate of Completion of Foreign Resident Registration, or your passport. You will also need your *inkan,* or you may be able to use your signature. Savings accounts include *futsū yo-kin* (regular accounts), *teiki yo-kin* (fixed period accounts), and *tsumitate cho-kin* (accumulated deposit accounts).

You may also be able to use your ATM card from a major American bank, such Citibank, at post office cash machines. This is a great convenience, as there are many more post offices than branch banks. In this case, a small fee is charged for each transaction—around ¥200 ($1.80).

Post Office Banking

The Japanese postal system is government-owned and offers savings accounts in addition to mail service. A pamphlet entitled "Make Your Life More Enjoyable" offers four reasons why citizens should take advantage of the *jidō furikomi* (automatic payment) system from their postal savings accounts:

1. Automatic payment is convenient.
2. You can check your withdrawals, just like a budget book.
3. You can rest easy because of *yūyū loan* (postal loans).
4. You collect interest.

If you pay your electric, telephone, NHK (public television), gas, water, credit card, and apartment fees automatically from your postal savings account, you don't have to worry about anyone coming by to collect, nor about going to the bank to transfer money. A record of each withdrawal is printed in your savings book, along with the category of payment (such as electric, gas, or water), so you can see a month's payments at a glance. If, for some reason, there are insufficient funds in your savings account to cover the fees—and you have a *pa-ru-ru* (comprehensive savings account) into which you make regular deposits—a *yūyū loan* will automatically cover your payments. All you have to do is pay back the amount into your regular account. You also collect interest on the account until the day before an automatic payment is made.

To set up a payment account, go to any post office with your comprehensive savings account book, your *inkan* (name stamp) that's on file with the bank, an application to set up automatic payments, and receipts for the bills you wish to pay automatically. If you don't yet have a comprehensive savings account, the post office will set it up for you. Also remember to bring identification, such as your driver's license or national health insurance card.

TRANSFERRING MONEY

Sending Money Abroad

You can transfer money overseas from both banks and post offices. To do so, you must present some form of personal identification, such as a foreign resident (alien) registration card, Certificate of Completion of Foreign Resident Registration, passport, or driver's license. To send money from a bank, you have three choices. Telegraphic transfer is the fastest method; notification of the transfer is sent electronically by telegraph. You will normally pay the cost of the transfer plus handling charges.

With an ordinary transfer, notification of the transfer is by airmail (5–7 days to the U.S.). The third way is a demand draft, which operates like a money order. It is purchased at a bank for a specific amount, then mailed directly to the recipient, who can cash it at a bank. Many banks also offer online financial services, enabling you to transfer money between accounts or to an overseas account—for a fee.

Within Japan, cash can be mailed easily at the post office. Just ask for a *genkin kakitome,* and they will give you a special envelope for sending cash (bills only, no coins). The envelope is sealed with a special stamp on which you affix your *inkan.* It's also possible to send money internationally through any post office that handles savings accounts. Again, there are three methods: sending money directly to the person's address, postal book savings, or bank account. For further information concerning sending money overseas, contact Japan's Customer Advisory Office (tel. 0120-085420), which is open 8:30 A.M.–6:00 P.M. Monday–Friday and has English-speaking staff.

Automatic Payments

Thanks to a highly developed system of *jidō shiharai* (automatic payments) in Japan, the easiest way to pay utilities and other bills is to have the money deducted from your bank or post office account each month. Several weeks before payment is due, you will receive monthly electric, gas, and telephone (domestic) statements through the mail (water/sewerage statements come every two months). Once your payment system is set up, the correct amount will be deducted from your account. Utility and other bills, such as national health insurance, can also be paid at a bank, credit association, post office, or convenience store.

CONSUMER RIGHTS

If you purchase something with a credit card or cash and later decide you don't want it, you're in luck—consumers in Japan are, by law, allowed a cooling-off period. In its *Guide to Living in Japan,* the metropolitan government explains that the cooling-off period allows consumers to cancel a contract, such as one finalized with a door-to-door salesman, even after the contract has been finalized. The consumer must write to the retailer in Japanese within eight days from the time the proper written contract was received from the retailer. Notify the retailer of your desire to cancel the contract by postcard. Keep a photocopy of the postcard and send it by registered mail or another certified delivery service.

The government provides a sample written notice to send via postcard, as follows:

On [date], I contracted to purchase [item] for [amount] yen with a salesperson of your company named Mr./Ms. [Name]. However, I now wish to cancel this contract. Accordingly, please send me a refund of [amount] yen (equal to the sum I paid) as soon as possible. In addition, please arrange to pick this product up promptly.

Date:　　　　　　　Address:　　　　　　　Name:
Address of Retailer:　　Name of Retailer:

If a credit contract has been finalized, the consumer must also write to the credit company. The cooling-off period applies only to unused merchandise. For more information, contact your local consumer center in Japan. At the Tōkyō Metropolitan Comprehensive Consumer Center (tel. 03/3235-1155), books and videos related to consumer life may be viewed on-site or borrowed. Consultations concerning problems with merchandise, services, and contracts are also conducted.

Taxes

JAPANESE TAXES

Everyone living in Japan, regardless of nationality, is obliged to pay *zeikin* (taxes). The 5-percent consumption (sales) tax is the most obvious daily tax. Two additional types include national taxes, which are levied by the national government; and local taxes, which are levied by prefecture and municipal governments. Each person in the country must pay an income tax (national tax) and a resident's tax (local tax).

Income Tax

For foreign residents in Japan, whether or not you will be taxed—and, if so, the income on which your taxes will be levied—depends on your residence status. There are three types of resident status, defined as follows:

A "resident" is someone who has lived in Japan continuously for more than one year. The two subcategories of resident include: 1) a nonpermanent resident who has lived in Japan for five years or less and does not intend to become a permanent resident; and 2) anyone who does not fit that first qualification, in which case he or she is regarded as a permanent resident. A "nonresident" is someone who has lived in Japan for less than one year.

Both types of residents are taxed on income generated in Japan, whether paid in Japan or outside Japan, as well as on income generated outside Japan and paid in Japan. Of the income earned outside Japan by nonpermanent residents, only the amount sent to Japan is subject to taxation. For income earned outside Japan, the amount kept outside Japan is not subject to taxation.

As a rule, nonresidents are taxed on income generated in Japan, whether paid in Japan or outside Japan. Nonresidents are not subject to taxation on income generated outside Japan.

Personal *shotokuzei* (income tax) is a national tax collected by district tax offices and levied on personal income earned between January 1 and December 31. It is assessed on the total income for the year, so you must file a tax return if you have earned any income. Personal income is calculated as total income minus "necessary expenses" (defined as expenses involved in gaining the income). Tax returns must be filed at the local municipal office between February 16 and March 15.

> *For foreign residents in Japan, whether or not you will be taxed—and, if so, the income on which your taxes will be levied—depends on your residence status.*

If your total income for the year is less than ¥380,000 ($3,550), an income tax report is not required. When a foreigner leaves Japan permanently and his income for the year exceeds ¥380,000, he must designate a proxy to file an income tax report during tax season, or file a return in person and pay any taxes before departure.

There are two methods of income tax payment, one for nonsalaried workers and the other for salaried workers:

1. Nonsalaried taxpayers must calculate their own income and tax for the year, submit an income tax report, and pay the necessary taxes. Income tax reports must be filed at the tax office administering to the area of residence during the period between February 16 and March 15 for the previous year.

2. Salaried employees must deduct their personal income tax from their salary (under a tax withholding system). Since the employer carries out a year-end adjustment every December to calculate excesses or shortfalls in taxes paid for the year, salaried taxpayers do not need to file an income tax report. However, the following persons must file a personal income tax report: 1) salaried employees with an annual income of more than ¥20 million ($182,000); 2) salaried employees with additional income amounting to more than ¥200,000 ($1,820) in the year; and 3) salaried employees earning separate incomes from two or more employers.

When filing income tax reports, taxpayers can claim deductions for the following items: 1) *not applicable to nonresidents*—If medical expenses for the previous year, excluding the portion covered by health insurance, totaled more than 5 percent of the individual's annual income or more than 100,000 ($910); 2) if the taxpayer suffered losses from disaster or theft; and 3) *not applicable to nonresidents*—If the taxpayer took out a loan to purchase a home. In addition, taxpayers can claim a spouse deduction and spouse's special deduction if the spouse's income for the year did not exceed a certain amount. To claim these deductions, the taxpayer must submit documented evidence, such as receipts for medical expenses, to the tax office.

Residential Tax

Jūminzei (residential tax) is paid to the municipality in which you resided on January 1. You must pay the tax if you were living in that municipality on January 1, lived in Japan for the previous twelve months, and earned income during that period. Taxes are based on the previous year's annual income and consist of two amounts—one proportionate to the level of income, and the another uniformly applied to all (on a per capita ratio) regardless of income level.

Nonsalaried workers usually pay the residential tax computed on the basis of the income tax report in four separate installments in June, August, October, and January. Notification is sent by the ward or municipal office, and payment can be made through banks, credit associations, credit unions, agricultural cooperatives, and post offices. The salaried employee's residential tax is computed by the ward or municipal office on the basis of the employer's report. The residential tax is deducted from the individual's salary in 12 installments from June through May of the following year.

For Tōkyō residents, a *Guide to Metropolitan Taxes* (in English, Chinese, and Korean) is available from the Consultation Section of the Metropolitan Taxation Office, or from the Tōkyō Metropolitan Citizens Information Room (3F, Main Bldg. No. 1, Tōkyō Metropolitan Government, 2-8-1 Nishi-Shinjuku, Shinjuku-ku, Tōkyō, tel. 03/5321-1111).

Asset-Based Tax

The *koteishisan-zei* (municipal property tax) and *keijidōsha-zei* (light motor vehicle tax) are based on assets. The former is paid by persons who own land, a house, or a depreciable asset, and is collected by the Tōkyō Metropolitan Government Tax Office (for Tōkyō residents). The amount of tax payable is based on the value of the asset. The Light Motor Vehicle Tax is paid by owners of motorcycles and light cars. Contact your local municipal taxation office in Japan for requirements.

U.S. TAXES

How about income taxes to the U.S. government for American citizens residing in Japan short- or long-term? The answer is yes, you must file an income tax return each year by June 15—a two-month automatic extension is granted to citizens living abroad. You may also be required to file a state income tax return with your home state.

The Bona Fide Residence Test requires that you have spent at least 330 days outside the U.S. in the previous year. If you have less than $80,000 in income, tax exemption is granted, but you still have to file. Detailed instructions and all the relevant forms are available online. A good starting point is IRS Publication 54, Tax Guide for U.S. Citizens and Resident Aliens Abroad (www.irs.gov/publications/p54/index.html). The U.S. Embassy in Tōkyō and U.S. Consulates throughout Japan can also answer your tax questions (see the Resources section for contact information).

Investing

The leading Japanese manufacturers, such as Toyota, Honda, and Sony, have become global household names. In recent years, many Japanese companies have made direct investments abroad, setting up manufacturing plants in North America, Southeast Asia, and Europe. They hire a local workforce and either sell products locally or export them. Partly as a result, Japan has begun importing more and more manufactured goods. The Japanese economy, which has been in a period of recession since the late 1990s, is finally showing signs of recovery.

© Ruthy Kanagy

Shinjuku noontime traffic

> *The leading Japanese manufacturers, such as Toyota, Honda, and Sony, have become global household names.*

The Japanese government wishes to promote more investments in Japan. One way to learn about the Japanese markets and get started in investing is through the Japan External Trade Organization (www.jetro.go.jp), an arm of the government that organizes seminars and individual consultations abroad to provide information about investing in Japan, including trends in the Japanese market, the regional investment climate, and laws and procedures. In addition, JETRO publishes an online journal, *Invest Japan!*, which offers detailed information on the investment environment in Japan, including macroeconomic data, laws and regulations, and foreign companies operating in Japan.

A LOOK AT THE MARKETS

Japan has five equities exchanges, located in Tōkyō, Ōsaka, Nagoya, Sapporo, and Fukuoka. The Tōkyō Stock Exchange (TSE) offers market information in real time. The Nikkei All Stock Index is a market value-weighted index that serves as a benchmark against which investment results can be measured. Stocks in the Nikkei 225 Stock Average can be found at www.nni.nikkei.co.jp. The Nikkei Stock Index 300 (also known as Nikkei 300), a representative gauge of the overall market, is a market value-weighted index of 300 major selected issues on the Tōkyō Stock Exchange. Finally, the Nikkei JASDAQ covers most over-the-counter issues.

HOW TO INVEST

Stocks

Nikkei Net Interactive online provides business news, market data, and current information on *kabu* (stocks), backed by Nihon Keizai Shimbun, Inc., publisher of *Japan Economic Newspaper*. Nikkei News and Nikkei Daily publish numerous articles online, including news from Kyōdō and Dow Jones. Markets Japan offers a comprehensive database of Japan's financial markets, including current market data, real-time Nikkei figures, and news.

Securities

Following are descriptions of some of the *shōken* (securities) companies in Japan. (See the Resources section for contact information.)

Japan Securities Agents, Ltd.: Established in 1950, this company is engaged in services related to securities transfer, custody, close inspection, clearing, and financing. The company is affiliated with Japan Securities Finance Co., Ltd. which holds 36.61 percent of issued stock.

Securities transfer, transit, and other related services accounted for 99 percent of the company's fiscal revenues in 2000; calculation and data processing services accounted for the remaining 1 percent. Japan Securities Agents has one consolidated subsidiary based in Tōkyō. The group's operations are entirely domestic.

Wakō Securities Co., Ltd.: Established in 1947, this securities house provides investors with financial products and services through 61 domestic offices. Commissions and fees accounted for 64 percent of fiscal revenues in 1999; trading income, 31 percent; and interest and dividend income, 5 percent.

Jafco Co., Ltd.: Established in 1973, Jafco invests in unlisted medium and small-sized companies with high potential, and offers related services, such as leasing, installment, and commercial loans. The company provides information, consulting, and other support services to investee companies to enhance their performance and provide assistance in their initial listing on the stock markets, as well as help them form investment enterprise partnerships and manage the collected funds. Operating investment securities revenues accounted for 68 percent of fiscal revenues in 1999; investment management fees, 22 percent; consulting fees, 5 percent; interest on operating loans, 5 percent; and other, nominal.

THE COMPANIES

The following descriptions are based on information from the website of each respective company. See the Resources section for contact information.

Ashigin Financial Group

Ashigin Financial Group comprises five companies, including the Ashikaga Bank, leasing, and credit card companies. The bank holds a 40-percent share of deposits and loans in Tochigi prefecture, and the company holds ¥50 billion ($455 million) in capital.

Mitsubishi Tōkyō Financial Group

The Mitsubishi Tōkyō Financial Group is a holding company that oversees the operations of The Bank of Tōkyō Mitsubishi, Ltd., The Mitsubishi Trust and Banking Corporation, and their subsidiaries. The group holds total capital of ¥1.26 trillion ($11.45 billion).

Nippon Steel

Nippon Steel is the second largest manufacturer of steel products in the world and holds ¥419.5 billion ($3.8 billion) in capital.

Nissan Motors

Nissan shares capital and operations jointly with Renault, and holds a 15-percent share of Renault stock. The company is ranked ninth in the world in auto sales, and is currently focused on expanding in the U.S. market; it holds ¥606 billion ($5.5 billion) in capital.

NTT DoCoMo

NTT DoCoMo is part of Nihon Denshin Denwa (the NTT Group), which holds an almost 60-percent share of the mobile phone market. The company is currently developing its i-mode and third generation mobile phone products, and holds ¥937 billion ($8.5 billion) in capital.

Prime Systems Corporation

Prime Systems Corporation provides enterprise engineering services, such as systems solutions, and is currently rebuilding its management. The company holds ¥2.8 billion ($255 million) in capital.

Resona Holdings

Resona Holdings is a financial company formed by the former Daiwa and Asahi Banks; its subsidiaries include Kinki Ōsaka Bank, Nara Bank, and others. The company holds ¥720.5 billion ($6.6 billion) in capital.

Tōshiba

Tōshiba is number two in Japan in total electronics manufactured; its top products include semiconductors, laptop computers, and heavy electrical equipment. The company holds ¥274.9 billion ($2.5 billion) in capital.

Toyota Motors

Toyota is Japan's top automaker, with a 40-percent share of the domestic auto market. In 2003, auto sales topped 7 million units, surpassing Ford as the second largest auto manufacturer in the world. The company is financially sound, with expanding overseas operations, and holds ¥397 billion ($3.6 billion) in capital.

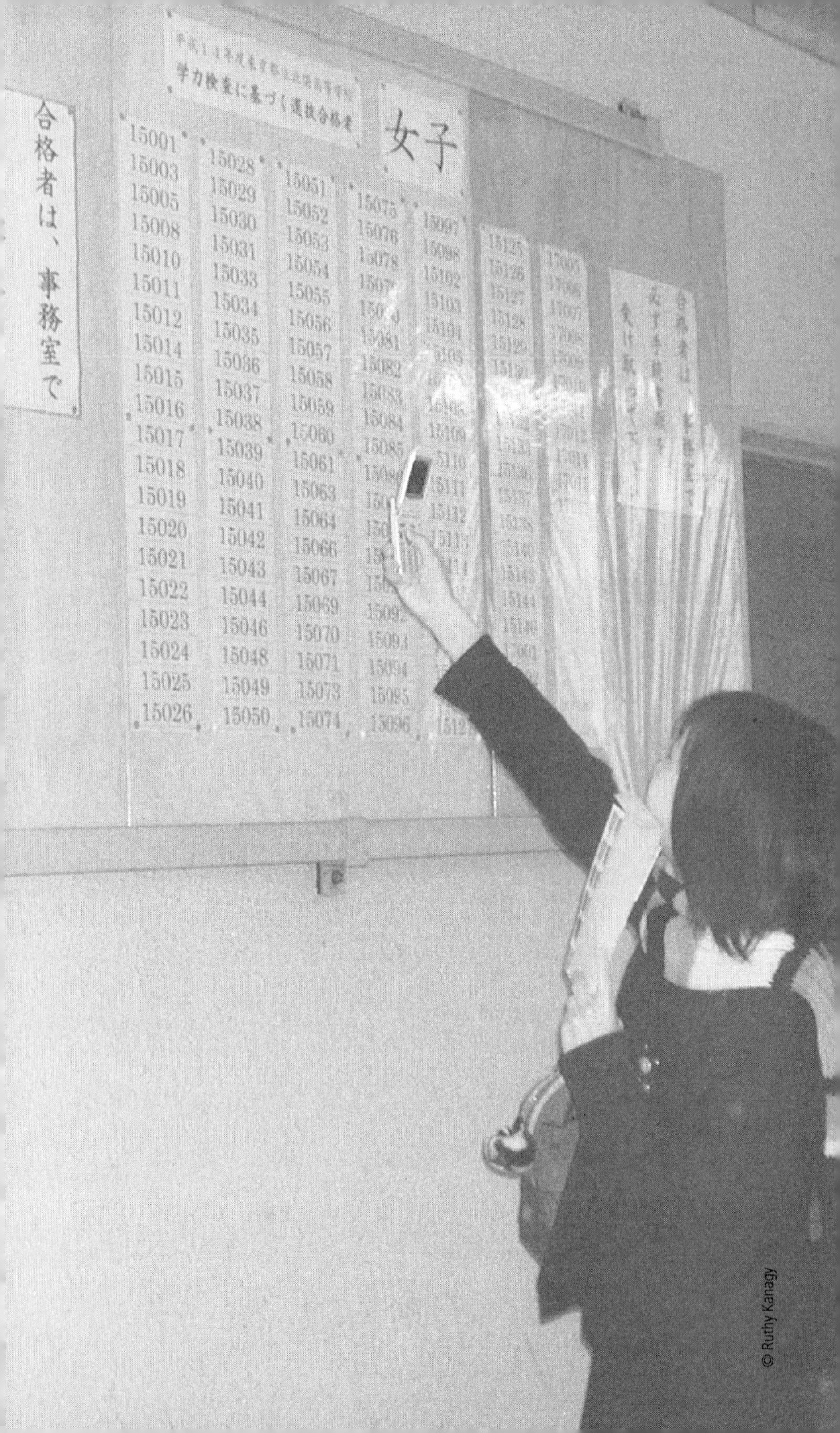

© Ruthy Kanagy

Communications

Communication has been an art form in Japan since ancient times, when itinerant monks narrated tales of warrior battles accompanied by *biwa* (stringed lute), and myths of the nation's founding were recorded in calligraphy. Today, the rate of communication has accelerated to the point that news and other information are conveyed almost instantaneously throughout the populace, from Hokkaidō to Okinawa. Newspaper circulation has dwindled as electronic communication takes over.

One of your first impressions upon arriving in Japan may well be how people communicate. It sometimes comes in the form of bowing, but it's just as likely to be cell phones snapping open, followed by the rapid tap-tap of email messages composed and sent in public. These days, it is not uncommon for Japanese family members to each keep a personal cell phone for the purpose of reaching each other. Because of their busy lives, keeping in touch through digital email and conversation may improve family communication, as reported in *Japan Media Review*.

However, cell phones have not yet fully replaced other forms of communication, such as the old-fashioned telephone, fax, postal service, print, and visual media. Read on for details on how to obtain such services, as well as access information and news, while you are living in Japan.

Telephone Service

LAND LINES

The standard way to obtain telephone service in Japan is to go to the nearest NTT office. NTT used to be a monopoly, but has now been broken into regions. In Tōkyō, the company is called NTT Higashi Nippon (NTT East Japan). Take along the following to purchase a *denwa* (phone line): identification (passport, alien registration card), the installation fee of ¥72,000 ($700), a contract fee of ¥800 ($8), and a labor fee of ¥10,000 ($100). That's right, the standard way of getting new phone service in Japan costs more than $800!

But there's another way. Next to every NTT office are shops that buy and sell phone lines at a discounted ¥40,000 ($364) or so. If you want to save even more, check online in the *Tōkyō Classifieds* (www.tokyoclassifieds.com) for people who are leaving Japan and desperate to sell their phone line (subscription) for ¥20,000–30,000 ($182–273). It's all legitimate. You decide on a date and time to meet the seller at an NTT office and both go inside. The seller will sign a form for NTT, you will sign some more forms, and the line is all yours (after you hand the seller cash for the sale). Next, schedule a date to have your new line installed. The phone subscription happens only one time in a lifetime. Once you own the right to a phone line, it goes wherever you go in Japan.

Now all you have to do is buy a phone or fax phone—new or used. You have a choice of long-distance companies. Frequently, the phone you buy will come with a card and coupons promoting a particular company, or the phone may already be programmed to use that company when a long-distance call is dialed. You are not obligated to any one service, however, and should shop around. Competing phone carriers typically list their rates in three-minute units, such as three minutes for ¥9 for local calls, or ¥20 for a wider area.

When making long-distance calls, dial the area code (which may be more than three digits), plus the city code and phone number. Every area code in Japan begins with zero. This zero should be omitted when calling Japan internationally.

Japanese Conversations

In Japan, it's not customary to look strangers in the eye, smile, or greet them in public. You just look ahead or down. If someone drops something or leaves it behind on the train, and you give it to them, it triggers a verbal interaction. They will probably bow slightly and say either:

Ah, sumimasen.	Oh, I'm sorry (for your trouble).
Dōmo.	Thanks. (Literally, "in every way.")

If you recognize a neighbor from your block, it's nice to say (while bowing slightly):

Konnichiwa.	Good day.

or mention the weather:

Atsui desu ne?	Hot, isn't it?
Samui desu ne?	Cold, isn't it?

People performing professional services never ask customers personal questions. Instead of "Hot enough for ya?," or "Have a nice day," the entire bank, store, or restaurant staff greets each customer formally as they enter and leave the establishment:

Irasshaimasse.	Welcome.
Arigatō gozaimashita.	Thank you very much.

Ask your neighbors how to find a local business:

Sūpaa wa doko desu ka?	Where is the supermarket?
yūbinkyoku	post office
ginkō	bank
yakkyoku	drugstore

They may answer:

Koko desu.	It's here.
Soko desu.	It's there.
Asoko desu.	It's over there.

MOBILE PHONES

Don't be surprised when you arrive in Japan and see almost every person on the streets, on the trains, and on bicycles busily tapping the keys of their cell phones. Japan now has more *keitai* (literally, "portable") than land lines. In 2001, 72 million people had cell phones, meaning that more than one in two Japanese citizens carries a *keitai*. And they're used less for talking and more for emailing and Web surfing. Built-in digital cameras are popular for instant visual communication, and some phones feature Webcams so you can see the person you're talking to in real time.

You will see hundreds of shiny *keitai* in rainbow colors everywhere. The big three telecommunications companies—NTT DoCoMo, J-Phone (Vodaphone), and AU—claim 60 percent, 20 percent, and 20 percent of the market share, respectively. They compete fiercely, advertise everywhere, and continually unveil new things you can do with your cell phone.

In Japan, more people connect to websites via cell phones (i-mode and others) than they do from personal computers. In 2000, there were 10 million Internet mobile phone users. Watching people on the trains or on the street tapping out messages to their friends with their thumbs is quite

© Ruthy Kanagy

Headphones and cell phones seem like part of the high school uniform.

amazing—especially when you consider that their phones have to handle complex Japanese scripts containing 2,000 *kanji* characters and two syllabaries. You can read the news, buy concert tickets, listen to the latest music, and download tunes to use as ring tones; some phones even come with GPS capabilities, so you can find recommended restaurants and shops when you're out on the town.

Remember that you won't be able to use your cell phone from the U.S. if you bring it to Japan. If you're not sure that you want to buy a new cell phone, renting is another option. You can rent cell phones at the airport, but that's fairly expensive. An inexpensive cell phone made by Tu-ka can be used with prepaid cards (called "Pretty Card"), available for ¥3,000 ($27) or ¥5,000 ($46) at a *conbini* (convenience store). They are good for two or three months, respectively, after which you can receive calls for 30 more days. Calls cost about ¥100 ($.91) per minute. Many companies offer family plans, late night plans, and many other variations.

To rent or buy a cell phone, take along your pass-

> *Don't be surprised when you arrive in Japan and see almost every person on the streets, on the trains, and on bicycles busily tapping the keys of their cell phones.*

port (or alien registration card) and a major credit card. Sometimes a deposit is required. For specifics, see the phone company websites listed in the Resources section.

PAY PHONES

With the spread of mobile phones, pay phones have become increasingly hard to find, but there are always a few in train stations. Green or gray rectangular pay phones take either ¥10 coins or ¥100 coins (but if you use the latter, you won't get change back). You won't hear a voice telling you the cost of the call; instead, a beep reminds you to add more coins. It's most convenient to buy a prepaid phone card for ¥1,000 ($9) or more, available from station kiosks and sightseeing spots. When you insert the card in the phone, it displays how many units of value are left on the card (100 units for ¥1000). There are also square gray pay phones that take ICC phone cards; many have analog outlets to connect to laptops. Telephones displaying an international telephone call sign can be used for domestic and international phone calls.

It's worth shopping around to find the cheapest long-distance and international rates. All phone companies offer night, weekend, and holiday

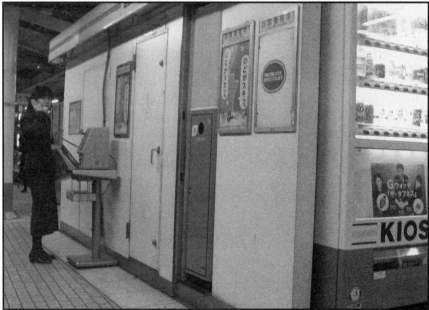

© Ruthy Kanagy

Pay phones on train platforms have become scarce since the advent of *keitai* (cell phones).

discounts. To make an international call, first dial your telephone company code (KDD is 001, JT is 0041, IDC is 0061, and so forth), then the country code (1 for the U.S.), followed by the area code and telephone number. See the Resources section for information on a few international telephone companies that handle inquiries in English.

Email and Postal Service

INTERNET ACCESS

There are a number of options when you want more heavy-duty Internet access than your mobile phone can provide. If you don't want to spend a lot of money, you'll be pleased to find that Internet cafés have begun to pop up in the larger cities. JR East operates a series of free Internet cafés; the one in Ueno station, on the Yamanote line in Tōkyō, is on the first floor. The coffee isn't great, but you get 30 minutes of Internet access on one of their dozen laptops for free.

I used to frequent a café called Love in the basement of Palroad II Bivio Store at the west exit of Akabane station (JR Saikyō and Keihin Tōhoku lines). The café membership card was ¥500 ($4.50) for a year, and the charge per hour was ¥300 ($2.70). They also had a library of magazines and stacks of thick comic books, creating a homey atmosphere.

In addition to locations in the train stations themselves, Internet cafés are frequently found in high-rise buildings near the station. These are also known as manga cafés for their selection of comic books and comfortable sofas. They usually charge by the hour (¥380 and up) and offer free hot and cold drinks and corn soup. Ask the officers at the *kōban* (police box) outside the station for an *"Intānetto café?,"* and they'll likely know the way to one.

Check with your Internet service provider (ISP) before you go to Japan to see if they have local access telephone numbers. If so, you can keep using your account while abroad. My ISP didn't offer such a service, so I signed up for a free account with freecom.ne.jp and started out using a dialup modem. After accumulating ¥20,000 ($182) in fees, plus phone bills, I decided to investigate a broadband company with fixed rates. Companies such as J-COM Broadband enable you to choose a cable connection for your TV, phone, or Internet service, and you can arrange for automatic payment of your monthly bill through your bank or post office account.

POSTAL SERVICE AND COURIERS

In Japan, post offices sell stamps, handle all types of mail, and offer savings

Deciphering Japanese Addresses

In the United States, we give each street a name, then number each block of houses on a given street. Under this system, once you find the correct street sign, you know the house you're looking for is on that street; you just have to drive up and down looking for the right block and the right number.

The Japanese address system, however, is organized spatially. It's like taking a pie and cutting it into six slices, then cutting each slice into smaller pieces, then cutting each of those into bite-sized morsels. A city or town is partitioned into areas, and each area is given a number. A Japanese address typically consists of three or four numbers connected with hyphens. When you're looking at a map to locate an address, first scan it to find the area with the number that matches the first number in the address. Then repeat this process to find the sub-area that matches the next number in the address. Finally, match the final numbers in the address to the building number (note that the buildings in each sub-area are numbered consecutively) and apartment number (if applicable).

Here's a typical address (specifically, of my residence in Tōkyō from 2000 to 2003) in Japanese order: 174-0051 Tōkyō-to, Itabashi-ku, Azusawa 2-23-10-101.

The first seven numbers are the *yūbin bangō* (postal code or ZIP code); followed by the largest geographical unit (generally the prefecture, but in this case, the metropolis of Tōkyō); then the ku (city ward)—one of 23 city wards in central Tōkyō. (Outside Tōkyō, the name of the ward would be replaced the name of the city or county.) The ward or city is divided into districts with names (such as Azusawa). Each district is divided and numbered (2); then further subdivided and numbered (23); and then each house or building has a number—in my case, my manshon was building 10. Last is the apartment number, 101.

accounts and insurance (see Chapter 9, Finance, for details). Postage stamps are also sold at train station kiosks, tobacco shops (sporting a red sign that reads *tabako* in *hiragana* letters), and stores displaying the Japanese postal mark (a "T" with a bar line over it).

To send stamped mail, drop it in a square red postbox marked with the word "Post" (and the "T" with bar line) along the street. Pickup times for weekdays and weekends are noted on the box. There are usually two drop slots—one marked Domestic and the other International and Special Delivery. You can also take your letters to the post office—a wise idea if you're not sure how many stamps to put on that birthday card to your nephew in Panama. A chart with detailed postal rates is available at the post office. Small parcels can be mailed from the post office or other agencies, such as *conbini* (convenience stores) displaying a Yū Pakku (sounds like "You Pack") sign.

Not many post offices have stamp-vending machines.

There are three rates for sending parcels overseas: *kōkūbin* (airmail), *funabin* (sea mail, which takes about four to six weeks to the U.S.), and *sarubin* (SAL). SAL means "space available basis" and travels a little slower than airmail, but faster than sea mail. You will be asked to fill out a small green form identifying the item you are sending and its value. When sending books, refer to the rate chart carefully, as there are restrictions on maximum weight for books and printed matter.

You can send international mail from your local post office, or use the Tōkyō Central Post Office or the Tōkyō International Post Office if you're in that city. Note that post offices also provide packaging services.

What happens if the mail carrier tries to deliver something that's too big for your mailbox and/or requires your signature, but you're not home? He or she (I've never actually seen a female postal carrier, but . . .) will take it back to the post office and leave a notice of delivery on your door. To pick up the item, you must take the notice of delivery, identification (alien registration card or something else verifying your address and name), and your *inkan* (name stamp; see Chapter 9, Finance, for details) to the designated post office. It's usually the largest one in your area. At my post office, attempted deliveries could be picked up 24 hours a day.

If you move within Japan, fill out a change of address postcard at the post office and either deliver it in person or mail it in. Mail to your old address will be forwarded for one year. As in the U.S., there is no forwarding overseas.

Media

NEWSPAPERS AND MAGAZINES
Several national newspapers are published in Japanese and English. *Japan Times, Asahi Evening Times, Daily Yomiuri,* and *Maichini Daily News* are sold in train stations and newsstands in larger cities, or you can subscribe to any of them and arrange delivery through branch offices in your neighborhood. Major economic newspapers in English are the *Asian Wall Street Journal* and *Nikkei Weekly.* There are also prefectural and local newspapers in Japanese. Weekly periodicals in Japanese are plentiful; they (and their buxom girl-of-the-week cover photos) spill out over the racks at bookstores and newsstands. *Time* and *Newsweek* in English and Japanese, along with other popular English-language magazines, are available in bookstores such as Kinokuniya and Junkudō.

TELEVISION
Television channels abound—if you subscribe to cable. The public (government-owned) channels are NHK and NHK education, with BS1 and BS2 available to subscribers. The latter two often carry NFL and NBA games from the U.S. If you buy a television in Japan, you can get one with bilingual broadcast reception (via cable or satellite) to view movies, NHK news, and other programs in English. NHK goes door-to-door to collect fees supporting the public station. There is no penalty for nonpayment, but the solicitors will keep stopping by. Basic television in Tōkyō has nine channels, with fewer channels in other areas, so many people subscribe to satellite or cable.

RADIO
The only English radio station is broadcast by the U.S. military (FEN) at 810 kHz in Tōkyō and 648 kHz in Okinawa. Japanese FM radio is broadcast at a lower frequency than in the U.S., 76 to 90 MHz, so you will need to buy a radio locally in order to access those stations. Wide-band radios, which cover both Japanese and U.S. frequencies, can be purchased at some electronics stores. (In Tōkyō, head to Akihabara station on the Yamanote and Sōbu lines, then follow signs to the Electric City—ten blocks of nothing but electronics). Some of the J-pop (Japanese pop) stations, such as J-WAVE (81.3 MHz in Tōkyō), have bilingual DJs who announce the tunes and chat in a mixture of Japanese and English.

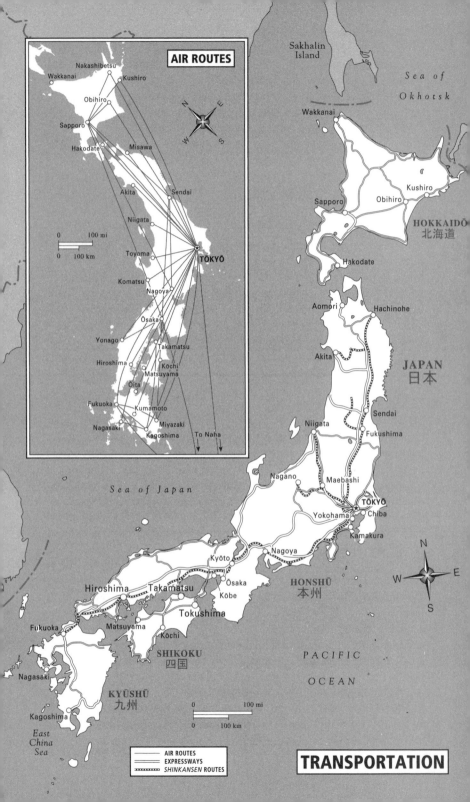

AIR ROUTES

Nakashibetsu
Wakkanai
Kushiro
Obihiro
Sapporo
Hakodate
Misawa
Akita
Sendai
Niigata
Toyama
TŌKYŌ
Komatsu
Nagoya
Ōsaka
Yonago
Takamatsu
Hiroshima
Kōchi
Matsuyama
Ōita
Fukuoka
Kumamoto
Nagasaki
Miyazaki
Kagoshima
To Naha

0   100 mi
0   100 km

Sakhalin
Island

Sea of Okhotsk

Wakkanai

Kushiro
Sapporo
Obihiro
HOKKAIDŌ
北海道
Hakodate

Aomori
Hachinohe
Akita

JAPAN
日本

Niigata
Sendai
Fukushima

Nagano
Maebashi
TŌKYŌ
Yokohama
Chiba
Kamakura

Sea of Japan

Kyōto
Nagoya
HONSHŪ
本州
Hiroshima
Takamatsu
Ōsaka
Kōbe
Tokushima
Matsuyama
Kōchi
SHIKOKU
四国

Fukuoka

Nagasaki

KYŪSHŪ
九州

Kagoshima

East China Sea

PACIFIC OCEAN

N
W   E
S

0   100 mi
0   100 km

AIR ROUTES
EXPRESSWAYS
SHINKANSEN ROUTES

TRANSPORTATION

Travel and Transportation

In Japan, the best ways to travel are by air, train, subway, bus, ferry, or bicycle. You can rent a car if you absolutely need one, but public transportation is very well developed, timely, and efficient. And no matter how you travel, you don't have to drag your suitcases with you on trains, buses, or subways. If you've been to Japan, you may have noticed how everyone seems to travel light. The secret lies in point-to-point delivery services, such as Yamato, Nittsū, and Sagawa. When you arrive in the country, give your suitcases and boxes to one of these companies at the airport, and the next day at a designated time, they'll deliver your bags to your hotel or home.

If you're taking a trip within Japan, you can arrange to have your luggage shipped to the airport, or even to your final destination. Give the delivery service a call a couple of days ahead, and they'll come to your door and take care of your luggage—even a bicycle in a suitcase. Pricing depends on the size and weight of each item, but usually costs between ¥1,600

($14.50) and ¥2,000 ($18) per piece. And it's well worth the price, since many train stations have only stairs—no escalators.

When planning your trips in Japan, refer to the thick transportation books published every month listing the schedules of all trains, airplanes, and ferries throughout the country, with maps and indexes (in Japanese). You can also find such information online by looking up the websites of each airline, train, or ferry operator. Some of this information is also available in English (see the Resources section for details).

By Air

The two major airlines in Japan are Japan Airlines (JAL) and All Nippon Airways (ANA). The former Japan Air System (JAS) has merged with JAL. There are a number of small airlines as well. JAL, pronounced *ja-ru* in Japanese, serves 59 domestic airports from Hokkaidō to Okinawa, as well as numerous airports around the world. ANA, pronounced *a-na,* serves an equal number of domestic and overseas destinations.

Major airports include New Tōkyō International Airport (Narita Airport),

Arriving in Japan

© Ruthy Kanagy

Tōkyō International Airport (Haneda Airport), Kansai International Airport (in Ōsaka), Ōsaka International Airport (Itami Airport), Komaki International Airport (in Nagoya), New Chitose International Airport (in Sapporo), and Fukuoka Airport (in northern Kyūshū).

Hokkaidō

JAL, ANA, and other airlines have regular flights to all the major cities in Hokkaidō. From Haneda Airport in Tōkyō, flight time to Hakodate City is an hour and a quarter, with seven flights daily. Traveling from Tōkyō to Sapporo (New Chitose Airport) takes just over an hour. In addition to ANA and JAL, the Hokkaidō-based Air Do also offers flights. Regular one-way fares to Sapporo often cost ¥20,000 ($182) or more, but may drop as low as ¥10,000 ($91) if you meet certain conditions, such as purchasing 21 days ahead or taking early morning or late night flights. Some also offer a birthday discount that allows you to fly round-trip anywhere in Japan during the seven days before and after your birthday for ¥10,000—and your companion pays the same price. See each airline's website for details.

You can fly directly to Obihiro Airport from Tōkyō (Haneda), Kansai, and Nagoya Airports. There are flights to Kushiro from Tōkyō, Ōsaka, and other cities in Honshū, each taking about an hour and a half.

Nagano and Gunma

From Tōkyō, Nagano and Gunma prefectures are easily accessed by *shinkansen* (super-express train). From Ōsaka, flights between Itami Airport and Matsumoto City in Nagao take just one hour. There are also flights from New Chitose and Fukuoka Airports.

Kansai

Kansai International Airport (KIX) and Itami Airport next to Ōsaka link the Kansai region, including Kyōto and Kōbe, to domestic airports throughout Japan. International flights from KIX take you around the world, and trains and buses link the airports to Kyōto, Kōbe, and other Kansai destinations.

Hiroshima

The New Hiroshima Airport is located 60 minutes from Hiroshima and offers domestic flights to Haneda (in Tōkyō) in 70 minutes, as well as to Sapporo, Hakodate, Aomori, Sendai, Miyazaki (in Kyūshū), and Naha and Ishigaki in Okinawa. New Hiroshima also hosts international flights to Seoul, Hong Kong, Singapore, Shanghai, Beijing, and Honolulu. In addition, Hiroshima Nishi (West Hiroshima) Airport has regular flights to five other regional cities in Japan.

By Train, Subway, or Ferry

Japan has a very efficient public transportation network, the quickest way to get around most metropolitan areas and between major cities. Trains and subways are punctual, convenient, and used by a great number of people.

TRAINS

Japan Railway (JR) operates about 70 percent of the 23,670 kilometers (14,709 miles) of railways in Japan; the remaining 30 percent is operated by private railway companies. Tōkyō is the hub of the nationwide network of trains. By convention, all trains headed in the direction of Tōkyō are called *nobori* (inbound) trains, even if they are operating far from Tōkyō, within Hokkaidō or Kyūshū. Similarly, trains headed away from Tōkyō are known as *kudari* (outbound) trains. When you look at train schedules or stand inside a train station trying to figure out your platform number, you will see *kanji* characters for *nobori* or *kudari* to indicate the direction of the train.

To ride a JR train or private train, buy a ticket at the ticket window or from the ticket vending machine inside the station. The ticket is stamped when you board the train, then collected by an official when you exit the gate. Most JR stations have a Midori-no-Madoguchi (literally, "Green Window") ticket office where you can book up to one month in advance for a *shitei-seki* (reserved seat) on any JR train route in Japan.

If you travel on a *tokkyū* (special express train) or *shinkansen* (the so-called bullet train; literally, "new trunk line"), you will need two tickets—a *jōsha-ken* (boarding ticket) and *tokkyū-ken* (special express ticket). In addition, you will need to purchase special tickets for a *shindai* (sleeper) train, or to ride *guriin-sha*, (first class, literally "Green Car"). In most cases, when you pay for your reservation you can ask for a seat in a nonsmoking car, other than on local and commuter trains.

The first *shinkansen* was completed in time for the Tōkyō Olympics in 1964. Traveling by *shinkansen* is fast, convenient, and expensive. The Tokaido Shinkansen line runs west from Tōkyō to Nagoya, Kyōto, and Ōsaka. You can continue west on the Sanyō Shinkansen through Hiroshima and western Honshū, and through a tunnel to the city of Fukuoka in Kyūshū. Going north from Tōkyō, you can take the Tōhoku Shinkansen as far as Hachinohe at the northern end of Honshū. You can also take a

The Yamanote loop train has a green stripe.

branch line, Akitan Shinkansen, west from Morioka to Akita on the Japan Sea coast. Similarly, you can travel on the Yamagata Shinkansen from Fukushima west to the city of Yamagata on the Japan Sea coast. The Jōetsu Shinkansen goes from Tōkyō to the city of Niigata on the Japan Sea coast, and the Nagano Shinkansen links Tōkyō and Nagano city in the central mountains. There is no *shinkansen* in Hokkaidō, but there is a network of special express trains linking all the major regions.

There are numerous other trains that travel slower and make more stops than the *shinkansen,* but cost less. If you have the time, you will see much more of Japan this way, as *shinkansen* spend more time inside tunnels than out in the open. If you want to travel to Hokkaidō, you can take the *shinkansen* from Tōkyō north to Hachinohe, then change to a special express that goes through the undersea tunnel to the city of Hakodate in Hokkaidō, and on to Sapporo in about 11 hours. You could also take a sleeper train from Ueno station in Tōkyō to Sapporo. Long-distance sleeper trains and regular express trains travel to every region of the country.

Japan Rail Pass
If you come to Japan as a tourist—for example, during your initial exploratory journey to the country (see Chapter 4, Planning Your

Trains and Planes

In Japan, you will have many opportunities to ride the highly developed rail transportation system. Japan Rail (JR), formerly the government-owned Japan National Railway, was privatized in 1987. Today, it's divided into six private regional companies: JR Hokkaidō, JR East, JR Central, JR West, JR Shikoku, and JR Kyūshū. (JR is pronounced "J-Aaru" in Japanese). The rail fleet consists of *shinkansen* (bullet trains), sleeper trains, commuter trains, and deluxe long-distance trains.

Try to become familiar with the following transportation terms, which will help you find your way at the station:

新幹線

shinkansen | "New Trunk Line"; high-speed trains that operate on wide, elevated tracks (don't worry— there haven't been any accidents since 1964).

特急

tokkyū | Abbreviation for *tokubetsu kyūkō* ("special express" or "limited express"); the fastest trains on regular rail lines.

急行

kyūkō | Makes more stops than a *tokkyū*, so it takes a bit longer—but it costs less to ride.

特別快速

tokubetsu kaisoku | Special express commuter trains operating between suburbs and cities.

快速

kaisoku | Express commuter trains.

普通

futsū | Local trains that stop at every station. Affectionately called *donko*, these are a popular local way to travel for students, the elderly, and others who don't have cars.

地下鉄

chikatetsu | Underground or subway.

きっぷ

kippu | Ticket, of which there are many kinds (see below).

乗車券

jōsha-ken | Regular ticket, the base fare point to point.

特急券

tokkyū-ken | Special express ticket (required in addition to the regular ticket).

一日乗車券

ichinichi-jōsha-ken | A one-day ticket good for travel in a specified area—a great bargain if you plan to be out and about town. Available for JR trains, buses, and streetcars in many cities.

定期

teiki | Commuter pass. If you buy for one month or three, you get a certain percentage off, but you must present a form stamped by your school or employer.

回数券

kaisūken | Multiple trip coupons available at a discount.

パスネットTカード

Passnet T-card | A common fare card used on the Toei and Eidan subway lines in Tōkyō, plus any private railway line associated with the Passnet system. Many trains and buses sell prepaid cards for ¥1,000–5,000 worth of rides at a slight discount.

上り

nobori | Inbound.

下り

kudari | Outbound.

1番線

1-bansen | Track number 1 (*sen* means line, so the Yamanote line is Yamanote-sen).

航空券

kōkūken | Airplane ticket.

割引

waribiki | Discount or sale.

特割り

tokuwari | Special discount (airlines offer these at specific times of the year with advance purchase).

Fact-Finding Trip)—the Japan Rail Pass (www.japanrailpass.net) offers significant savings over purchasing individual tickets, if you plan to travel extensively for one to three weeks. The pass is valid for JR-operated trains, buses, or ferries. (The one exception is the fastest *shinkansen,* called the Nozomi, for which you will have to pay a surcharge). Only temporary visitors—meaning those who will stay in Japan for 90 days or less—may buy and use the pass, which must be purchased in your home country before entering Japan. If you are entering Japan with any status of residence (e.g., on a working visa, student visa, research visa) you will *not* be able to use the pass.

The cost of a one-week pass is around ¥28,300 ($257). Your local travel agency should be able to sell you the Exchange Order that you must take to Japan and exchange for the actual dated Rail Pass. Most JR ticket offices at major stations (such as Sapporo, Tōkyō, Yokohama, Kyōto, Ōsaka, Hiroshima, or Hakata) and JR Travel Service Centers handle the pass. Take your passport and Exchange Order along. If you arrive at Narita Airport in Tōkyō, you can exchange the Order for the Rail Pass on-site and begin using it immediately on JR transportation. The pass covers the Narita Express train to Shinjuku in Tōkyō, which normally costs ¥3,500 ($32).

If you have a working visa or student visa and are not eligible for the rail pass, JR offers other discount travel deals. The Seishun 18 ticket is the cheapest way of traveling by slow train, allowing you to ride local and rapid JR trains anywhere in Japan for five days for ¥11,500 ($105). It goes on sale once each season for a period of about 40 days. Numerous other rail and bus passes for different regions of Japan may be purchased in Japan with no visa restrictions.

SUBWAYS

Subways are the fastest way to get around major cities such as Sapporo, Sendai, Tōkyō, Yokohama, Nagoya, Kyōto, Ōsaka, Kōbe, and Fukuoka. You don't have to worry about weather or traffic conditions, and can usually get across town faster than by bus or car. Tōkyō has twelve subway lines, all color-coded and operated by the metropolis (Toei lines) and private companies (Eidan lines). A comprehensive guide to subways in Japan, with route maps, is available at http://us.metropla.net/index2.htm.

FERRIES

If you have enough time and want to save money, consider taking a ferry from Tōkyō to any port in Japan. Sometimes you can take your motorcycle, bicycle, or car on board, a popular option in the summer for college students going to cooler Hokkaidō for a tour. A ferry from Ōarai

Taking the ferry across the Inland Sea from Hiroshima to Matsuyama

near Tōkyō takes you to Tomakomai in Hokkaidō (south of Sapporo) in 20 hours. Major seaports in Japan include Chiba, Himeji, Hiroshima, Kawasaki, Yokohama, Tōkyō, Muroran, Tomakomai, Ōsaka, and Kitakyūshū.

By Bus or Bicycle

BUSES

City and private buses operate in most cities and towns in Japan. In addition, long-distance highway buses offer an alternative to *shinkansen* for half the price. In cities and towns, complete timetables are usually posted at each bus stop. The charts show the schedules for *heijitsu* (weekdays), as well as *doyōbi* (Saturdays) and *nichiyōbi/shukujitsu* (Sundays/Holidays). In some places, you board from the front of the bus (on the left side), and exit from the rear. In other locations, the rear door is the entrance and the front door is the exit.

Some buses have fixed fares, while on others, the fare is determined by the stop where you get on and off. When you board from the rear, there is often a machine with a numbered boarding ticket. Take a ticket and check your fare on the chart by matching the number on your boarding ticket. To indicate that you wish to disembark, push one of the buttons near the window or on the ceiling.

For buses and trains, children aged 6–11 are half fare, and if accompanied by an adult, one child under age six is free. On city buses and streetcars, the fare box is at the front next to the driver. Put your boarding ticket and the correct change into the coin slot. If you need to make change, you can put a bill or coin in the change machine attached to the fare box. If you are paying with a *kādo-kaisūken* (prepaid card), place it into the prepaid card slot. If you have a *teiki-ken* (commuter pass), show it to the driver.

Bus Passes

On city buses, you may use a prepaid card. This is handy because you don't need correct change each time your ride, and you also receive a discount with a card. You can buy these cards, along with *ichinichi-jōsha-ken* (one-day pass) or *futsuka-jōsha-ken* (two-day pass) from bus drivers or at the bus terminal. *Teiki-ken* (1–3-month commuter passes) are also available at a discount.

The cheapest long-distance travel is by intercity highway bus. Some are operated by JR, and others by private regional companies. Often you travel at night between cities, such as Tōkyō to Ōsaka. If you are trying to save on lodging, an overnight bus is an easy way to avoid paying for a hotel and get to your destination at the same time.

BICYCLES

Like cars, bicycles are officially regarded as vehicles in Japan. However, in reality, bicycles are not taken seriously—they are seen as an extension of your legs, except that they get you there more quickly. Thus, riders are very casual about operating their bikes, and often don't pay attention to pedestrians and other vehicles. Likewise, pedestrians and cars tend to brush off bicycles. As a result, accidents involving pedestrians, bicycles, and automobiles are fairly common, and sometimes fatal. Cyclists often ride on the wrong side of the street while preoccupied with their cell phones, cigarettes, or umbrellas. At night, few people use lights on their bikes, and many riders wear dark clothing.

Where I lived in Tōkyō, the following bicycle regulations were distributed by Itabashi-ku:

- Be sure to observe traffic rules and ride a bicycle that is properly inspected and maintained.
- Keep to the left side of the street when you ride your bicycle.
- Bicycles can be ridden on sidewalks if there is a sign that reads "Bicycles

© Ruthy Kanagy

A large apartment complex doubles up on bike racks.

and Pedestrians," or the like. Generally, however, pedestrians have priority on sidewalks. When trying to move along a crowded sidewalk, it is best to get off your bicycle and push it.

- It is usually illegal to park your bicycle in front of a station with a lot of foot traffic. Illegally parked bicycles may be removed, and will be disposed of after two months if not reclaimed. There are usually free or inexpensive bicycle parking lots available near the station, so make good use of them.

- Bicycle Crime-Prevention Registration: All new bicycles must undergo crime-prevention registration after being purchased. Even if you receive a used bicycle from a friend or acquaintance, you must reregister the bicycle. If you leave a bicycle registered under the name of the previous owner, you may face problems. The fee is ¥525 ($4.75), and most bicycle shops handle crime-prevention registration.

If you can, bring or buy a high-performance folding bike to ride in Japan. Most of the bikes you see in Japan for running errands are the heavy, steel *mama-chari* ("Mom's bike") variety. Too big and heavy to bring inside, they are left at train stations and on side streets with thousands of other bikes to rust in the rain. By contrast, a folding bike can be stored in the smallest Tōkyō apartment and gives you a two-wheeled advantage

Like cars, bicycles are officially regarded as vehicles in Japan. However, in reality, bicycles are not taken seriously—they are seen as an extension of your legs, except that they get you there more quickly.

anywhere in Japan. Of course, you can use it for grocery shopping, trips to the convenience store, river-path riding, and more. I took a custom, foldable, packable bicycle from Bike Friday (www.bikefriday.com) to Japan, and it's the best thing I did. Bike Friday bicycles either fold or disassemble easily to take on a bus or train (in a bag), then unfold quickly at your destination to ride again.

Urban streets are crowded, and you must stay aware pedestrians. The sidewalks and shoulder of the street are shared by bicycles, pedestrians, and illegally parked cars.

By Car

DRIVER'S LICENSES

If you have an international driver's license from your home country, it can be used in Japan. An international license is valid for one year from the date of issue, and not more than one year from the date you enter Japan. To change a foreign driver's license to a Japanese license, go to the Driver's License Testing and Issuing Center of the police department. Note that applicants must have spent at least three months in the country in which they obtained their license, starting from the date the license was issued.

Required items include:

1. A foreign driver's license.
2. A copy of a resident register listing your permanent address (or alien registration card, for those not subject to the Family Register Law—see the sidebar in Chapter 3, People and Culture).
3. One photograph (3 cm by 2.4 cm) for identification.
4. A certified translation into Japanese of your driver's license from your embassy, consulate, or the Japan Automobile Federation.
5. Your passport (showing date entry into Japan).
6. The ¥4,150 ($38) fee for ordinary vehicles—fees vary according to type of license.
7. Written and driving skill tests are also required.

Obtaining a Japanese License

To obtain a driver's license in Japan for the first time, you must pass a driver's license examination (aptitude test, skills test, and knowledge test).

The written examination is available in English or *hiragana,* as well as in Japanese. Anyone who attends an approved driving school, completes a full course of instruction (skills and knowledge), and passes a graduation test will be exempted from the skills test of the driver's license examination.

Driver's licenses are valid for three years from the date of issue. However, those under 70 years of age who have had a Japanese driver's license for more than five years with no accidents or citations in that five-year period will receive a license valid for five years.

To get a Japanese translation made of your foreign driver's license, contact your embassy, consulate, or the Japan Automobile Federation (JAF). If you are not a resident of Tōkyō, contact the JAF of your prefecture. Japan Automobile Federation Translation Telephone Service has a 24-hour information service (tel. 03/5976-0055) with a taped message in Japanese.

BUYING AND REGISTERING A CAR

Car owners in Japan are required to pay taxes (acquisition tax, tonnage tax, and automobile tax) and buy compulsory insurance. Compulsory insurance only provides personal compensation, and the compensation ceiling is quite low, so it is a good idea to have additional insurance for personal protection in case of an accident. When purchasing a car, you contract with the car sales company. The vehicle must then be registered with the District Land Transport Bureau or an automobile inspection and registration office before you can drive the car.

Items required for car registration are:

1. A certificate of signature issued by your embassy (or a Seal Registration Certificate for Japanese citizens).

2. A parking space certificate issued by a police superintendent providing evidence that a parking space has been secured.

3. Alien registration card.

When you purchase or scrap a car, change your address, or transfer ownership, you must notify the District Land Transport Bureau or an automobile inspection and registration office, as well as the ward or municipal office. If you are planning to leave Japan, you must complete ownership transfer and other necessary paperwork before leaving the country.

The location to register a car differs by the type of car:

1. For ordinary cars (over 2,000 cc), small cars (2,000 cc or under), small two-wheeled vehicles (over 250 cc), and light two-wheeled vehicles (over 125 cc and 250 cc or under), contact the District Land Transportation Office or automobile inspection and registration office in your area.

2. For light three- or four-wheeled cars (660 cc or under), contact the Light Car Inspection Association or branch office in your area.

3. For motor scooters (up to 125 cc), contact the local ward or municipal office (inquire at your local branch office).

TRAFFIC LAWS

Drivers who violate traffic regulations imposed under road traffic laws must pay a fine or face criminal punishment. In addition, they receive penalty points according to the seriousness of the violation. When penalty points accumulate to a certain level, offenders will have their licenses suspended or cancelled, and will be banned from driving (or riding) on the roads. Foreign drivers should pay special attention to the following traffic rules in Japan:

• Drive on the left side.
• Drivers and passengers are required to fasten seatbelts.
• Children under six years of age are required to use child seats.
• You must not drive while using a mobile phone.
• Driving under the influence of alcohol is prohibited. Even if no accident occurs, it is still against the law to drive after drinking alcohol.
• Park only in proper parking spaces.
• Cars parked on the street may be towed away if they violate parking laws.

Don't touch that taxi door! It opens automatically.

There is a Mutual Aid System for Traffic Accidents in most areas that offers low-cost premiums to provide a financial benefit if you are involved in a traffic accident. For more information, contact the traffic casualty counter of your local ward or municipal office.

TAXIS

Scores of *takushii* (taxis) cruise city streets. All you have to do is stand on the left side of the road and raise your hand. There are also taxi stands in front of train and bus stations, or you can call ahead for a ride. All taxis are metered, and there is no custom of tipping—just pay the amount displayed. Some drivers are reluctant to open the trunk for luggage, so you may have to put your bags in yourself. And be sure not to touch the rear door handle, because it opens automatically! Japanese businesspeople often use taxis after a night on the town, since the trains stop running soon after midnight.

Housing Considerations

I f you've heard anything about the cost of living in Japan, you've probably been warned that prices in Tōkyō, Ōsaka, and other large cities are out of sight. A two-room apartment in Tōkyō can cost anywhere from $800 to $8,000, and the price of buying a home? Well, don't even ask! As in New York and San Francisco, space is at a premium in concentrated urban areas. Smaller living spaces are the result of continuous urbanization and centralization of the populace in industrial zones along the Pacific seaboard. One out of five Japanese residents reportedly lives in the greater Kantō plain, where Tōkyō—the political, economic, financial, and educational center of Japan—is situated. The average Tōkyō family with a salaried wage earner can never hope to own a detached house, even with a yard the size of a *tatami* mat (3 by 6 feet), so many opt for a *manshon* (condominium) in one of the high-rises sprouting like shiitake mushrooms above the traffic-choked highways. Others move to the suburbs an hour or two away from the city, or even to a neighboring prefecture, where housing is more affordable—but the family rice earner must get used to a two- to three-hour commute on packed trains. The good news is, once you get away from the metropolis to the small towns in outlying regions, housing prices drop by 30 percent or more. It is also possible to build or buy a traditional house in the country.

Housing Options

JAPANESE- OR WESTERN-STYLE ROOM?

In the past, Japanese houses have been described through Western eyes as "paper houses," and this stereotype contains a kernel of truth. Traditional houses were built of wood, with sliding *amado* (literally, rain-doors) on all sides that could be opened to air the house in hot, humid climates. Inside, rooms were partitioned off with ingenious *fusuma* (wood-framed paper doors) that, when slid back, could open up three or even four rooms into a combined great room when relatives gathered. In place of curtains, windows were fitted with pairs of sliding *shōji* (wooden lattice frames covered with white Japanese paper, smoothed on with homemade rice glue) for privacy. The inevitable tears and rips children made poking fingers through the delicate *shōji* panes were patched with white, cherry-petal-shaped cutouts, then repapered completely at year's end. Floors were covered with *tatami* (thick, rectangular woven rush mats), and cooking areas with earthen floors. *Tatami* are still used in *washitsu* (Japanese-style) rooms, imparting a fresh scent of grasses.

> In the past, Japanese houses have been described through Western eyes as "paper houses," and this stereotype contains a kernel of truth.

If you decide to live in a small town in the rural areas of Honshū (the main island), Kyūshū (southern island), or Shikoku (western island), you may be lucky enough to rent or even buy such a traditional house. Rarely, it may even have a thatched roof, though very few such houses remain, other than as historical museums (as in Takayama, in central Japan). Many Japanese have abandoned traditional houses as too difficult and costly to maintain, and instead have fled to the cities. In modern Japanese housing, stucco or reinforced concrete walls have replaced sliding doors, and lace curtains flutter in place of opaque *shōji*. These days, *onsen* (traditional hot springs inns) may be one of few places you can sleep surrounded by traditional Japanese architecture.

APARTMENT OR CONDO?

In a place where land is at a premium and has been fully developed for

Typical home in the Itabashi neighborhood

more than 400 years, the only direction to build is up. Every day, scores of single-family homes 20 or 30 years old are razed, then replaced with high-rise buildings known as *manshon* ("mansions"), meaning something quite different than a million-dollar estate. How do you tell a *manshon* from an apartment? A *manshon* is a newer, multi-unit, reinforced concrete, high-rise building with units for rent or purchase—like a condominium complex. The fancier ones come with nice landscaping, a lobby, a security guard, and an elevator. Because of its sturdy construction, a *manshon* unit keeps out noise from other units more effectively.

An *apāto* (Japanese abbreviation of apartment), on the other hand, is typically located in an older two- or three-story wood building with thin walls and cheaper rent. There is also public housing subsidized by cities or the Tōkyō metropolis. So many people apply for such units that they are awarded through a lottery, and the wait may be five years or more.

The Housing Search

WHILE YOU'RE LOOKING

Where will you stay while searching for a place to call home? There are several alternatives less costly than paying for a hotel room.

Common Housing Terms

Note that each Japanese vowel is pronounced separately and always sounds like: a = papa, i = pizza, u = put, e = pet, o = port. An "r" in Japanese is *not* pronounced like the English "r," but with a Spanish-style flap of the tongue against the palette.

Number of Rooms

ワンルーム

wan-rūmu | studio/one room

ワン

wan | one

ツー

tsū | two

スリー

surii | three

ワンK

1K | *wan-K* | one room and a tiny kitchen

ツーDK

2DK | *tsū-DK* | two rooms and a dining room-kitchen

ツーLDK

2LDK | *tsū-LDK* | two rooms and a living-dining-kitchen area

スリーSLDK

3SLDK | *surii-SLDK* | three rooms, a storage room, and living-dining-kitchen area

Style of Room

洋室

yōshitsu | Western room

和室

washitsu | Japanese room

畳み

tatami | woven mats; roughly three by six feet, counted in units called *jō*

Type of Unit

賃貸

chintai | rental

売り

uri | for sale

アパート

apāto | apartment

マンション

manshon | condominium or newer apartment

分譲住宅

bunjō-jūtaku | house and lot

都営住宅

toei-jūtaku | city housing

一軒家

ikken-ya | single house

コンクリート

konkuriito | concrete

木造

mokuzō | wood frame

Features

インターホン

intāhon | intercom

エレベーター

erebētā | elevator

オートロック

ōto rokku | automatic lock

玄関

genkan | entry

キッチン

kitchin | kitchen

ガスコンロ

gasu konro | gas stove

電子レンジ

denshi renji | microwave

(continued on next page)

Common Housing Terms (cont'd)

トイレ
toire | toilet

ウオシュレット
uoshuretto | bidet

バス
basu | bath

シャワー
shawā | shower

収納
shūnou | storage

ベランダー
berandā | veranda

バルコニー
barukonii | balcony

エアコン
ea kon | air conditioner

[BS] アンテナ
BS antena | TV antenna

テレビ
terebi | television

カーテン
kāten | curtains

シーツ
shiitsu | sheets

Negotiable

子供
kodomo | children

ペット
petto | pets

ピアノ
piano | piano

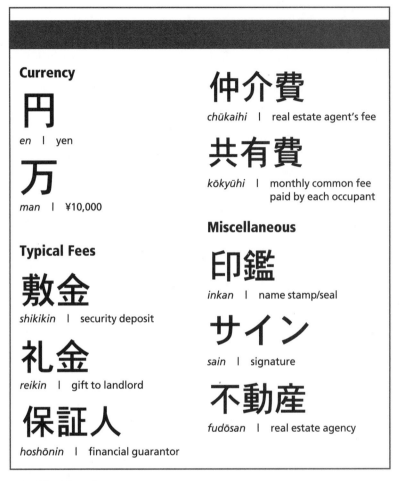

Currency

円
en | yen

万
man | ¥10,000

Typical Fees

敷金
shikikin | security deposit

礼金
reikin | gift to landlord

保証人
hoshōnin | financial guarantor

仲介費
chūkaihi | real estate agent's fee

共有費
kōkyūhi | monthly common fee paid by each occupant

Miscellaneous

印鑑
inkan | name stamp/seal

サイン
sain | signature

不動産
fudōsan | real estate agency

Weekly Mansions

One option is a short-term "weekly mansion," a furnished apartment that includes linens, TV, and basic kitchenware and rents for as low as ¥3,500 ($32) per day. Weekly or monthly *manshon* are popular among Japanese businesspeople and single workers who are transferred to another city short-term. Posters advertising furnished units are common on the trains and subway, as well as online. There are also cheaper hotels that cater to foreigners. You can find these in English weeklies, such as the *Tōkyō Classifieds*.

Japanese Host Families

Another option is to find a Japanese family to stay with for several nights—or even the duration of a school year, if you're a student. If you plan to enroll in a Japanese university, the housing office can likely match you with a host family. Be aware that living in a Japanese home may come with constraints, such as a curfew, lack of personal space due to tight living quarters, scheduled bathing order, and requests to teach English to children or neighbors. If you live with a Japanese family, you should not expect to come and go as you please, returning home only to eat and sleep. You will experience Japanese customs and cultural events as a member of the family, and you can learn a lot firsthand. For instance, observe how the family's shoes are arranged in the *genkan* (entryway)—in which direction do they point?; the order in which family members take baths—where do you fit in?; and how trash is sorted and when it is taken out. Bring small gifts from your hometown or state to present to your host family. These will be greatly appreciated as a token of thoughtfulness, as will pictures of your family, school, and hometown.

In most towns and cities, there are volunteer international organizations waiting to help visitors find everything from housing to jobs to Japanese language lessons. Inquire at your local city or town hall for information, or consult the *Multilingual Living Guide,* available online in fourteen languages.

Renting

PRICES

How much do rentals cost? A two-room apartment in Tōkyō can cost anywhere from ¥88,000 ($800) to ¥880,000 ($8,000) per month. In housing ads, a unit's total dimensions are expressed in square meters, but the size of each room is indicated by number of *tatami* mats, or *jō* (one mat is roughly 3 by 6 feet). Room sizes in mat equivalency—4.5-mat, 6-mat, 8-mat, and so on—represent total floor space, whether or not the floor is actually covered with *tatami*. (See the sidebar "Common Housing Terms" for details.)

RESOURCES

Where do you start looking for a place? English sources include the four daily English newspapers in Japan *(Japan Times, Mainichi Daily News, Asahi Evening News,* and *Yomiuri Daily News),* but most housing advertisements target foreigners of economic means, such as corporate or diplomatic transfers, and are quite expensive. *Tōkyō Classifieds* and other free weekly papers for English-speaking tourists are another source. A search of the Internet will lead to housing sites that cater to "foreigners" (large, expensive units) or to Japanese college students (tiny, cheap units).

© Ruthy Kanagy

Apartment building in Tōkyō

You can also learn from the locals. How do Japanese people find a place to live? Pick up a rental magazine at any bookstore or kiosk. The thick, oversized magazines are a compendium of *chintai* (rental) *apāto* or *manshon* and are organized by region, town, and train line. Say you work near a station on the metropolitan Mita subway line, and you don't want to fight crowds by changing trains during rush hour. If you don't read Japanese, you will need a friend to help you look up the section of the magazine labeled "Mita Line" (in characters). Grouped under each train station along that line, rentals are listed from cheaper to more expensive and from fewer to greater number of rooms, with details on rooms and a phone number to call. If you know Japanese characters, you can get some good information from such books. You can also find similar information from the Japanese websites of the companies who put out the rental magazines *Isize, Chintai, Able,* and *Home Adpark.*

If you've gotten this far and found an apartment that interests you, the next step is to call one of the real estate agents in the magazines. Some may take calls in English, but it's a good idea to have a Japanese friend call for you. Ask about availability and whether you can see the unit. You will probably be asked to visit the office first and fill out an application. Many real estate agents in the cities have branch offices—in Tōkyō, there may be offices around the Shinjuku, Shibuya, Ikebukuro, and Tōkyō stations. You may need a guide to navigate this process.

While you're in the neighborhood of an appealing property, let everyone you meet know that you're looking for a room. The corner greengrocer, stationary store owner, dry cleaner, *yakitori* (grilled chicken on skewers) vendor, your Japanese language teacher, post office worker, or bank teller may know someone with an available room—or may even have one themselves.

RENTAL AGENTS

Another, and perhaps even better, way to find housing is to head to the area where you would like to live and walk up and down the main shopping streets looking for real estate agent's offices. Even if you don't read Japanese, you will be able to identify a real estate agent by the large glass windows papered with rows of housing ads to catch the attention of passersby, indicating price and floor plans. Most neighborhood real estate offices are quite small and carry listings only for buildings in the immediate vicinity. The notices displayed outside the windows indicate whether the property is a *chintai* (rental) or *uri* (sale) and *apāto* or *manshon,* along with details

© Ruthy Kanagy

Two rooms in my former 2DK apartment

such as date of construction, material, number of stories, address, number of minutes' walk to the nearest train station, perhaps a map, and features, including direction (important if you want sunshine), price (including move-in fees), floor plan, and size (counted in *tatami* mats—see the sidebar "Common Housing Terms"). Even if you cannot read all the characters, you should be able to decipher the floor plan and monthly rent. For example, if you know the character for yen, then you can figure that a one-room unit listed for ¥64,000 is roughly $582 per month. Rents are often listed in ¥10,000 units (called *man* in Japanese); thus an apartment advertised for 8.85 *man-en* costs ¥88,500 ($805) per month.

After perusing the housing ads from the sidewalk, you might want to go inside. You can simply point to the apartment listings that interest you—the agent may even give you a photocopy—and ask to see some of the properties. If you can communicate in Japanese (*"Apāto o sagashiterun desu ga"* means "I'm looking for an apartment") or by gestures, great; otherwise, bring a Japanese friend along. The neighborhood agent may make a few phone calls and take you to see the properties immediately, by foot or by bicycle.

Here I must pause to break some unhappy news. When you poke your head through the door, the real estate agent may take one look and shoo you away wordlessly, or cross his or her forearms in the shape of an X and say something that means, "Terribly sorry, but the landlord doesn't rent to *gaijin* (foreigners)." If this happens, nothing you say or do will make any difference. You may have been born and raised in Japan, have lived there for 25 years, be fluent in Japanese, and work for the Japanese government—who promised to be your financial guarantor (see below for more on financial guarantors). I said all of the above and more, but it didn't change a thing. When I called ahead to make an appointment, everything was fine—no one can tell my nationality on the phone, since I'm a natural bilingual. But when I stuck my "high nose" into the office, a wall came between us. If you aren't part of the majority, wishing doesn't make you so. It seems that some bigots are that way by nature, and others may have given a *gaijin* a chance once, only to find that he didn't pay the rent, had raucous parties, emitted strange odors, fed the crows, put out non-burnable trash on burnables day, and eloped with their daughter.

If you get the *gaijin* wave-off, just turn, take a deep breath, and walk out the door. Then reflect on how minorities and those we call "aliens" experience life in our country. On the positive side, although one real estate agent rejected me, I found most to be friendly and helpful. Use your Japanese connections if you can, and also your employer, if you are lucky enough to have one. Then head for the next neighborhood agent with a smile.

REVIEWING YOUR OPTIONS

So, you've picked out three or four apartments and have followed the real estate agent up the stairs to a unit on the fifth floor (considering how you're going to move 30 boxes of books and a queen-size bed). The real estate agent unlocks the door of the vacant unit, steps inside the *genkan* (entryway), and removes her shoes—and so do you. She whips out two pairs of slippers from a bag and lines a pair up for you (never mind that the only time you've worn slippers is after taking a bath in winter).

You step inside and look at four bare walls. The room has potential as a kitchen, even though the only item it contains is a freestanding sink unit with a single faucet—oh, and a round hole bored into the floor next to the entry where you left your shoes. The hole, the agent explains, is where the hose goes to drain cold water from your washing machine (if you decide to buy one). There may or may not be cupboards and, of course, you provide your own stove for cooking—one or two gas rings set on the counter by the sink. You must also supply a refrigerator and sometimes a heater/air conditioner, if you want to be comfortable in seasons other than spring and fall. *Manshon* units tend to come with a small heating/air-conditioning unit on the wall. When I didn't see one in the apartment I wanted to rent, I asked my agent if she could persuade the landlord to provide one—and he did! I also asked for high-speed Internet access and, several months later, it was installed in the whole apartment building (for a fee, of course).

While you're poking about the other rooms—if it's not a *wan-rūmu* (studio)—note the number and sizes of closets and storage areas. Japanese-style *oshiire* (traditional closets) have a very deep shelf splitting the closet in two horizontally—handy for storing futons (cotton-filled mattresses) by day, but not so handy for hanging clothes (you can buy spring-loaded adjustable rods for that purpose). Note how the bathroom area is arranged. Are the bath, sink, and toilet all in one room—perhaps a compact, molded plastic unit like airplane bathrooms—or are the bath and toilet entries separate? (The latter is handy if you have a roommate.) If there are two or more rooms in addition to the kitchen, does each of them have direct access to the kitchen, or do you have to walk through another room each time you go to the bathroom? Notice the size and direction of windows: Do they face a gray wall one foot away, or can you see a parking lot or a small patch of blue?

Also note the floor covering: Is it *tatami* (comfortable enough to walk on, and soft enough to lay futons on to sleep) or *furōringu* (flooring, usually laminate wood)? Do the *tatami* look and smell new? (New *tatami* have a slightly green color and smell of rush grasses.) In better apartments, *tatami* are recovered or even replaced after a tenant moves out. Sunlight

© Ruthy Kanagy

Bedding and laundry airing over balconies

fades and dries *tatami,* so newspapers may be covering the *tatami* if the unit is unoccupied). Is the apartment unit above or below occupied? If so, you might want to arrange to see the unit again at night or on Sunday, to check the noise level when the neighbors are home. As noted above, concrete *manshon* have thicker, more soundproof walls than wood-frame apartments. Ask how many minutes it takes to walk to the bus and train station, as well as the nearest convenience store, supermarket, post office, and hospital—important information if you'll need to cover this distance twice a day. Proximity to public transportation is particularly important if you plan to walk to trains and buses, but less so if you have a trusty bicycle (highly recommended).

CLOSING THE DEAL

Financial Guarantors and Key Money

You've now spent several days, weeks, or even months searching for your home in Japan. You found one you really like and have filled out an application at the real estate agent's office (again, help from a Japanese-speaking friend is valuable). Whether it's a house or an apartment, the real estate agent will not finalize the agreement without a paper signed by a financial guarantor. This is a form that has to be signed—or rather, stamped with an *inkan* (name seal)—by a Japanese citizen who trusts you enough to put her or his financial resources at risk on your behalf. If you stop paying rent or damage the apartment, your guarantor is ultimately liable. If you already have a job and an employer who will be your guarantor, you're very fortunate.

When the final papers are signed and sealed, be prepared to hand over—in cash—the equivalent of six months' rent (sometimes less). Discrimination? No, that's how renting works in Japan—the not-so-hidden costs include a *shikikin* (security deposit) equivalent to one–two months' rent (refundable); *reikin* (literally, gratitude money) to the landlord, also one–three or more months' rent (nonrefundable). In addition, the real estate agent takes one month's rent as a fee for handling the contract (nonrefundable). In addition, there may be a *kōkyūhi* (public or common fee) assessed from each tenant in a building.

When renting an apartment, you will typically have to sign a lease for two years, but usually there's no penalty for moving out sooner. The rent can't be raised during the lease period, but it can be raised when you renew. In addition, renewing the lease often requires another "gift" to the landlord equal to one month's rent.

In your apartment, you will find information on utilities—gas, electric, and water—with instructions on how to request service by telephone. Your real estate agent also has this information and may be able to help you arrange for utilities to be turned on promptly when you move in. The gas company will come after you've installed the gas kitchen ring to check for leaking tubes and to turn the gas on. There are two valves attached to the gas tubing: one is the main valve, which should be shut off in an earthquake; and the other should be turned on and off each time you use the stove. The water company will check the water flow and quality from your kitchen faucet and read the meter. The electric company will read the meter outside. In each case, you have the option of paying your monthly bill at the corner *conbini* (convenience store), or you can go to your bank to arrange automatic payment of utility bills from your bank account. In either case, you will receive bills in the mail with your meter reading and balance due. Perhaps because personal checks are not used in Japan, the automatic bank payment system is widely used, highly efficient, and reliable. (See Chapter 9, Finance, for more information.)

Buying

After several years in Japan, you may become attached to the culture or to someone from the culture. You might start thinking about buying a house

A House in the Central Mountains

What is involved in building a house today? A former high-school classmate, Phil Bennett, lives in the mountains of Gunma prefecture. He and his wife, Akiko, built a combination home and restaurant, Café Manna, on the banks of the Tone River. The village of Kamimoku (part of Tsukiyono-chō, population 10,000) is three hours north—and many lifestyles removed—from Tōkyō. Phil describes their experience as follows:

"A friend of Akiko's found the spot on the riverbank where we are and introduced us to the landowner, who agreed to lease 100 *tsubo* (330 square meters/3,550 square feet) for ¥10,000 ($91) a month. Since most of the land sloped down to the river, in order for us to have some flat land to build on, our contractor [had to haul] in huge preformed L-shaped concrete slabs as retaining walls for the filled-in land. Building the base for the house cost ¥6 million ($54,500), and our contractor spent a lot of time at the Numata Civil Engineering Bureau trying to persuade the inspectors that the project was safe. Given that we were building on a riverbank, the Bureau was very skeptical and delayed construction for several months until they finally gave

the OK. The next year, we learned the civil engineers had good reason to be cautious when the river flooded and washed away two-thirds of the river-bank below our house.

The building cost ¥11 million ($100,000), and the interior and restaurant fittings cost about ¥2.5 million ($22,700). There are no restrictions that I know of on foreigners buying land or building per se, but it is hard to get a bank loan if you don't have permanent resident status. In our area, many landowners are reluctant to sell land that has belonged to their families for many generations and would rather rent it instead. Akiko got a ¥10 million ($90,900) loan from her bank, payable in 10 years at an interest rate of about 1.5 percent, [with a] monthly payment of about ¥60,000 ($545)."

Plenty of Americans and other internationals from Tōkyō want to escape to a summer home in the mountains—but most are married to Japanese spouses who serve as the registered heads of the household, so everything is done in their names. The resulting collection of cabins in Phil and Akiko's part of the country is referred to as *gaijin-mura,* meaning "foreigner village."

and making it more permanent—especially when your two-year apartment lease is up and the landlord raises the rent (and you're charged one month's rent to renew). So, what are your options for buying a home? In urban areas, such as Tōkyō, the price of a detached house and land is so out of reach that many Japanese families opt to buy a *manshon* instead.

To advertise high-rise condos, builders usually construct model rooms near high-traffic streets, put flags up, and hand out brochures at the station to attract buyers before the *manshon* is built. The model room is made of plywood and cheap material, then torn down after a suitable time. The price depends on the location, size, year of construction, and amenities.

Where I lived in northern Tōkyō (Itabashi-ku, where the cost of real estate is less than in the core *ku*), a three-room unit built in 1985 with compact floor space of 49 square meters (about 527 square feet) was selling for ¥15.3 million ($139,000). You could live in a four-room *manshon* with 109.5 square meters (1,179 square feet) of space for ¥37.8 million ($344,000). These are the low-end prices. New construction closer to the center of the city is priced considerably higher.

To North Americans used to living in 2,000 or more square feet, a home this small may be a shock. Personally, living in two 9- by 12-foot rooms plus a tiny kitchen for three years with my daughter had a positive effect—it puts an end to hoarding. Plus, you don't have to walk anywhere to fetch something—just reach.

If you want more space or wish to live in a pricier neighborhood, it will take ample resources. Many Japanese families take out 75-year or even 100-year mortgages to buy a house (meaning the mortgage will be passed on to their grandchildren). For this reason, the actual home ownership rate in urban areas like Tōkyō is less than 40 percent. In outlying prefectures, home ownership is higher: 70 percent in Gunma prefecture and 60–70 percent in Hiroshima and Shikoku to the west. The national average rate is 60 percent, and the average amount of floor space per home is 92 square feet.

While as a foreigner, you encounter no legal restrictions on buying property, it's very difficult for a foreigner to obtain a bank loan. You have to be a permanent resident, and you will usually need a guarantor. Banks will not loan more than three times your annual salary. However, if your spouse is Japanese, a mortgage can be taken out in his or her name.

BUILDING

Yes, it is possible to build a home in Japan. Is the process easy? No. Buying land is quite a complex process, and you're advised to engage professional assistance in the transaction to make sure it proceeds according to Japanese real estate laws. The Japanese Civil Code is sometimes confusing and difficult even for Japanese legal experts to interpret. Often it's wiser to simply lease a lot from the owner for a certain length of time. Many Japanese are reluctant to sell land that's been handed down for generations, but are willing to rent it out. You can build a home on a rented lot without too much difficulty. Many Japanese houses are not built to last more than 20 or 30 years, after which they are torn down and rebuilt, or sold to the highest bidder (who constructs a twelve-story *manshon* on the lot).

Back in 1951, when my parents sailed from Seattle to Yokohama on the

Neighborhood real estate office

President Wilson, many American missionaries were settling in small towns and building churches and homes (since so many buildings were destroyed in the war, rentals were scarce). My parents built a small church and a house in eastern Hokkaidō out of cement blocks. I remember watching the cement being mixed, poured into a mold, and set out on boards to dry. The house in Nakashibetsu that Lee and Adella built stood solid for nearly four decades before yielding to a modern house more in keeping with prosperity.

Moving In

FURNISHINGS

To outfit your apartment or house, you will need to purchase such things as shower and window curtains and possibly curtain rods, light bulbs, and ceiling lights—and furniture, of course, which you can buy relatively inexpensively at any number of *risaikuru shoppu* (recycle shops, or secondhand stores). *Risaikuru shoppu* have become quite popular and well-stocked in recent years. Some are very large and will deliver for a fee. You will find the best selection in March, national moving month.

Many cities have a *shōhisha sentaa* (consumer center) to handle complaints and give advice regarding shopping commercial goods, door-to-door sales, etc. They may have a *risaikuru sentaa* (swap shop) of used clothing and furniture.

NEIGHBORHOOD PROTOCOL

Once you've moved in, there are several things you can do to break the ice with your new neighbors. Tradition dictates that you present a small gift, such as a hand towel, to your neighbors living on either side and in the three houses across the street. However, in a 20-story *manshon,* only the sky or a view of distant mountains (if you're lucky) will be across from you; more likely, you'll see a solid wall. In these close quarters, it goes without saying that you should avoid making excessive noise (e.g., talking in a loud voice or playing loud music) in your apartment, especially at night.

But even if you never see your neighbors, be sure to follow the system for putting out trash on designated days, or you'll risk annoying your neighbors, as well as the trash collectors. Divide trash into burnable items (paper, wood, clothing, and kitchen garbage), nonburnable items (plastic bags and containers, metal, and anything that would be toxic to burn), and recyclables (glass bottles, tin, aluminum, newspaper, magazines, and cardboard). The local supermarket usually has bins to recycle plastic drink bottles, white Styrofoam food trays (from the grocery store), and washed and flattened milk and juice cartons. Burnables are generally collected twice a week, and nonburnables and recyclables once a week, at a designated spot along the street. At many collection sites, stacks of white plastic trash bags are covered with blue netting to prevent pesky crows, which is why your neighbors will not look at you kindly for putting the trash out the night before official pickup day.

Doing your wash at the local coin laundry, which may double as the neighborhood public bath (mine did), is another creative way to meet the neighbors, if you are adventurous. Most of your neighbors will do the wash at home on days that it's not raining, then hang the laundry out to dry on poles strung horizontally across the balcony. On sunny days, don't be surprised to see thick futons, mattress covers, sheets, and blankets hanging out of windows and balconies, and even draped over bicycles to catch some rays. Due to the humid climate, bedding gets damp and musty unless aired out. Giant spring-loaded clothespins prevent the family bedding from leaping off 13th floor balconies.

One reason people may not initiate conversations with you is that they may be self-conscious about not being able to speak English well, even though everyone in Japan studies English starting in grade seven. On occasion, take the initiative and strike up a conversation with someone. You can ask your neighbors for help finding a supermarket, post office, bank, or drugstore. Hopefully, you will develop some friends over time, but don't be surprised if they don't invite you to their home. Most homes are simply too small to entertain. Instead, people go out to eat or drink together and enjoy karaoke.

Give yourself at least three to six months to feel acclimated to your new home and neighborhood. The *Daily Living Guide,* published by the Itabashi-ku in Tōkyō, has some tips for settling in, including the following: "Japanese are traditionally community-oriented, and it is important to have good relationships with your neighbors. Even though you may not be able to speak Japanese fluently, you will find that you can get a lot of support from your neighborhood. By exchanging information and helping each other, your life will become more fulfilled and enjoyable, so try to initiate contacts with your neighbors."

Prime Living Locations

© Ruthy Kanagy

RUSSIA

Sakhalin
Island

*Sea of
Okhotsk*

145°

45°

Wakkanai

Rebun Island

HOKKAIDŌ

HOKKAIDŌ
北海道

Kurile
Islands

CHINA

Obihiro

Kushiro

Sapporo

40°

Hakodate

Aomori

NORTH
KOREA

JAPAN
日本

14

Sendai

Sea of

Japan

**CENTRAL
MOUNTAINS**

Maebashi

Nagano

TŌKYŌ

THE WEST

Kyōto

Nagoya

TŌKYŌ

SOUTH
KOREA

INLAND SEA

Takamatsu

Ōsaka

HONSHŪ
本州

*PACIFIC
OCEAN*

Hiroshima

Matsuyama

Kōchi

Tokushima

Fukuoka

SHIKOKU
四国

30°

Nagasaki

KYŪSHŪ
九州

135°

140°

*East
China
Sea*

30°

AMAMI

Amami
Islands

**PRIME LIVING
LOCATIONS**

OKINAWA

130°

135°

140°

0   150 mi
0   150 km

© Ruthy Kanagy

Overview

T he following prime living locations offer contrasts in climate, environment, industry, population density, history, cultural traditions, and dialects. We start with Tōkyō, the nation's capital; fly north to Hokkaidō, the last frontier; south to Gunma and Nagano, in the central mountains of Honshū; west to the ancient capital, Kyōto, and to Ōsaka, center of commerce; and finally to Hiroshima and the four prefectures of Shikoku, squared off along the Inland Sea.

TŌKYŌ

When we think of Japan, most of us think of Tōkyō—that megalopolis where crowds of dark-haired people in suits are jammed onto trains by hired pushers; a city of skyscrapers where everything is digital and high-tech, and sushi and anime abound. True, Tōkyō has the highest population density in the country (Ōsaka is second) and has hot, sultry summers and cold winters with snow (even blizzards—I was born during one). But Tōkyō also has

Colors and costumes on a Harajuku Sunday

© Ruthy Kanagy

mountains, gorges, hot springs, and eight semitropical islands with active volcanoes. There's a great deal of tradition in Tōkyō, if you look for it, such as neighborhood festivals at shrines and temples. If you're looking for English-language resources, a large English-speaking community, and a job where you need only minimal Japanese, you may find it in Tōkyō—among 12 million neighbors. If you decide to live in the Eastern capital, take the time to explore the six other prefectures that make up the Kantō region— Chiba-ken (location of Narita Airport), Kanagawa-ken, Saitama-ken, Tochigi-ken, Ibaragi-ken, and Gunma-ken (*ken* means prefecture).

HOKKAIDŌ

Hokkaidō, the frontier island to the north, is strikingly similar to the U.S. Pacific Northwest in geography and climate, with cool summers, snowy winters, open spaces, and largely unspoiled nature.

Hokkaidō is the largest prefecture in Japan in terms of land area (about the size of the state of Indiana), but with only 5.7 million people (less than 5 percent of the population of Japan) living near mountain ranges, lakes, wetlands, and plains. The land is 70 percent forested, 16 percent used for agriculture, and only 1.8 percent used for residences. The three characters in the word Hokkaidō mean North, Sea, and Circuit.

People in Hokkaidō often say that the island's open space creates communities less bound to tradition, with more open attitudes. Based on my experience growing up in eastern Hokkaidō, I would say this is true. You're allowed to be an individual and move off the beaten track. If you have an idea for a business related to food, agriculture, nature, or outdoor sports, Hokkaidō might have room for you. If you enjoy cosmopolitan city life, Sapporo (the island's main city) has 1.5 million people and scores of foreign entrepreneurs, teachers, and housebuilders. By airplane, you can be in Tōkyō in an hour; by train, it's a scenic 10- or 12-hour journey to the capital; and by ferry, a leisurely 20 hours on the waves. That is, if you need to go south at all, once you've made your home in Hokkaidō.

> *Hokkaidō, the frontier island to the north, is strikingly similar to the U.S. Pacific Northwest in geography and climate, with cool summers, snowy winters, open spaces, and largely unspoiled nature.*

CENTRAL MOUNTAINS: GUNMA AND NAGANO

What if you want it all—to live close to Tōkyō, but go rafting on rushing rivers, snowshoeing in the mountains, and *sansai*-gathering (wild vegetables) in the spring? All of these activities await in the mountains of Gunma-ken, just two hours north of Tōkyō by special express train. A fair percentage of the Tōkyō foreign contingent heads for the mountains during the sweltering summer months. One enterprising local town even rents rice paddies out to Tōkyōites who want the experience of planting seedlings by hand in the mud and harvesting it in the fall. Less urbanization and more traditions are what you'll see here, although most of the young people head for the city lights as soon as they're old enough.

Nagano prefecture, the gateway to the Japan Alps and host of the 1998 Winter Olympics, is west of Gunma. If you'd like to live surrounded by snow-capped mountains, you can find a place here. Some areas of Nagano are summer resorts for city folk, such as Karuizawa. You can experience a rural lifestyle, connected to the earth and strikingly scenic, yet only two hours from urban Tōkyō—thanks to the *shinkansen* (high-speed train) tracks laid down in time for the Olympics.

THE WEST: KYŌTO AND ŌSAKA

The Kansai area contains three major cities—Ōsaka, Kōbe, and Kyōto. Kansai is the other end of the continuous industrial zone that stretches from Tōkyō along the Pacific coast, where almost 70 percent of the Japanese population lives. Economically, Kansai plays a vital role second only to Tōkyō. The three Kansai cities have distinct characteristics, yet

Shintō assistant at a shrine on Miyajima Island

are only an hour or less apart. Kyōto has a 1,200-year-old historic and cultural heritage, Ōsaka is the commercial center, and Kōbe has a multinational feel. In this region, you'll find historic spots, many designated as World Heritage Sites, as well as skyscrapers, business districts, restaurants, shopping malls—and Universal Studios.

> *If you choose to live in Kyōto, you'll have traditional culture all around you—countless Buddhist temples, Shintō shrines, thousand-year-old festivals, and numerous universities.*

In Ōsaka, the legend goes, people greet each other by asking, *"Mōkatte makka?"* ("Making any dough?"). This supports the common notion that Ōsakans are supposedly more direct, pragmatic, practical-minded, and also impatient. These qualities have nurtured many products and ideas. Ōsakans speak Ōsaka-ben (*ben* means dialect), and are the only dialect-speakers in Japan who don't switch to standard Japanese when they're around Tōkyōites—or so I've heard. In other words, they're proud of their dialect and don't try to hide it, as too often happens with speakers from other regions.

If you choose to live in Kyōto, you'll have traditional culture all around you—countless Buddhist temples, Shintō shrines, thousand-year-old festivals, and numerous universities where you might possibly teach. The

Kyōto dialect is considered refined—or a soft touch. In Kyōto, people welcome you saying, *"Oideyasu"* (instead of *"Irasshai"*), and thank you with *"Ōkini"* (rather than *"Arigatō"*). Kansai food is flavored differently than Kantō; the latter is more salty, with a soy flavor, while Kansai cuisine tastes sweeter. Kansai is only three hours away from Tōkyō, thanks to the *shinkansen.*

INLAND SEA: HIROSHIMA AND SHIKOKU

Two hours further west from Kansai, you arrive in the Hiroshima prefecture. This is western Honshū, influenced by the Setonaikai (Inland Sea)—the scene of many fierce battles during the feudal period. The climate is also milder, with less wind and rain. Hiroshima is a regional city and very international, with a message for the world. Every head of state ought to visit the Peace Memorial Park and listen. Hiroshima also has mountains, small towns, and superb oysters in winter, cooked a dozen ways. Hiroshima dialect is spoken here, but so is standard Japanese.

Whether you cross the sea by ferry, train, bus, or car, in an hour you've piggy-backed over the Inland Sea islands and landed in Shikoku. Shikoku means "four countries" or districts, which make up the smallest of Japan's main islands. From the northeast corner, they are Kagawa, Tokushima, Kōchi, and Ehime. Shikoku is rural, with a slower pace, leaving time to enjoy the mountains, gorges, rivers, and beaches. Resident Americans and other English-speakers are active in their communities, producing English newsletters, radio programs, and websites. Many universities have native English speakers on the teaching staff.

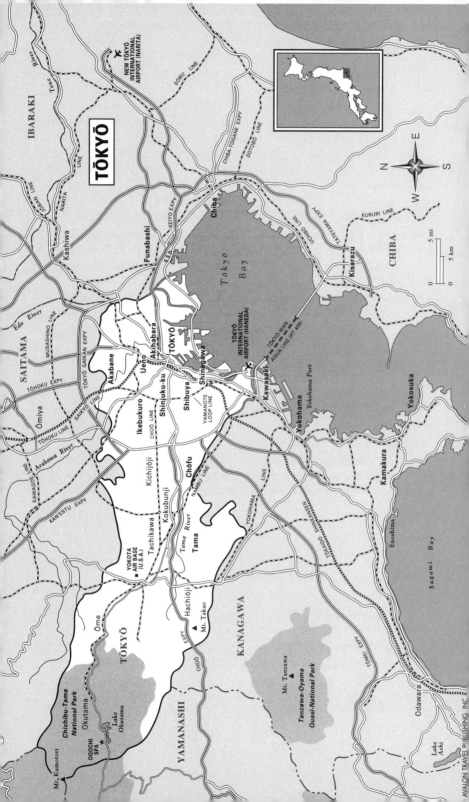

Tōkyō

Situated on the Kantō plain in the middle of Honshū, Tōkyō (pronounced "To-o-kyo-o," in four syllables)—home to 12.7 million people—is the geographic center of Japan. Including the population of the neighboring prefectures of Saitama, Kanagawa, and Chiba, one out of every five Japanese resides in the Kantō region. Tōkyō is also the political, economic, commercial, transportation, educational, cultural, and psychological center of Japan. Almost all major corporations have their headquarters in Tōkyō. All the prestigious universities are here, including renowned Tōkyō University. The emperor and his family reside on the Imperial Palace grounds—a green oasis in the middle of the capital city. And although the idea of moving the capital elsewhere has been debated in recent years, the national government and ministries are firmly planted in the Kasumigaseki district. Loud, exciting, and filled with concrete, neon, museums, concerts, theater, and sports, Tōkyō is the ultimate consumer's paradise. It's as if Washington D.C., New York, Chicago, and

Los Angeles were blended into a giant megalopolis in the middle of Kansas, and 26 percent of the U.S. population took up residence there.

Although Tōkyō is commonly referred to as a "city" in English, it is actually a prefecture (like a state) with a governor, and officially called Tōkyō-to (Tōkyō metropolitan prefecture). This narrow piece of land, measuring 25 kilometers (15.5 miles) from north to south and 90 kilometers (56 miles) from east to west, is divided into 23 core *ku* (city wards) and 26 cities, five towns, and eight villages extending west. Included in the villages are the Izu and Ogasawara Islands, dotting the Pacific like skipping stones.

Sound a little crowded? Certainly, when you're rubbing elbows with eight million people in the core *ku*. Even so, most Tōkyōites—or New Yorkers or Parisians—would very likely say, "So what if it's crowded? It's convenient," and disparage the countryside as too far out of the way. If you love noise, lights, crowds, trains, and a full palette of choices for how to spend your time, then Tōkyō may be the place for you. (If, on the other hand, you love solitude, gardening, and animals, suffer from asthma or allergies, or play the trumpet, you might prefer to live elsewhere in Japan—see the other prime living location chapters for ideas.)

ADVANTAGES AND DRAWBACKS

Is Tōkyō the right place for you? More than 12 million Japanese have said, *"Hai"* ("Yes"). If you love 24-hour amenities, enjoy being carefree and car-free, and adore art museums, theater, live concerts, and crowds, you will thrive in Tōkyō—or Ōsaka or Sapporo or Fukuoka. And if you're not keen on learning Japanese, you will be closer to English resources in Tōkyō than anywhere else.

However, if you have health problems, such as allergies or asthma, Tōkyō's exhaust (though much reduced of late) and cedar pollen season (January–March) may be aggravating. In addition, Tōkyō has relatively few trees and green spaces, though the rows of potted trees and planter gardens lining street curbs evidence residents' love of nature (there's nothing like a plum tree in a pot, blooming with all its might). If you have children, there are few safe places to play or ride bikes with them, unless you live next to a large park. And if your goal is to immerse yourself in traditional Japanese arts, Kyōto may be more to your liking, although there are some artisans and craftspeople in Tōkyō.

History

In my travels, I've found that the more I know about a place, the more

© Ruthy Kanagy

Visitors to the East Garden of the Imperial Palace

pleasurable my stay, whether for a few days or a year. If you know where to look, evidence of Tōkyō's long history is abundant. In 1603, the spotlight fell on the village of Edo, when Tokugawa Ieyasu ascended to the shōgunate (military general) and established political rule over Japan. Tokugawa set about building a castle city, and the population grew rapidly to more than one million by the 1800s. To maintain a grip on the *daimyō* (regional lords) who might have designs on him, the shōgun instituted a system of *sankin kōtai* (alternate attendance). All *daimyō* were commanded to pay a visit to Edo every other year, leaving their wives and children behind, effectively as hostages. Long processions of *daimyō*, samurai retainers, and servants carrying household goods from outlying regions to the capital became a common sight. The routes leading east from Kyōto to Edo included the Tōkaidō (east sea way) and the Nakasendō (middle mountain way). The journey took three months on foot.

Four hundred years later, one of these ancient routes is called the Tōkaidō train line, which Japan Railway (JR) began operating in 1914 with service to Kōbe, west of Kyōto. Now, the trip to Kyōto is just two hours and 40 minutes by the Tōkaidō *shinkansen* (high-speed train). Nakasendō is now Route 17, a major truck route commencing at Nihonbashi, east of the present Yamanote loop. Just as mile markers stand along the old

Former samurai cut off their topknots and replaced their swords and kimonos with Victorian-style bowler hats, suits, and walking sticks; women donned high collars and full skirts.

highway linking Philadelphia and Lancaster, Pennsylvania, a stone marker stands where the ancient highway began; another marker stands in Itabashi-ku, beside the busy highway. In 19th-century Edo, new cultural forms became popular. Flamboyant Kabuki developed as the first theater for the common people, and mass production of *ukiyo-e* (wood-block prints) made art accessible to everyone. (See Chapter 3, People and Culture, for more information on the arts in Japan.)

During the 250 years of the Tokugawa era, the emperor remained in Kyōto, which had been the capital city for a thousand years. This changed in 1868, when the rule of the shōgun ended, and the emperor was "restored" and brought to the new "Eastern capital"—Tōkyō. 1868 to 1912, known as the Meiji period, saw the introduction of brick buildings, paved roads, telecommunications, public education (first for boys, later for girls), and steam locomotives. In 1885, the first prime minister was selected and a cabinet form of government (with a constitution) established. Former samurai cut off their topknots and replaced their swords and kimonos with Victorian-style bowler hats, suits, and walking sticks; women donned high collars and full skirts. The nation's first zoo opened in Ueno in 1882—you can still visit today.

In the early 1900s, more people moved into the city for work, and the consumer lifestyle was born. In 1923, the earth shook, and the Kantō region experienced its worst natural disaster. More than 140,000 people died or disappeared, and 300,000 houses were destroyed in fires. Following the Great Kantō Earthquake, the city formulated an urban reconstruction plan, but did not have the budget to implement it. This may account for the mixture of residences, factories, schools, and commercial establishments that make up Tōkyō neighborhoods. Starting in 1926, during the Showa era, the first subway line opened between Asakusa and Ueno. In 1931, the airport at Haneda (now mostly used for domestic flights) was built, and in 1941, the Port of Tōkyō opened. By this time, Tōkyō was a city of 6.3 million, on the scale of New York and London.

In 1943, Tōkyō-to was formed, and the first governor appointed. During the last two years of World War II, Tōkyō was bombed 102 times by U.S. forces. (March 10, 1945, was the worst day; more than 100,000 people perished.) Five months later, Japan surrendered and the war ended. During the war period, schoolchildren were evacuated to the countryside with their teachers. Tōkyō's population dropped to 3.4 million. Today, you can see documentary accounts of the firebombing, along with pictures

drawn by children about their experience of *sokai* (evacuation), at resource centers maintained by many of the *ku* (city wards).

The 23-*ku* system of Tōkyō was organized in 1949. The next three
decades saw economic growth and mass production. By 1962, Tōkyō's population reached 10 million. Japan hosted the Olympics in 1964, and in
preparation built the first *shinkansen* line (Tōkyō to Kōbe, paralleling the
Tōkaidō route) and the Metro Expressway. As a result of rapid industrial expansion, Tōkyō suffered the effects of congestion and air, water, and
noise pollution. During the late 1980s, land prices and stocks shot up
in a bubble economy, then crashed in the early 1990s. Economic recession
and the financial crisis of banks and government continue today, although the beginning of 2004 has seen some positive change (see Chapter 9, Finance). Tōkyō is looking to attract more tourists and residents as
a partial solution. But despite tough economic times, Tōkyōites do not just
stay at home. In 2000, according to the Tōkyō Metropolitan Government Bureau of General Affairs, one out of every four metropolitan residents traveled abroad. The largest number visited Asia and North America;
other destinations included Europe, Africa, South America, and the South
Pole (by 63 scientists!).

The Lay of the Land

NEIGHBORHOODS
The saying "All roads lead to Edo" rings as true today as it did 200
years ago, when Edo (now Tōkyō) was an overgrown castle town of
one million. Every day, hundreds of *shinkansen* depart and return to
Tōkyō station, scores of planes depart and land at Haneda and Narita airports, and close to 100 ships dock at Tōkyō Port. Unlike car travel in the
U.S., where interstate highways are designed to bypass cities, Tōkyō's
highly developed transit system takes you through multiple layers of
densely populated metropolis. If you're not used to urban areas, it can
be a bit overwhelming. However, once you understand how the metropolis is organized and linked to the transportation system, it won't
seem so confusing.

If you look at a transportation map of Tōkyō, you will see a looped train
line called Yamanote-sen (*sen* means line), usually marked green. The
loop encircles the four busiest *ku*—Bunkyo-ku, Chiyoda-ku, Minato-ku, and
Shinjuku-ku. From the Yamanote hub, dozens of train lines radiate in
all directions. At every point where a train line intersects with the loop are
the major stations, which also serve as transfer points to outlying areas.

One Day in Tōkyō

As of February 2003, there were 6.13 million men and 6.16 million women living in Tōkyō in 5.6 million households. Every day, 1,213 more people moved into Tōkyō and 1,016 people moved out; 275 babies were born and 233 people died; 243 couples were married and 78 pairs divorced.

In an average day, Tōkyōites ate 1,700 tons of rice, 4,700 tons of vegetables, 1,800 tons of fruit, 1,900 tons of fish and seafood, and 230 tons of meat. They drank 4.5 million bottles of beer and happōshu (brewed with less than 67 percent malt), 140,000 bottles of sake, 400,000 bottles of shōchū (distilled spirits), 240,000 bottles of wine, and 80,000 bottles of whiskey.

They sent 19 million pieces of domestic mail.

In an average day, there were 8.5 million Japan Railway (JR) riders, 7.3 million private train line passengers, 7.2 million subway riders, 2 million bus riders, 80,000 plane passengers, 2,000 ferry passengers, and 5.9 million automobile drivers.

In an average day, Tōkyōites lost ¥20 million ($182,000), found ¥6.8 million ($62,000), lost 2,400 items, and turned in 4,500 items.

They committed 802 crimes (arrests), stole ¥14 million ($127,300), and caused 242 traffic accidents—injuring or killing 280 people. The police rescued 44 lost children, helped 25 drunks, and fielded 3,500 emergency phone calls.

They took out 13,000 tons of trash for collection and produced 5.9 million square meters (63.5 million square feet) of sewage.

In an average day, 19 fires caused ¥26 million ($236,000) in damage, 2,900 people reported fire emergencies, and 1,600 emergency vehicles were dispatched.

In an average day, 10,000 people visited Ueno Zoo, 5,800 visited Kasai Rinkai Aquarium on Tōkyō Bay, 4,700 visited Edo Tōkyō Historical Museum, and 67,000 went to the movies. 210,000 books were checked out from libraries.

In an average day, Tōkyō exported products worth ¥34.9 billion ($317 million) and imported products worth ¥38.8 billion ($353 million). Trucks transported 550,000 tons of goods, JR trains transported 17,000 tons, and 91 ships docked at the Port of Tōkyō.

Source: Tōkyō No Ichi-Nichi (A Day in Tōkyō), Tōkyō Metropolitan Government Bureau of General Affairs, 2003

Viewing the Yamanote line as a clock, Ueno is at 2:00, Tōkyō station at 4:00, Shinagawa at 6:00, Shibuya at 8:00, Shinjuku at 9:00, and Ikebukuro at 10:00. Underground there are 12 color-coded subway lines crisscrossing 23 *ku* in every direction.

Imagine that your train has arrived in Shinjuku. No matter what direction you exit from the station, you will see large department stores, high-rise office buildings, theaters, and restaurants, some of them built into the train station itself. By contrast, if you exit at any of the smaller stops, you will find yourself in the middle of a Tōkyō neighborhood fanning out from the train station. Buses and taxis are lined up to take you wherever the trains don't. Shopping streets in several directions are lined with specialty shops, such as the greengrocer, baker, and butcher, as well as seafood, tea, rice, sake, and tofu shops. There are also multiple *conbini* (convenience stores), fast food places, beauty salons, Pachinko (pinball) parlors, restaurants, real estate offices, and a post office. These streets are unnamed and impossibly narrow, with concrete telephone poles jutting into the lanes—in short, a jumble of pedestrians, bicycles, motorcycles, cars, buses, taxis, and trucks. The white lines painted at the edges of the streets are not only bicycle lanes—they also take the place of sidewalks.

The farther west you travel away from the Yamanote loop, the closer you get to rural Tōkyō, and the more greenery you see. The westbound Chūō (central) line traverses the broad Tama region above Tamagawa (Tama River), with stops at major stations, such as Ogikubo, Mitaka, Kichijōji, and Kunitachi. After an hour or more, you will notice fewer high-rise buildings and a bit more space between houses, maybe a vegetable garden or two; and then the houses yield to green trees entirely, and you reach your destination deep in the mountains of Oku-Tama (*oku* means interior). Hiking trails, hot-springs inns, and rushing streams abound, and it's hard to believe that you are still in Tōkyō. If you picked a weekday to visit, you may have a quiet outing. But if it's the weekend or a national holiday, don't turn around, because half of Tōkyō will be gaining on you!

DEMOGRAPHICS

It should come as no surprise that not everyone living in Tōkyō is Japanese. In 2003, just over 344,000 city residents were "registered foreigners," that is, those living in Japan longer than six months who registered their status at city hall. Of these, 33 percent were Chinese and 30 percent Korean—most Chinese and Koreans in Japan are second-, third-, or even fourth-generation residents, but are not granted citizenship. Almost 9 percent were from the Philippines, 5.4 percent from the U.S., and fewer from Britain, Thailand, and Brazil. Short-term visitors are not included in these figures. Depending on their country of origin, temporary visitors may stay in Japan up to 90 days with no visa. (See Chapter 5, Making the Move, for detailed visa information.)

> *It should come as no surprise that not everyone living in Tōkyō is Japanese.*

CLIMATE

Tōkyō is cold in winter, and generally hot and muggy from July to September. The average temperature in February, the coldest month, is

Lunchtime in the metropolis

6°C (43°F) and in August, 28°C (83°F). Also in February, dark pink plum trees bloom. In late March, *sakura* (cherry trees) unfurl. The rainy season begins about the same time as iris season in June, while typhoons in late summer and fall bring rain and strong winds. In November, when the air turns chilly, rows of gingko trees lining the Tōkyō University campus and many city streets turn golden, and December is so busy with "forget-the-old-year" parties and gifts that even teachers have to run. (*Shiwasu* is the old name for December, and literally means "teachers run.") Oshōgatsu (New Year's) is the biggest holiday of the year. Millions desert the metropolis for their annual visit to the homestead or a junket overseas, and for three short days, you can hear the *hashi* (chopsticks) drop in Tōkyō.

ENTERTAINMENT AND RECREATION

Tōkyō offers many places to explore, including parks, historic neighborhoods, museums, antique shops, live shows, and at least 13 amusement and theme parks (including Tōkyō Disneyland and Disney Sea). There are also many places for spiritual fulfillment—numerous temples, shrines, synagogues, mosques, and churches (Tōkyō Union Church in Shibuya has English services).

As you begin to explore Tōkyō, you might enjoy some of the following places. They are listed below going clockwise around the Yamanote loop, starting at Ueno (in the 2:00 position).

Ueno and Vicinity

Ueno is for museum buffs: the National Science Museum, National Museum of Western Art, Tōkyō National Museum, Tōkyō Metropolitan Festival Hall, and the Shitamachi Museum are here, and this area also contains Ueno Zoo and Shinobazu Lake, with *sakura* in the spring, water lilies, and row boats.

Asakusa Kannon Temple, with the great Kaminarimon (Thunder Gate), souvenir arcade, temple, and throngs of people, is several blocks east of Ueno. Just east of Asakusa is Sumidagawa (Sumida River), a favorite spot since Edo times for viewing the 1,200 *sakura* that bloom in spring. In midsummer, millions stand on the shores of the river to see the Sumidagawa Fireworks. You can take a riverboat ride down to the Odaiba waterfont on Tōkyō Bay.

Ameya Yokochō (American Corner) is a shopping street extending from Ueno south to the Okachimachi station on the Yamanote line, and it's always lively with bargain-hunters. Akihabara Electric Town, with a concentration of electronics stores and secondhand bargains, is two stations south of Ueno. The Edo-Tōkyō Museum and Kokugikan Hall, where *sumō* wrestling takes place in January, May, and September, is two stops on the yellow Sōbu line going east from Akihabara. Two more stops south of Akihabara is Tōkyō Station. The Renaissance-style, redbrick station was built in 1914; there's also an elegant restaurant upstairs. Walking west from Tōkyō Station, you soon come to the moats and gates of the Imperial Palace, attesting to the former Edo Castle. The Gaien Gardens are open to the public, and the wide boulevards make it an ideal place for cycling. South of the Imperial Palace is the Diet (National Assembly) building, erected in 1936 in a blend of European and Japanese styles. Note the bronze statues of famous Meiji politician Itō Hirobumi and others. The closest subway stop is Kokkai-Gijidō Mae.

Ginza and Vicinity

Curious about Kabuki? Take the Hibiya subway east to the Higashi Ginza stop. Kabuki-za (*za* means theater) was built in 1951 in the style of the Momoyama period. The cheapest tickets are for the fourth balcony, where you can rent a radio and earphones to listen to an English explanation of the drama. Ginza is a shopper's paradise, with many department stores and name-brand shops selling everything from pearls to handbags. From Ginza, you can walk southwest to the Shinbashi station and board the Yurikamome transit line. The train goes over the Rainbow Bridge and makes a stop at Odaiba Seaside Park on Tōkyō Bay. The shops, boutiques, and a waterfront atmosphere make Odaiba popular with young people. There is a Statue of Liberty replica from France, and the night view of Rainbow Bridge, Tōkyō Bay, and the giant Ferris wheel at Palette Town is memorable.

Shibuya and Beyond

A major stop on the southwest side of the Yamanote line is Shibuya, where boutiques, cinemas, cafés, and people meet at the "scrambled crossing" under a huge video screen. The statue of the dog *Hachikō* in front of the station is a popular meeting spot. Harajuku is one stop north of Shibuya on the Yamanote line, and another great place for people-watching. You can mingle with the crowds of Japanese young people dressed in costumes, and watch impromptu band performances. Or head west of the station to Yoyogi Park and Meiji Shrine (built to honor the Meiji Emperor). Two stops north on the Yamanote line brings you to Shinjuku station, which is always crowded with commuters and shoppers. Walking west from the station, you will pass shops, restaurants, hotels, and a cluster of skyscrapers. Giant gray towers 202 meters (663 feet) tall rise from the Tōkyō Metropolitan Government Building, designed by architect Kenzō Tange and open to the public. The courtyard of the Metro building is also the starting point for the Tōkyō City Cycling event in September, with over 2,000 participants. Go east from Shinjuku station, and you will arrive at Shinjuku Gyoen (the Shinjuku Gardens), covering 58 hectares and incorporating Japanese, French, and English styles. People come to view pink *sakura* in the spring, purple iris in June, and red and yellow leaves in autumn. The wide expanse makes this a favorite spot for walkers, couples, families, and photographers.

Oku-Tama

Far west of Shinjuku on the Chūō line is Oku-Tama, a green mountain hideaway that is still part of Tōkyō. Like Takao-zan (Mount Takao), Oku-Tama is popular with hikers on weekends and holidays. You may find yourself jostling people like it's Shinjuku station during rush hour, and end up standing the whole way back on the return train. On weekdays, however, it's a pleasant getaway.

Housing

If you've already lined up a job in Tōkyō, it will simplify your housing search. Ask yourself the following key questions: How far am I willing to commute? (The average Tōkyōite commutes an hour each way to work or school, and two hours is not unusual.) What's my budget? What kind of neighborhood do I want to live in? How close do I need to be to the train station, parks, rivers, airport, and schools? Housing decisions often come down to a question of convenience versus affordability. Japanese listings always specify how many minutes it takes to walk to the nearest train station and how many minutes it takes by train to central Tōkyō. When calculating your own commuter fatigue factor, keep in mind how many times you will have to transfer to another line. A 90-minute commute on a single train is less tiring than three 25-minute rides with three transfers, especially if one involves a 15-minute hike underground—and you must repeat it all on the way home. Note if there are elevators, escalators, or only stairs in the closest station. Unfortunately, Tōkyō transit has many barriers for people in wheelchairs and those who can't walk the many stairs. If you have the luxury of flextime and can avoid rush hour, that makes a longer commute much more tolerable.

The pole man sells his wares for drying laundry on your balcony.

Tōkyō Street Peddlers

It's your first Sunday in Tōkyō. While trying to catch a few extra winks, you are awakened by a loud commotion. A high-decibel speaker is blasting your apartment—the raucous Japanese, you discover, comes from a recycling truck that traverses the neighborhood, repeating its endless call: "Got any broken TVs or video decks, CD radio-cassette players, mini-stereos, or amps? We'll take them off your hands for free whether they play or not."

You crawl out of bed and hear another chant: "Long poles, laundry poles—at a price you can trust." You peek between the curtains and see a man with a towel tied around his head pedaling slowly up your street. A sidecar attached to his rusty bicycle carries half a dozen poles. A woman from a nearby 14-story *manshon* waves down the salesman, handing him money in exchange for two eight-foot poles. The pole man tips his hat and peddles away singing. Soon you notice that all your neighbors hang their laundry, blankets, and bedding on the balcony on long poles. So, you listen for the pole man to come by your apartment complex again, buy two of his wares for ¥1,000 ($9), and fasten them to your balcony.

As the weather turns chilly, a tinkling melody from a music box wafts up from a silver tank truck rumbling by. After a melancholy tune in a minor key, the speakers blare a Japanese message: "Fuel oil, fuel oil. Put your poly-containers outside your door. We're fast, we're safe, we fill your home with warmth."

Later, while exploring Chidorigafuchi (the moat of the Imperial Palace), you see half a dozen trucks with barrel drum stoves in the bed. Chimneys spew black smoke. Inside are red-skinned yams buried in sizzling red stones. A child asks for one, and the entrepreneur plucks a yam from the hot stones and wraps it in newspaper. The flesh is yellow and piping hot, warming the hands and stomach.

Late in the afternoon, a tooting truck stops in the street. Homemakers with aprons and plastic containers in their hands approach the truck. The tofu man scoops one or two silken squares into each container. The tofu is destined for *miso-shiru* (soybean-based soup) at the dinner table.

At six o'clock, chimes ring out familiar tunes from every school. A cheerful female voice announces over the speaker, "This is Itabashi City Hall. It's time for all good children to go home. Watch out for cars in the street."

After catching the evening news, you hear a quiet, haunting tone, almost like a sea horn. You step out onto your balcony to investigate. It's the revolving ramen truck, a tempting midnight snack. If you take your biggest soup bowl out to the truck, the vendor will fill it with steaming golden noodles and char-shu pork floating on a rich brown broth, all for ¥600 ($5).

Noise pollution? Certainly, if you're trying to sleep in on a weekend. But what might disturb the peace in one culture is familiar, convenient, and even nostalgic in another. Despite the prominence of "public noise" in Japan, street peddlers are a reminder that some traditions continue—even in high-tech urban settings like Tōkyō.

RENTING

High End

If your company transfers you to Tōkyō with all expenses paid, or if cost is not an issue, an attractive array of housing is available in the center of Tōkyō. Roppongi, Azabu, Hirō, and Ebisu stations are close to American-style supermarkets, private international schools, and fancy nightclubs where you will meet many other expatriates. However, the downside of living among concentrations of foreigners is the lack of urgency to learn Japanese, as well as fewer opportunities to interact with Japanese neighbors and gain a new perspective on Japan and the world.

Chiyoda-ku, Minato-ku, and Shibuya-ku, in the center and southwest of the Yamanote loop, are considered prime real estate because of their proximity to the political, economic, and financial districts. Chiyoda-ku occupies 11.6 square kilometers (4.5 square miles) in the center of Tōkyō and contains the Imperial Palace grounds, government buildings, and Marunouchi business district. At night, Chiyoda-ku has 39,297 residents (of which 1,400 are foreign), a population that swells to almost one million during the day. Minato-ku (Port City) occupies 20 square kilometers (7.7 square miles) in southeastern Tōkyō, facing Tōkyō Bay to the east. It shares borders with Shinjuku-ku and Chiyoda-ku to the north, Shibuya-ku to the west, Shinagawa-ku to the south, and Chūō-ku and Koto-ku to the east. Minato-ku's resident population of 159,000 (as of 2001) expands to 850,000 people by day with the influx of commuters. As of 2001, Minato-ku also had the fourth largest registered foreign population with 15,701.

Rental housing in these areas can be found in the classifieds in the weekly *Metropolis* (http://classifieds.japantoday.com). Rentals are grouped as over ¥200,000 ($1,820) and under ¥200,000 per month. H&R Consultants (www.japanhomesearch.com) also lists properties in Tōkyō. Another agency that leases Western-style apartments and houses is Century 21 SKY Realty (www.century21japan.com). Their prices start at ¥200,000 ($1,820) per month and go up to ¥2.5 million ($22,727) per month. When you pay this kind of rent, you're paying for a fashionable address in the middle of Tōkyō with a minimal commute to your downtown job.

Midrange

If you're looking for more affordable housing, check out the eastern, northern, and northwestern areas of Tōkyō, as in Arakawa-ku, Kita-ku, Itabashi-ku, and Nerima-ku. Cheaper apartments are older and smaller, but you may be close to a river with a cycling path or small neighborhood parks with cherry trees, and be within walking distance of all the essential shops—and you can see the sky. In the downtown districts, the sky never touches the ground; out here, the sky is all around you.

In 2000, I moved to Itabashi-ku in northern Tōkyō and was puzzled when several people told me, "Itabashi-ku is rural Tōkyō." Looking up at the 13-story *manshon* facing truck-choked Route 17 (not a good place to live for allergy and asthma sufferers), it didn't seem like country living. But after looking at several apartments with an agent from Kimura Shouji, I found a suitable unit in a fairly new, three-story, reinforced concrete *manshon*. Tucked away on a side street, the apartment was only five minutes from the Shimura-Sakaue station. That meant I could catch the Mita subway line and be in the center of Tōkyō in less than 30 minutes. My daughter and I moved into our apartment and each took a six-mat-size (9- by 12-foot) room—one covered with *tatami* (woven mats) and one with a laminate floor. There was a tiny kitchen and bath and ample storage, for which I considered the rental fee of ¥83,000 ($755) per month to be reasonable. (I also paid several types of move-in fees; see Chapter 12, Housing Considerations, for details.)

As I explored the neighborhood, I noticed many shops specializing in the same single item: rice, sake, tofu, and fish, repeated every few blocks. I learned that each shop had been in the same family for generations, from the time the *daimyō* made their procession down the Nakasendō. Itabashi was their final overnight stop before entering Edo for an audience with the shōgun, so multitudes of people needed food and lodging. It was hard to believe that just a hundred years ago, the last Tokugawa shōgun came to Itabashi to hunt wild boars on horseback. Today, a stone *ichiri-zuka* (marker) along Route 17 is silent testimony to that era.

In Nakano-ku and Suginami-ku, west of the Yamanote loop, it's possible to find an apartment for ¥80,000–100,000 ($727–909) per month, if you don't mind a one-room or very small two-room apartment 15–20 minutes' walk from the station. My brother lives in Suginami-ku along the Chūō line, with quick access to Shinjuku to the east and to the west as far as the Oku-Tama mountains. He has a tiny apartment about a 15-minute walk from the station in a three-story wood and stucco building that his landlord built in his backyard 20 years ago. He pays ¥85,000 ($772) per month, about the same as I did, but one of his two rooms is only 4.5 mats (9 by 9 feet), and the building is aged and has thinner walls than most reinforced concrete *manshon*. In other words, proximity to the popular Chūō line and Yamanote loop requires a larger housing budget—or it may mean settling for less space in a wood-frame apartment that may be less fireproof and earthquake-proof.

Bargains

If your budget is extremely tight, can you still live in Tōkyō? Maybe, if you're willing to be frugal, like many Japanese college students. There are plenty of older, very small apartments and boardinghouses that offer one room and a toilet, but no bath, with a shared kitchen down the hall (and sometimes even shared toilet). These types of accommodations rent for ¥30,000–50,000 ($272–455), even in prime areas inside the Yamanote loop. Many are close to universities. But how do you take a bath, you ask? That's where the *sentō* (public bath) comes in handy, and there's one in every neighborhood (males and females bathe separately). To find it, look for someone carrying a basin and towel in the evening, and follow him. For ¥400 ($3.50) or so, you can bathe daily, and even wash your clothes at the attached coin laundry.

> *If your budget is extremely tight, can you still live in Tōkyō? Maybe, if you're willing to be frugal, like many Japanese college students.*

You can find minimalist rooms for rent in rental magazines such as *Chintai* or *Isize* (published in Japanese) at bookstores and train station kiosks. Another option is perusing vacancies posted on the windows of real estate offices in the locale of your interest.

The final option for cheaper housing is to head north to Saitama-ken (*ken* means prefecture), east to Chiba-ken, or south to Kanagawa-ken (near Yokohama), and endure a longer commute to work or get a local job. In Toke, in Chiba-ken, an hour east of the Tōkyō station on the JR Sotobō line, a two-room place with an eat-in kitchen, bath, storage, and balcony in a 10-year-old reinforced concrete *manshon* runs around ¥54,000 ($490) per month, with a refundable security deposit (equal to two months' rent) and a realtor fee (one month's rent).

BUYING

The price of real estate in Tōkyō in 2000 averaged ¥357,000 ($3,245) per square meter. In that same year, the average price of a *manshon* was ¥45 million ($409,000). That's 5.8 times the yearly income of the average Tōkyōite. Conditions have actually improved since 1991's bubble economy, when the average cost of a home was 10.6 times the average yearly income of a Tōkyō resident. To give you an idea of space limitations in the metropolis: the average land area per house in Tōkyō is 157 square meters (1,690 square feet), and the average floor space of a home is 62 square meters (667 square feet). Or, to take it down to a personal scale, Tōkyō residents have, on average, 9.5 *tatami* mats to call their own, which is 19 square meters (205 square feet) per person.

If you're seeking property in the core of Tōkyō, inside the Yamanote loop line, and can afford the price, Shinjuku-ku has many attractive *manshon*. A very spacious 2LDK maisonette (duplex) in Higashi (East) Shinjuku with 243 square meters (2,616 square feet) of floor space will set you back ¥88 million ($800,000). Many *manshon* were built and sold by speculators during the bubble economy of the 1980s.

In northern Tōkyō, where the Arakawa River separates the metropolis from Saitama prefecture, there are family-size *manshon* at an affordable price. The older the *manshon,* the lower the price. In a 16-unit building constructed in 1985, a 3DK (three rooms plus a dining room-kitchen) with 49 square meters (527 square feet) of floor space costs ¥15.3 million ($139,000). Older *manshon* are often advertised as "renewal" (remodeled), with a "system kitchen" (built-in cupboards), DK (dining room-kitchen) with flooring (wood laminate), and carpeted Western-style rooms. Such places come with an additional ¥11,310 ($103) per-month management fee and a ¥10,400 ($95) charge per month for upkeep. A slightly larger 3LDK with 66 square meters (710 square feet) in a 52-unit building with an elevator runs ¥21.8 million ($198,000). Need more space? A 4LDK with 109.5 square meters (1,179 square feet) lists for ¥37.8 million ($344,000) on a plot of land measuring 62 square meters (667 square feet).

Want something brand-new? Less expensive new *manshon* are available northwest of the Yamanote loop line in Itabashi-ku, if you're willing to go compact. In Ōyama, a 2LDK with 50 square meters (538 square feet) goes for ¥13 million ($118,200); Ōyama is just three stops from Ikebukuro on the private Tobu Tojo line. A bit farther west in Nishi-Takashimadaira, a city of giant apartment complexes, a 75-square-meter (785-square-foot) 3LDK lists for ¥32.8 million ($298,200) about 35 minutes out from the Yamanote loop on the Mita subway line.

If you're tired of elevators and the 13th floor, you may want to live in a detached house. Single-family homes in Tōkyō have become scarce, most of them torn down and replaced with as many as *four* houses on a postage-stamp size plot. The results are tall, skinny, three-story houses, each floor barely wider than a minivan, with the walls almost touching the houses on either side. One of these narrow homes, a 3DK totaling 60 square meters (646 square feet) sells for around ¥29.8 million ($270,900). Each house stands on a plot of land measuring 41 square meters (441 square feet). There is no yard, but you can be a Tōkyō homeowner!

If you have your heart set on buying a single-family home with room for a vegetable garden, you will probably have to move to Saitama-ken to the north or Chiba-ken to the east, or to far western Tōkyō. You must resign yourself to a one- to two-hour commute each morning and evening if you work in central Tōkyō. This is the choice many Japanese families have made, such as my friends the Inoues, who built a home near the city of Chiba, not far from Narita airport. Each morning, Mr. Inoue rises at 4:30 A.M., eats breakfast, and leaves the house at 5:15 A.M. After a brisk walk to the train station, he boards the 5:35 for Tōkyō, rides for an hour and 15 minutes, changes to another train, walks to his office, and arrives at 7 A.M. He repeats this process in reverse in the evening. Many children of "salary-men" (white-collar workers) only see their fathers on Sundays.

REAL ESTATE AGENTS: TŌKYŌ

Century 21 Real Time
Suginami-ku, Tōkyō
tel. 03/3396-1620
realtime@century21ace.co.jp

Chōtarō Fudōsan
Heiwadai Ekimae Store
4-26-4 Heiwadai
Nerima-ku, Tōkyō
tel. 03/3550-0002
www.choutarou.co.jp (in Japanese)

H&R Consultants
5F Toranomon Rich Bldg.
5-11-13 Toranomon
Minato-ku, Tōkyō
tel. 03/5776-6611
fax 03/5776-6613
contactus@japanhomesearch.com
www.japanhomesearch.com

Watco Realty Inc.
1-8-1 Higashi
Shibuya-ku, Tōkyō
tel. 03/3400-3232
fax 03/3400-2595
info@c21watco.com
www.c21watco.com

Week Lease Mansions Kurumi
1-1-9 Saga
Kōtō-ku, Tōkyō
tel. 03/3820-3331
fax 03/3820-5700
www.tmb.co.jp/~kurumi (in Japanese)

Online Real Estate

ADPARK
http://home.adpark.co.jp (in Japanese)

English TownPage
http://english.townpage.isp.ntt.co.jp (click on Real Estate and search for agents in English)

ISIZE
www.isize.com/house

Getting Around

RAILS AND HIGHWAYS

Tōkyō's consolidated network of public and private trains, subways, and buses makes it easy to get around without a car. According to the national census for 2000, there is a daily influx of 2.7 million commuters from surrounding prefectures (Saitama, Kanagawa, Chiba) into Tōkyō, along with almost 400,000 students commuting to school in the metropolis. Headed in the opposite direction, almost 500,000 Tōkyōites go to work or school in outlying prefectures. Commuters like these accounted for 8.3 billion train and subway passengers in 2000. Shinjuku station alone is a transit point for one million people daily, and it's an easy place to get lost (look for signs with circles in the color of your train line).

As for driving in Tōkyō, here are some sobering statistics. In 2001, there were 90,000 traffic accidents and 359 deaths. Due to the lack of street signs, the slew of illegally parked vehicles, and plentiful pedestrians and bicycles, driving is difficult—even hazardous. Even if you manage to reach your destination, parking spaces are as rare as cherry blossoms in August—the subway is much faster. Owning a car is also very expensive.

© Ruthy Kanagy

Horizontal space between the dikes of the Arakawa River

You will pay $300 a month or more for a parking space near your apartment. Gasoline costs about ¥100 per liter, roughly $4 a gallon. In Japan, the older the car, the higher the inspection and registration costs. Despite these obstacles, many Tōkyō families do own a car or two and use them for family outings. Personally, I prefer pedal power.

Intercity expressways link Tōkyō to north, central, and western Honshū; but on weekends and holidays, when Tōkyō empties out, they offer only kilometers of traffic jams. This is particularly true during the famed *kisei rasshu*, the mass exodus that occurs at New Year's and during Obon (Buddhist festival in mid-August). There are millions of drivers on the highways, and millions more people on trains carrying 300 percent capacity—but at least you know your arrival time, instead of facing road rage. On summer weekends, so many people head for the nearest beach (Enoshima) that some end up sitting in traffic jams all day, just to turn around at night without having reached the beach.

© Ruthy Kanagy

Hokkaidō

You know you're in Hokkaidō by the
Straight roads, wide shoulders,
Sugar beets and potatoes;
Cattle grazing calmly as you pedal past
Houses lined with larch trees
And inhale the northern air.

Struck by the differences between Hokkaidō and Tōkyō, I penned the
lines above while touring the region by bicycle, dodging sugar
beets and potatoes along the shoulder of the roads. Life in Hokkaidō
feels different from the rest of Japan because of its wide-open spaces
and great opportunity. Historically, the island was called Ezo and served
an outpost of the Tokugawa shōgun. The land actually belonged to the
indigenous Ainu people until the late 19th century, when they were
pushed further inland and most of their territory taken by the Japanese.
Homesteaders from southern prefectures, who saw Hokkaidō as a new

frontier, continued to migrate as recently as the 1960s to clear brush and forests for agriculture.

Hokkaidō's proximity to Russia also differentiates the area from southern Japan. Geographically, Russian Sakhalin Island, just north of Hokkaidō, and the four Russian-held (and disputed) northern territories off eastern Hokkaidō are closer to the region than Honshū and the rest of Japan. Throughout the region, wildlife includes the brown bear, *tanchō-tsuru* (red-crested crane), seal, northern fox, Ezo deer, and many birds, salmon, and other varieties of fish. There are many types of indigenous high-elevation wildflowers.

The primary industries in Hokkaidō are agriculture, forestry, fishing, manufacturing, construction, and distribution. Housing costs are 30–50 percent lower than in Tōkyō, and the language is standard Japanese. Foreigners don't create much of a stir, in part due to more than a century of interacting with native Ainu, Americans, and Russians.

The prefectural government has a long-term comprehensive plan for Hokkaidō. Begun in 1998 and expected to run through 2007, the plan aims to create a society where everyone can live safely, where men and women participate on equal status, and where Ainu pride is respected, their language and culture promoted, and their social and economic status improved. Hokkaidō strives to encourage tourism, creative technology, and the information industry, and to support small and medium-sized enterprises that plan to expand to a global scale.

Where to Live

The following four cities deserve consideration as places to live and work: Hakodate, population 300,000, is on the tip of the southwestern peninsula shaped like the "boot" section of Italy. Four hours north by train is Hokkaidō's capital, Sapporo, with a population of 1.8 million. Three hours east is Obihiro, a city of 170,000 in the middle of a fertile agricultural plain. Finally, travel two more hours east and you'll arrive at Kushiro, a major eastern fishing port with 200,000 residents.

If you like Seattle, cosmopolitan Sapporo is a near twin (albeit with 5 meters/16 feet of snow, rather than rain). If you're drawn to the wild seacoast, Hakodate or Kushiro fit the bill. If admiring pastoral vistas and digging potatoes with your bare hands are more your style, Obihiro might be just the place.

What about jobs? Commerce and industry abound in Sapporo and Hakodate. Foreign entrepreneurs have small businesses in these cities and also in Obihiro. Teaching and research opportunities are widely available in Sapporo's eleven universities, Kushiro's four universities, and Obihiro's agricultural university. Teaching English is also possible in all of these cities, and all are good candidates for self-employed translators, writers, editors, and naturalists.

Hokkaidō is an outstanding destination for summer hiking, camping, and cycling, but the ocean is too frigid for swimming (which is why I never learned to swim growing up here). There is no rainy season as such in Hokkaidō, and some summers can be cool and rainy, others hot and dry. Sapporo has lots of snow, but is not as cold as the east (-14°C/7°F in winter). Kushiro has far less snow than Sapporo, but winters are cold and summers are cool. Obihiro temperatures can drop to -25°C (-13°F) in winter, but the skies are blue and the sun is brilliant. Obihiro has more sunny days than elsewhere in Hokkaidō (Kushiro has the least sun). The roads are straight, smooth, paved, and less trafficked, but speeding is a problem, sometimes resulting in major accidents. Deep snow in the central and western regions requires chains, and the heavily salted roads are hard on cars.

HAKODATE

Hakodate is the southernmost city at the bottom of the Italy-shaped boot in southwest Hokkaidō, and it's your gateway to Hokkaidō if you're crossing over by train through the undersea tunnel linking the region to Honshū. Hakodate was the northernmost outpost of the shōgun's military government in the 18th and 19th centuries.

In 1859, Hakodate, along with Yokohama and Nagasaki, was opened as an international trade port. As a result of a long tradition of international exchange and cultural contact with many countries, Hakodate has an exotic atmosphere, with many historic areas and buildings in various foreign architectural styles.

In recent years, the city of Hakodate has promoted exchanges with its sister cities (Halifax, Canada; Vladivostok, Russia; and Lake Macquarie, Australia), as well as with other foreign cities. Many promotion groups in Hakodate have been actively involved in international exchange, and the city has numerous foreign residents.

> *As a result of a long tradition of international exchange and cultural contact with many countries, Hakodate has an exotic atmosphere, with many historic areas and buildings in various foreign architectural styles.*

Tourists are drawn to Hakodate for its historic Western architecture and the beautiful night view from Mount Hakodate. During the bubble

Konbu (kelp) drying next to a shrine in Hokkaidō

economy of the late 1980s to early 1990s, many of Hakodate's old buildings were demolished to make way for condominiums. Funded by investment capital from Honshū, these buildings create an unseemly spectacle. 1992 was particularly difficult for Hakodate—dismantling the old Yachigashira Elementary School and arguing over the Hakodate-no-Hito and Squid Monument were typical of the year. The city tree is the yew; the city flower is the azalea; the city bird is the varied tit, and the city fish is the squid (though it's not very fishlike).

Hakodate has three universities (all potential employers): Hakodate University, Hokkaidō Education University Hakodate Campus, and Future University-Hakodate. Future University-Hakodate (FUN; a great name!) is the newest, established in April 2000 with an emphasis on communication technology.

Climate

Hakodate's average temperature in August is 22°C (77°F); average for January is -3°C (27°F). Hakodate in winter is sparkling white, and you can admire it from a hot spring. Fish and other seafood are abundant and fresh, as is the clear winter air. Roads are icy in January and February, necessitating caution when walking.

Housing

The Hakodate train station is the geographical center of Hakodate city (this is true of most cities in Japan); within walking distance are the bus terminal, city hall, fish market, and numerous department stores and hotels. Western Hakodate spreads out on a peninsula jutting into the sea, with Hakodate Port, the waterfront, and a ropeway taking you up Mount Hakodate. There are many historic buildings clustered in the area, including Catholic churches, a Harrist Church, former Russian and British consulates, historical museums, and the foreigners' cemetery. Eastern Hakodate has Goryōkaku Park and Tower as a backdrop, with the Northern Regions Museum, the Prefectural Art Museum, and *Hokkaidō Newspaper* offices in the area. In southeastern Hakodate, you'll find the Yunokawa Hot Springs, the City Cultural and Sports Center, a tropical arboretum, a beach, race tracks, and a nearby Trappist monastery. The choice of where to live is wide open, perhaps influenced by your work location.

While you're looking for a place to rent, you might consider staying at a hotel, *ryokan* (Japanese-style inn), or youth hostel. Hakodate has many facilities, such as a municipal spa, library, city museum, fort museum, historical museum, community center, women's center, northern sea fishery museum, literature museum, art museum, gym, swimming pool, baseball stadium, and track.

In Hakodate, rent for a 1DK (one room plus dining room-kitchen) runs from ¥38,000 ($345) per month in a 17-year-old building to ¥53,000 ($482) per month in a three-year-old building. A 2DK rents for ¥55,000 ($500), while a 2LDK costs around ¥60,000 ($545). A family-size 3LDK in a 15-year-old building can be rented for ¥67,000 ($609). Most places are convenient to buses or streetcars. As for buying a place, lots near a park suitable for building a house are available for ¥11 million ($100,000). A 17-year-old 4LDK house went on the market for ¥12 million ($109,100), and a 5LDK built 25 years ago sells for ¥13.8 million ($125,454).

Real Estate Agents: Hakodate

Alive
2-46-10 Tomioka
Hakodate 041-0811
tel. 0138/42-1620
fax 0138/42-1621
www.alive-f.com (in Japanese)

Hakodate Fudōsan Web
(Hakodate Realtor's Web)
www.hbf.ne.jp/real (in Japanese)

Getting Around

Hakodate is easy to get around by bus, streetcar, taxi, or train. The two bus companies are *shiei basu* (City Bus), in a two-tone orange color; and *Hakodate basu* (Hakodate Bus), in gray with a red stripe. There are also streetcars. Timetables are posted at each stop for *heijitsu* (weekdays), *doyōbi* (Saturdays) and *nichiyōbi/shukujitsu* (Sundays/Holidays). Enter at the rear of most buses and streetcars, and exit from the front. Take a *seiri-ken* (boarding ticket) from the machine at the rear when you get on. Before your stop, push a button near the window and check your fare on the chart in front.

On city buses and streetcars, you can use a prepaid card or one-day and two-day tickets, as well as *teiki-ken* (commuter passes). If you need a *takushii* (taxi), either phone ahead or hail one on the street or at taxi stands in front of the station.

You can buy Japan Railways (JR) tickets at the ticket window, or from the ticket vending machine at the station. JR Hakodate Station has a Midori-no-Madoguchi (Green Window) office where you can make *shitei-seki* (seat reservations) a month in advance for any JR train. Sapporo is four hours north on the "Hokuto" special express, while Tōkyō is around eight or nine hours away by special express train and *shinkansen*.

Landing at Hakodate

© Ruthy Kanagy

Hakodate Airport is 20 minutes by bus from the city and serves major airports in Hokkaidō and points south. Hakodate to New Chitose Airport (Sapporo) takes 35 minutes, while the trip to Haneda Airport (Tōkyō) is an hour and a quarter, with seven flights daily.

Recreation

Hakodate holds a Winter Festival in February, a Goryokaku Festival in May (when *sakura*/cherry trees are in bloom), a Port Festival and a Yunokawa Spa Fire Festival in August, Open Air Theater from July through August, and a Half Marathon in September. Mount Hakodate is known for its outstanding night view, and historic Goryōkaku Park is a popular tourist destination.

Ōnuma Quasi-National Park is administered by the Hokkaidō government. Some years ago, lava spewed from Mount Komagatake (1,131 meters/3,710 feet) and blocked a river, creating big and small lakes with numerous islands. Fall colors are spectacular here. The park is a 50-minute drive from Hakodate and three hours by train from Sapporo.

SAPPORO

Four hours north from Hakodate on the Ishikari plain is the seat of the capital, Sapporo. More than one in four *Dosanko* (an affectionate nickname for people from Hokkaidō) live in the capital city. Sapporo is the fifth largest city in Japan, and the third largest in land area, which is 57 percent forested and 12 percent buildings. The city started as an agricultural outpost and has become the pivotal urban area in northern Japan.

The main industries in Sapporo are wholesale and retail, construction, transportation and communication, manufacturing, government, finance, and insurance. Seventy-eight percent of Sapporo employees work in the tertiary sector, 20 percent in the secondary sector, and only one half of one percent in the primary sector.

As of 2000, Sapporo had 11 universities with 48,000 students and 11 junior colleges with 7,400 students. The most prestigious is Hokkaidō University, a national college with agricultural roots. In 1877, William Smith Clark came from Massachusetts to establish what was then the Agricultural College of Sapporo. After teaching for a year, Clark returned to the U.S. and left with the parting words, "Boys! Be ambitious!," a phrase known and admired by most Japanese.

Climate

Sapporo has an average annual temperature of 9°C (48°F), with summer temperatures in the mid-20°Cs (mid-60°Fs). The first snow falls in late

Boys, Be Ambitious!

In 1876, William Smith Clark, President of the Agricultural College of Massachusetts (now the University of Massachusetts), was invited by the Japanese government to come to Hokkaidō and establish an American-style university. Clark accepted the offer and became vice president of the new college, which had only 50 students. Clark had a positive impression of Japan and the climate of Hokkaidō, and he wrote to his family that it was pleasant to teach hard-working, polite, and grateful Japanese students.

When Clark departed Sapporo in 1877, he left these farewell words with his students: "Boys, be ambitious! Be ambitious not for money or for selfish aggrandizement, not for that evanescent thing which men call fame. Be ambitious for the attainment of all that a man ought to be." You can see these famous words next to the statue of William Clark at Hokkaidō University today. Students throughout Japan read about this 19th-century American, one of the many foreigners who contributed to modern Japan, in their textbooks.

Among Clark's students were Paul Nitobe Inazō, author of the book *Bushidō (The Code of Samurai),* Christian activist Uchimura Kanzō, and other prominent Meiji-era figures.

October, and from December to April, up to one meter (3.3 feet) of snow covers the ground. In January and February, temperatures drop below 0°C (32°F). Ice and snow begin to melt in April (mud season), and green vegetation flourishes in May and June. July and August are summer, September to October fall. Highest summer temperatures range around 36°C (97°F), while winter's lowest reaches -15°C (5°F). Annual total snowfall is around 500 centimeters (16.4 feet).

Housing

Sapporo stretches 42 kilometers (26 miles) east to west, from the Ishikari River and Nopporo forests to the Teine mountain range. Sixty percent of the city is covered in mountain forests. Streets in Sapporo are wide, laid out north–south and east–west, and numbered so that it's easy to find your destination. If you want to learn Japanese, there are many Japanese language schools in town. Foreign-owned businesses include a bagel bakery, several restaurants, the Gaijin Bar, and owner-operated English schools.

Each area of Sapporo has its attractions. The Fukuzumi residential area to the south boasts a new Sapporo Dome; a bus and subway transportation hub provides easy access to downtown and to New Chitose Airport. In southwest Sapporo, urban activity is concentrated around the Toyohira River that flows through the city, becoming increasingly hilly toward the mountains. Hiragishi in Toyohira-ku (*ku* means city ward) is the

© Ruthy Kanagy

Hokkaidō prefecture building in Sapporo

home of Hokkaidō International School. If you will be teaching or studying at Hokkaidō University, you might consider living near the campus, north of Sapporo station. Your choice of where to live will depend partly on your job location (and, if applicable, your child's school) and how long a commute you can handle.

One of the best resources for English-speakers moving to Sapporo is *Hokkaidō Insider News,* an email newsletter available through Sapporo resident Ken Hartmann (www.ne.jp/asahi/hokkaido/kenhartmann). Subscribers frequently post apartments or houses for rent, furniture for sale, and information on jobs. For example, a 3LDK 130-square-meter furnished house with two bathrooms, a basement, a garage, and a garden—located near a university—costs ¥90,000 ($818) per month; in Tōkyō, it would likely rent for four times that. Another smaller house near a park, 2LDK with a garden, rents for around ¥45,000 ($409) per month. Many rentals are listed in real estate agents' magazines—pick one up at the train station or purchase it at a bookstore.

Public housing units managed by the city or prefecture are available at reasonable rates. Because of high demand, occupants are selected by lottery. If you work or live in Sapporo and have an alien registration card, you can apply to Sapporo Housing Management Corporation. Information on prefecture-managed apartment houses is available from the Hokkaidō Housing Management Corporation, and there are also public apartment houses operated by the Hokkaidō Housing Supply Corporation.

If you are planning to build or renovate a house, an application must be submitted in advance for approval. Keep in mind when purchasing land that housing construction is prohibited in urbanization control areas. For details, contact the Building Permit and Inspection Section, tel. 011/211-2846 (in Japanese); for land purchase, contact the Housing Land Section, tel. 011/211-2512 (in Japanese).

Real Estate Agents: Sapporo

Elm Fudōsan (Elm Real Estate)
5-3-10 Misono 5 jō
Toyohira-ku, Sapporo-shi,
Hokkaidō
tel. 011/821-5885
fax 011/821-5879
elm.f@aq.wakwak.co
www.oba-q.com/elmf (in Japanese; scroll down and click on "English Page" for a translation)

Peace
1F Maruta Building
4-1-1 Kikusui 3-jō
Sapporo-shi, Hokkaidō
tel. 011/811-7758
fax 011/811-7754
kikusui@peace-v.co.jp
www.peace-v.co.jp (in Japanese)

Getting Around

Sapporo is easy to reach by plane from Tōkyō and other cities down south. Tōkyō (Haneda) to New Chitose Airport near Sapporo takes just over one hour. In addition to All Nippon Airways (ANA) and Japan Airlines (JAL), Hokkaidō-based Air Do offers flights. Regular one-way fares are at least ¥20,000 ($182), but may be discounted as low as ¥10,000 ($91) if you meet certain conditions. From New Chitose, you can fly direct to Seoul, China, Russia, Hawaii, and Guam. Six regional airports in Hokkaidō have flights to Sapporo's Okadama Airport in the suburbs.

In the old days, when air travel was a luxury, most people took the sleeper train from Ueno station in Tōkyō to Aomori at the northern tip of Honshū; then transferred to a ferry for four hours across the Tsugaru Straights to Hakodate; and then boarded a northbound train to Sapporo and points east and north. During my high school years in Tōkyō, the journey home to Hokkaidō took 26 hours. Now, you can take a *shinkansen* from Tōkyō to Hachinohe in northern Honshū, then board a special express to Hokkaidō through an undersea tunnel (40 years in the making), reaching Hakodate in six hours and Sapporo in just under 10 hours.

Contemporary house in eastern Hokkaidō

If you have plenty of time but not a great deal of money, consider taking a ferry from Tōkyō to Hokkaidō. The trip from Ōarai (near Tōkyō) to Tomakomai (south of Sapporo) takes 20 hours.

Sapporo has a superb transportation system, with three subway lines, JR lines, a streetcar, a network of buses, and two airports (New Chitose and Okadama). The subway links the main business, commercial, and entertainment areas, along with Sapporo station and residential areas. Shuttle buses operate between shopping areas and event venues, as well as between the two airports. Discount one-day passes are available.

Recreation

In Sapporo, as in all of Hokkaidō, outdoors is always in fashion. Sapporo, site of the 1972 Winter Olympics, holds an International Snow Festival in February that draws millions. You can explore the Winter Sports Museum and take a chairlift to the top of Okurayama Ski Jump, and you can even cross-country ski for free at Nakajima Sports Center in Nakajima Park (near Horohirabashi subway station). In the summertime, you can go hiking, mountain climbing, cycling, or spa-hopping, and take a trip to the beach in Otaru.

Sapporo is close to numerous national parks, mountains, and spas, all

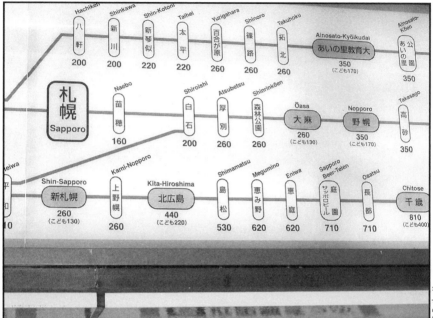

Sapporo train map

within an hour or two. Lake Shikotsu and Lake Tōya are both surrounded by volcanoes; Mount Usu erupted in 2000 and is still steaming; and Niseko ski area, with its Olympic ski courses, is just an hour away.

OBIHIRO

Three hours east from Sapporo through the Hidaka Mountains is Obihiro, situated in the center of the patchwork Tokachi plain, with the snow-capped backdrop of the Daisetsuzan Mountains. Obihiro, the "pastoral city building the new century" (according to the city's website; my translation). is known for agriculture, food processing, construction, and transportation. The first Japanese settlement in Tokachi formed 120 years ago, although the Ainu were already living here.

Climate

Winters are cold (down to -27°C/-17°F) and covered in snow, and summers are comfortably warm, but not humid. Obihiro has more days of sunshine than any other city in Hokkaidō, making it a great location for solar power.

Housing

Obihiro's wide streets are laid out like a grid, so it's easy to find your way around. Addresses consist of the east–west block first, followed by the north–south. Go to Nishi 5 (west five blocks), Minami 7 (south seven blocks), and you will find City Hall—blocks are counted from Ōdōri (Main Street).

> *Obihiro, the "pastoral city building the new century," is known for agriculture, food processing, construction, and transportation.*

In Obihiro, you can rent a 1DK (one room plus dining room-kitchen) apartment for as little as ¥30,000 ($273) per month, and a 3DK for ¥55,000–60,000 ($500–545) per month.

In addition to regular rentals, the city owns about 3,000 public housing units, varying in size, location, age, price, and conditions for entrance. Foreigners are allowed to rent public housing under the same conditions as Japanese, if they meet the following three conditions: a need for housing, a family (single elderly or handicapped persons allowed), and certain income requirements. Contact the Public Housing Section to apply.

Community Resources

The Obihiro International Center was built to enable people from around the world to study agricultural technology and other fields. You can get information on living in Obihiro and the Tokachi district from the International Relations Section of Obihiro City Hall. They handle phone calls in English and Chinese.

The "U-turn" phenomenon refers to Hokkaidō-born young people who travel to Tōkyō for higher education and stay there for a job. After several years of toeing the company line, some of them get wise and return to Hokkaidō, where the air is clear. One such young man, Urashima Hisashi, worked for a big-name car manufacturer down south, them came back to Obihiro and started his own English school, English House Joy. That was 20 years ago. Today, Joy English Academy has a translation service and a full curriculum for everyone from children to adults, with several native speakers of English on the staff.

Another good contact is Obihiro Chikusan Daigaku (Obihiro University of Agriculture and Veterinary Medicine). A national university with 1,000 students, the school offers degrees in agriculture and veterinary medicine. There are around 50 foreign students, many of whom live in the International House on campus. In the 1980s, I taught English conversation to freshmen at the university. They may have openings for a foreign teacher.

A cheap source for household items are the many recycle shops in Obihiro. Every October, the Obihiro Autumn Recycle Festival takes place at the Public Sanitation Section. Reusable goods collected during the year are for sale.

Chōnaikai (neighborhood committees) are groups of residents that provide information on festivals and other events, trash pickup days, and other daily needs. When you move into a new house or apartment, don't be surprised by a visit from your local chōnaikai representative; or ask a neighbor how to join.

Obihiro has six TV channels, including two NHK (National Broadcasting Corporation) bilingual channels. If you own a television, you must pay an NHK reception fee. With a parabolic antenna and BS decoder, three additional channels are available (NHK Satellite 1, NHK Satellite 2, and WOWOW). In addition, OCTV is a cable television provider. Radio stations include FM-Wing 76.1, FM-JAGA 77.8, Air-G 78.5, North Wave 82.1, NHK-FM 87.5, NHK-CP 603, STV 1071, NHK-Q 1125, and HBC 1269. English-language newspapers published by Japanese national dailies *(Asahi Evening News, Daily Yomiuri, and Japan Times)* are available by subscription through a local newspaper agent for around ¥4,000 ($36) per month. *Mainichi Daily News* is available online.

Financial institutions in the Tokachi region include *ginkō* (banks), *shinyō kinko* (trust banks), and *shinyō kumiai* (trust unions). You can exchange money at the main post office and several local banks, wherever you see the sign Authorized Foreign Exchange Bank. When changing from yen to foreign currencies, only U.S. dollars are available on demand. Travelers checks are available in U.S. dollars and other currencies. The maximum daily exchange limit of $1,000 or equivalent.

Real Estate Agents: Obihiro

Chien, Inc.
1-11 Minami 14-chōme Nishi 15-jō
Obihiro-shi, Hokkaidō
tel. 0155/36-2477 (rentals)
tel. 0155/36-4946 (real estate)
chintai@chien.co.jp
www.chien.co.jp (in Japanese)

Hokkaidō General Homes
6 Minami 25-chōme Higashi 1-jō
Obihiro-shi, Hokkaidō
tel. 0155/20-5288
fax 0155/20-5277
staff@generalhomes.co.jp
www.generalhomes.co.jp
(in Japanese)

Getting Around

You can fly directly to Obihiro Airport from Tōkyō (Haneda), Kansai, and Nagoya. The airport is just 30 minutes south of city center. An airport bus takes you from the bus station next to Obihiro Station and leaves from the airport after each arrival. Parking is available. There are no international

Snow-shovel train in Kushiro

flights from Obihiro, but New Chitose Airport near Sapporo is only 2.5 hours away by train. Obihiro is on the major JR line Nemuro Honsen, halfway between Sapporo and Kushiro. Each day, a dozen super-express trains travel in each direction. "Tokachi" and "Super Tokachi" super-express trains go west to Sapporo, and "Ozora" and "Super Ozora" super-express trains go east to Kushiro. Bus routes traverse the city and the Tokachi area from the central bus terminal adjacent to Obihiro Station, operated by three bus companies: JR, Tokachi, and Takushoku. The cheapest long-distance travel is also by bus. Obihiro to Sapporo takes just over four hours, and to Kushiro, 2.5 hours. Taxis are readily available downtown or just a phone call away.

Recreation

The Tokachi area is ideal for cycling, hot-air ballooning, kite flying, and other recreation. All winter, you can cross-country ski everywhere and ski downhill at Memuro or on the advanced slopes at Karikachi Pass to the west. Ice hockey, skating, and curling are also popular winter sports. Obihiro has an Ice Festival in January and a homemade river-rafting race in the summer. In the fall, you can watch salmon swim up the Tokachi River to their spawning grounds. Tokachigawa Onsen (Tokachi River Hot Springs) is a spa resort with many traditional inns, popular for New Year's parties.

The Daisetsuzan mountains north of Obihiro are only an hour or two away. The whole area, dominated by Kurodake (Black Peak), is an outstanding hiking and wildflower-viewing destination. Pristine Lake Shikaribetsu is hidden among the mountains, with two quiet hot springs inns. In the winter, when the lake freezes over, an igloo and snow and ice sculptures are built on the lake.

KUSHIRO

Kushiro is situated on the eastern Pacific seaboard of Hokkaidō. In this city, you can expect to hear foghorns and smell fisheries and pulp/paper factories. The Port of Kushiro opened in 1899, and one of the Pacific's preeminent fishing grounds, just off the coast, feeds the city's marine food-processing industry. In the West Port area, a multipurpose international terminal is under construction. Offshore, Kushiro Coal Mine is the last domestic mine in Japan, located hundreds of meters below the sea floor, with untapped reserves estimated at 300 million tons.

Kushiro's paper industry began in the Meiji period and produces

Kushiro Wetlands National Park

© Ruthy Kanagy

newsprint, corrugated paper, and other paper products. In the 17th century, the Matsumae clan of Hakodate established posts to trade with the Ainu living where the city now stands. The first Japanese settlers came in 1870 from northern Honshū and Hakodate.

Kushiro citizens are reaching out and becoming more internationally-minded through a variety of exchange programs.

As is true all over Japan, Kushiro faces the dual challenges of an aging society and a declining birth rate. In addition, young people continue to leave rural areas for the big city lights of Sapporo and Tōkyō. However, Kushiro citizens are reaching out and becoming more internationally-minded through a variety of exchange programs. Kushiro's sister cities include Burnaby, Canada, and Kholmsk, Russia. Economic exchanges link the port of Kushiro with the ports of Seward, Alaska, and New Orleans, Louisiana. Kushiro Public University is affiliated with Simon Fraser University in Canada, and the city has an official relationship with Kooragang Nature Reserve in Australia.

Kushiro has a prominent hill—Tsurugadai—with a view of the port, Pacific Ocean, and mountains of Akan National Park. Hokkaidō University of Education's Kushiro Campus is located on this hill. The Kushiro Public University of Economics may have possibilities for teaching positions.

Climate

Kushiro is situated at 43 degrees north latitude between the Pacific Ocean and a large wetlands area and mountains. The average annual temperature is 5°C (41°F), compared to 6°C (43°F) in Obihiro, 8°C (46°F) in Sapporo, and 17°C (63°F) in Tōkyō. Spring and summer are cool, with a high of 20°C (68°F), and sometimes damp due to fog rolling in from the ocean. Fall and winter are crisp and sunny, with a low of -15°C (5°F); though the cold can be intense, total snowfall averages only 90 centimeters (3 feet), far less than Obihiro and Sapporo.

Housing

Downtown Kushiro is bordered by the Kushiro River to the west, the Old Kushiro River to the east, and Kushiro Harbor, Fisherman's Wharf, and the Pacific Ocean to the south. Southeast of Kushiro station, across the Nusamai Bridge and the Old Kushiro river, is a bluff called Tsurugadai (Crane Hill) that overlooks the city. Hokkaidō Educational University, Kushiro City Hospital, and Tsurugadai Park are in this area. East of the hill lies Lake Harutori, a popular spot for relaxing and strolling, and the Kushiro City Museum. The city expands west to the Tottori district, with shops, residences, and factories—the largest is a paper mill. Further west are the airport and zoo, and to the north are the Kushiro wetlands and roads leading to Akan National Park. Choosing where to live depends on whether you like to live in the hills, near the sea, near a university, or out in the countryside north and east of the city. Public transportation covers all parts of the city.

When it comes to rental prices, a brand-new 1LDK unit with 36 square meters (388 square feet) of space rents for ¥56,000 ($509) per month. Units in older buildings rent for ¥40,000–50,000 ($364–455) per month. Depending on age, 2DKs with similar floor space range ¥45,000–60,000 ($409–450) per month.

Getting Around
You can fly to Kushiro from Tōkyō, Ōsaka, and other cities in Honshū in about 1.5 hours. Flying from Sapporo (both New Chitose and Okadama Airports) to Kushiro takes less than an hour, and from Hakodate takes slightly longer. JR trains link Kushiro to Obihiro in two hours, and to Sapporo in four hours. The city is served by bus, JR train, and taxis.

Recreation
On the downtown waterfront, Kushiro is constructing a Fisherman's

© Ruthy Kanagy

Lake Mashu in Akan National Park, Hokkaidō

Wharf to hold events, part of its efforts to attract more international travelers. Kushiro is also the gateway to two national parks.

Kushiro Shitsugen National Park is a newly designated wetlands park that can be accessed by bus, car, or bicycle (via a cycling path from the city). Kushiro Marsh Observatory overlooks the wetlands, which are inhabited by many species, including the once almost extinct *tanchō-tsuru* (red-crested crane) found only in eastern Hokkaidō and Siberia.

Akan National Park encompasses three volcanoes and three caldera lakes in a relatively untouched wilderness. It takes about 1.5 hours by bus or car north from Kushiro. The inhabitants of an Ainu village called Kotan, on the shore of Akanko (Akan Lake), perform authentic dances and music for visitors and offer many shops with wood-carvings and other handcrafts. In January, Akan Lake freezes over, and people set up tents on the ice for smelt fishing. In the summer, this park is a hiker's and cyclist's paradise.

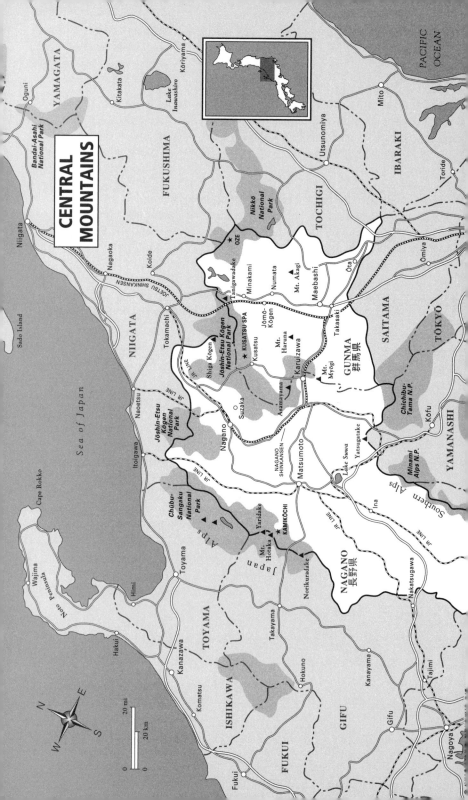

Central Mountains:
Gunma and Nagano

Gunma

One hundred kilometers (62 miles) north of Tōkyō lies the *furusato* (rural homeland) of everyone who doesn't have another to return to during the mass migration of the New Year's and Obon holidays. In Gunma, you'll find mountains, hot springs, pine trees, rivers, villages, and farms where grandmothers and grandfathers work in fields with their backs bent over. Industry and urbanization have crept north from the megalopolis below. Vegetables, arrowroot, and rice flow south. The mountains that used to form barriers are now sliced with highways; *shinkansen* tunnel through the backbone of Japan, emerging as silver flashes. And bit by bit, the old ways of life have begun to erode, and the old farmhouses rattle with space as their young people head south. But on weekends and holidays, the mountains and spas fill with urbanites speeding north to ski, hike, and soak.

Located in the northwestern part of the Kantō plain, close to the consumer market of metropolitan Tōkyō, Gunma is the primary vegetable basket for the urban population to the south. While silk, wheat, and rice were the primary agricultural products in the past, today the region produces the most *konyaku* root, cucumbers, and shiitake mushrooms in Japan. The cooler climate fosters high-quality vegetables, such as cabbage, leeks, and spinach.

As in neighboring Nagano prefecture, silk production was Gunma's major industry during the latter half of the 19th century. As Japan's economy took off in the 1950s, Gunma experienced rapid economic growth based on industry and commerce—so much that by the mid-1960s, revenue from manufacturing surpassed agriculture. Today, eastern Gunma's industry is based on the manufacture of transport machinery and electronic goods and is concentrated in the eastern area, primarily the cities of Ota and Oizumi. Isesaki and Kiryū are the center of traditional textile and clothing-related industries. In the mountainous northern area, tourism is the main industry, with numerous *onsen* (hot spring) resorts and ski areas. The capital of Maebashi is in the southeast plains on a direct line to metropolitan Tōkyō.

CLIMATE

Gunma's plains have a Pacific climate, meaning a great deal of rain in summer and very little in winter. The mountainous regions in the north, with a climate resembling that of the Japan seaside, also see a lot of rain and snow. The frequent occurrence of thunder in the summer and strong winds in winter, known as "The Dry Winds," are characteristic of the area.

HOUSING

Gunma prefecture is home to just over two million people in 11 cities, 33 towns, and 25 villages. Maebashi, the capital, is at the foothills of Mount Akagi, with a population of 280,000. The city of Takasaki is just west of Maebashi, with views of Mount Akagi and Mount Haruna to the north and Mount Myōgi to the west. Takasaki was a castle town in the Edo period and is now a center of transportation and commerce, with a population of 240,000. Minakami, in the northeast mountains, is a hot springs resort and outdoor mecca—visitors raft on the Tonegawa, climb Tanigawadake, and ski (both Alpine and Nordic) in the winter.

A *gaijin mura* (foreigner's village) of sorts has sprung up over the years in the neighboring town of Tsukiyono-machi (population 10,000). Some permanent exiles from the urban scene stay year-round, while others come to escape Tōkyō's sweltering summers. One enterprising

Gunma in fall

American and his Japanese wife operate a homemade pizza and pasta restaurant called Café Manna. If you'd rather be outdoors, there are plenty of places to explore, including two-story sericulture farmhouses with no one left at home.

For a sense of housing prices in this area, consider the following examples: a 1DK (one room plus dining room-kitchen) in Takasaki city starts at ¥35,000 ($318) per month, and a 2DK goes for ¥40,000 ($364) and up per month. You can even rent a spacious 3LDK (63 square meters/678 square feet) for a reasonable ¥55,000 ($500) per month or more.

Would you like to teach at a total immersion English school? Ota is an industrial town in eastern Gunma with an enterprising mayor. He recently announced a new type of school, Ota International Academy, at which most subjects will be taught in English by native speakers. Due to open in 2005, the school is taking applications from Japanese parents eager to have their children get ahead by acquiring a black belt in English. Apparently, the mayor became convinced that not being able to communicate in English (i.e., learning only the grammar and translation skills required to pass entrance exams) is a handicap.

Mozaemon, Peasant of Tsukiyono

Probably the most famous person to come out of Tsukiyono was Mozaemon, a wealthy 19th-century peasant and village leader who went to Edo (now Tōkyō) to protest to the shōgun about excessive taxes in his area. Despite crop failures and near-famine conditions, Sanada, the lord of Numata Castle, insisted on taxing the rice crop as if it were a bumper year. Mozaemon knew it meant death to be insubordinate and to break the law forbidding peasants from leaving their home district, and he ended up being crucified. However, the shōgun heard his complaint, deposed the Sanada clan, and tore down Numata Castle. Mozaemon's spirit is revered at a large shrine near Gokan station.

Real Estate Agents: Gunma and Nagano

Asia Real Estate Co., Ltd.
3040-53 Sasaga
Matsumoto-shi, Nagano-ken
tel. 0263/86-7822
fax 0263/86-5252
info@asia-fudosan.co.jp
www.asia-fudosan.co.jp
(in Japanese)

Kobayasi Fudōsan
2139-2 Shin-machi
Tano-gun, Gunma-ken
tel. 0274/42-8213
mail@kobayasi-fudosan.jp
www.kobayasi-fudosan.jp
(in Japanese)

ERA Cosmo City
63-1 Yanagihara-chō
Isesaki-shi, Gunma-ken
tel. 0270/40-6655
fax 0270/40-6656
www.erajapan.co.jp (in Japanese)

GETTING AROUND

From Tōkyō station, you can get to Takasaki in 60 minutes on the JR Jōetsu *shinkansen*. From Narita or Haneda Airports, there is a limousine bus to Takasaki and Maebashi that takes 3.5 hours. To reach the Minakami spa and ski area, you have two options: take the Jōetsu *shinkansen* from Tōkyō or Ueno (on the Yamanote loop) to Jōmōkōgen, then transfer to a bus for a 20-minute ride to Minakami; or, for a less expensive fare, take a JR tokkyū (special express train) from Akabane (on the Saikyō line) in Tōkyō to Minakami, a ride just over two hours long, with no transfers. There are local trains and buses serving every city in Gunma.

RECREATION

Two thirds of the prefecture are mountainous, and mountains also range across the northwestern border. At the western border of Gunma and Nagano prefectures is Asamayama (Mount Asama, a 2,500-meter (760-foot), highly active volcano. When Asama erupted in 1783, it spewed forth lava that formed a hardened field known as Onioshidashi (Goblin Rocks). Directly north of Asamayama is Kusatsu *onsen,* known throughout Japan for its abundant hot springs. Kusatsu has many traditional *ryokan* (Japanese-style inns) and fills up with skiers in the winter.

Northeast of Kusatsu is another well-known hot springs resort. Minakami *onsen* is nestled along the upper reaches of the Tone River, backed by the majestic Tanigawa Mountain Range. On the north side lies Niigata prefecture. You can take the easy way up Mount Tanigawa by ropeway, but every summer, scores of hardy mountaineers start at the foot. In November, Suwa Forge in Minakami is a blaze of red and yellow, leading to weekend traffic jams. One of the three longest rivers in Japan, 322-kilometer (200-mile) Tonegawa (Tone River) springs from Mount Ominakami in northeast Gunma. Most rivers in Gunma merge into the Tonegawa River Basin, which, at 16,840 square kilometers (6,502 square miles), is the largest basin in Japan.

On the northern border of Gunma is a fragile, high elevation marshland called Oze. At 2,000 meters (6,561 feet) above sea level, Oze is filled with rare flora and fauna. Crowds flock to Oze, especially in the spring to see the expanse of white and green *mizubashō,* and to sing about the beloved flower—which is, sadly, called skunk cabbage in English. (Every child in Japan learns the "Mizubashō" flower song about Oze in elementary school).

Nagano

Nagano prefecture is situated in the Chūbu region in the middle of Honshū, the main island, surrounded by eight other prefectures—Gunma, Saitama, Yamanashi, Shizuoka, Aichi, Gifu, Toyama, and Niigata. Nagano is called the "roof of Japan" for a good reason—sixteen of its mountains tower 3,000 meters (9,842 feet) or higher. It is the fourth largest prefecture in Japan, with a population of around 2.2 million. The number of foreign residents was 42,000 in 2000—a high percentage of them workers from China, Thailand, and Brazil.

Nagano's history is closely tied to the rise and fall of the silk industry. Before World War II, most farmers were engaged in raising silkworms and the mulberry plants they fed on. Both silkworms and mulberry leaves were

> *Nagano is called the "roof of Japan" for a good reason— sixteen of its mountains tower 3,000 meters (9,842 feet) or higher.*

prone to disease and damage by the weather, thus affecting the fortunes of silkworm farmers from year to year. The silk-reeling industry peaked in the 1920s but, due to the depression that began in 1929, the silk industry collapsed and farmers were hard-hit. The silk industry also floundered because of poor working conditions, salaries, and living conditions for factory girls, who were little more than indentured slaves.

Currently, the main industry besides agriculture is the manufacture of computer-related electric machinery. Tourism is actively promoted, with around 100 million people coming to Nagano each year. Three locations of note are Karuizawa (highland resort), Nagano (the prefectural capital), and Matsumoto (castle city).

CLIMATE

Nagano prefecture is one of the few in Japan that do not touch the sea. Because it is inland and at high elevation, summers are exceedingly refreshing (as in Hokkaidō), and winters quite cold. The average annual temperature of both Nagano and Matsumoto is 12°C (54°F), while Karuizawa is a cooler 8°C (46°F). The highest temperature is 36°C (97°F) for the first two cities, and the lowest temperature is around -12°C (10°F). In Karuizawa, the warmest temperature is 32°C (90°F) and the coldest -18° (0°F). Nagano and Matsumoto have an annual precipitation of 930 millimeters (37 inches), while Karuizawa receives nearly 1,600 millimeters (63 inches).

HOUSING

Karuizawa

Karuizawa is in eastern Nagano, with active volcano Mount Asama to the north and Yatsugatake in the south. The town originated as a retreat for foreign missionaries, headed by English missionary A. C. Shaw, who recommended the development of Karuizawa as a summer resort in 1886. In the 116 years since its inception, it has grown into an international health and tourist resort in a lush green environment. Both the resort owners and year-round town residents share a desire to preserve the culture in a setting where low buildings blend into the landscape. The imperial family summered in Karuizawa for many years, and this is where, in the 1950s, the present Heisei Emperor and Empress met playing tennis. The town is surrounded by farms raising highland cabbage, lettuce, and other crops.

Karuizawa's highland resort environment is considered an important asset to Japan. To respond to the high demand for condominiums in

Karuizawa and to ensure that the town's natural environment remains unblemished, the Nagano prefecture government passed an amendment in 2002 regulating the constructions of condominiums. The amendment stated that new condominiums cannot stand more than two stories high, and a single complex must contain less than 20 units. Without such environmentally sensitive regulations, any town could become Tōkyō.

A real estate agency called Home AdPark recently listed 1DKs and 2DKs at ¥45,000–55,000 ($410–500) per month and a newer 3LDK for ¥75,000 ($681) per month. A 2DK in Karuizawa rents for ¥55,000 ($500) per month, and a 3DK for ¥55,000–65,000 ($500–591) per month. Want to buy a condominium? In Karuizawa, a tiny 12-year-old studio *manshon* is priced at ¥4.4 million ($40,000), and a slightly larger 1LDK lists for ¥7.8 million ($70,900).

Nagano

The city of Nagano, the capital of Nagano prefecture, has a population of 350,000. It is surrounded by the mountains of Joshinetsu National Park and Zenkōji Plain, at the confluence of the Chikuma River and Sai River. The area, the home of Zenkōji Temple, is rich in historical and cultural assets (it started out as a temple town). In the same region are castle towns with old storehouses, such as Suzaka; Koshoku, known as Apricot Country; Obuse, a town of Japanese chestnuts; and Hokusai, home of the famous *ukiyo-e* (wood-block print) artist of the same name. The main industries include electrical and general machinery, food, and printing, along with agriculture and forestry. The 1998 Olympic Winter Games were held here, triggering an increase in international culture and sports exchanges.

Matsumoto

The city of Matsumoto is bordered on the west by the Northern Japan Alps and surrounded by tourist and outdoor destinations, such as the Utsukushigahara Highlands, Kamikōchi, and Norikura Highlands. As of 2002, almost 210,000 citizens lived here, surrounded by hot springs, galleries, museums, historical sites, and other attractions. About 4,500 registered foreign residents from 51 countries live in Matsumoto. Matsumoto has flourished as a castle town since the 16th century; the five-story Matsumotojō castle tower was built in 1592. The region, known as Shinano, had its capital in Matsumoto. In those days, the Nakasendō Highway was used by samurai traveling between Kyōto and Edo (Tōkyō).

Major industries include precision and agricultural machinery, furniture, food, medical supplies, and tourism. A wide variety of fruits and vegetables is produced, such as apples, grapes, watermelons, tomatoes, rice, and

Japanese horseradish. Matsumoto is the home of Sinshū University and the Talent Education Research Institute, better known as the Suzuki method of violin playing. Matsumoto has sister-city relationships with Salt Lake City and Katmandu.

Public Housing

Public housing is available for residents, including foreign residents, of Nagano. Foreign residents must have resided in Japan for one year or longer, or have a status of residence of one year or longer, or have permanent resident status. In addition, they must live or work in Nagano, earn a low income, and need housing. There is also public housing managed by cities and towns—apply at the local municipal office.

GETTING AROUND

The Hokuriku *shinkansen* line and Hokuriku Expressway through Nagano were completed in 1997, just in time for the 1998 Winter Olympics. From Tōkyō, you can get to Karuizawa via *shinkansen* in 70 minutes (at a cost of $50). The bullet train replaced the old Shinano Railway to

Buddhist statues

Karuizawa. The only cheaper option is an infrequent bus. Tōkyō–Karuizawa, via the Kanetsu Expressway, is 142 kilometers (88 miles), and the time it takes is governed by the number of cars on the road.

Japan Railway (JR) lines running through Nagano prefecture include the Chuo, Shin-etsu, Iida, Koumi, Iiyama, and Oito. There are also private lines—Shinano Railway and the Nagano, Matsumoto, and Ueda Electric Railroads. Three expressways—Chuo, Nagano, and Joshin-etsu—provide easy access to Nagano prefecture. To get around Karuizawa, Matsumoto, or Nagano, you can ride the bus, catch a taxi, or rent a car or bicycle. Matsumoto is about 2.5 hours by express train (Azuza or Super-Azusa) from Tōkyō. The flight from Ōsaka (Itami Airport) to Matsumoto is one hour, and there are also flights from Sapporo (New Chitose) and Fukuoka (northern Kyūshū) Airports. Matsumoto Airport, at 657 meters (2,155 feet) above sea level, is the highest airport in Japan.

RECREATION

Seventy-eight percent of Nagano's land area is forested, and 21 percent is designated as natural parkland. The four tallest mountains are Okuhodaka (3,190 meters/10,466 feet), Yarigatake (3,180 meters/10,433 feet), Akaishi (3,120 meters/10,236 feet), and Kitahodaka (3,106 meters/10,190 feet). The prefectural bird is the ptarmigan, its flower the gentian, its animal the Japanese serow (slightly smaller than a goat), and its tree the white birch. Nagano's primary resource is snow. The deepest snow recorded at a municipal office in Nagano was 4.34 meters (14.3 feet). The longest river is Shinano (or Chikuma) River (367 kilometers/228 miles). Nagano built the first ski lift in 1946 and manufactured the first snow plow in 1896. The city was also the first to build a *kemonomichi* (underpass) in 1923 to allow wild animals to pass under the road. Nagano welcomes tourists, offering old-fashioned hospitality at thousands of Japanese-style inns.

Each spring, Karuizawa holds a "Young Leaves" festival, with horseback riding, an international women's tennis tournament, and other events. Fireworks take place in the summer, there's a colored leaves festival in the fall, and winter brings ice-sculpting and international curling events. With golf, tennis, hiking, camping, skiing, hot springs, and churches aplenty, Karuizawa is the nearest mountain getaway for millions of city-dwellers.

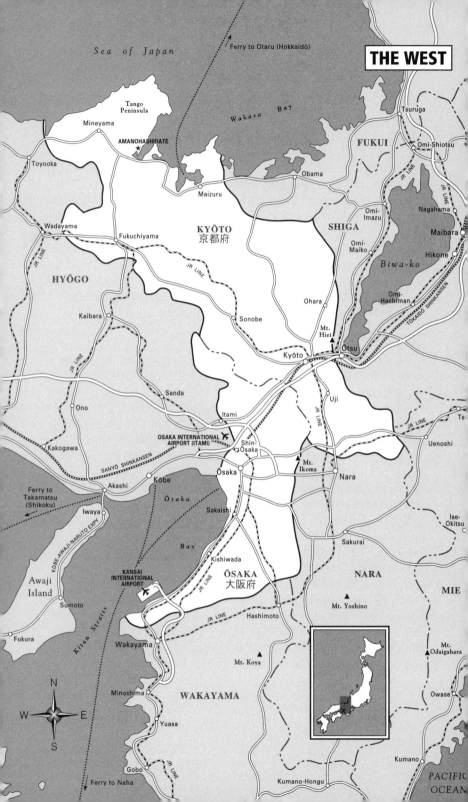

The West: Kyōto and Ōsaka

K yōto and Ōsaka, along with Kōbe, are three major cities in the Kansai district of Honshū, west of Tōkyō and Nagoya. The Kansai region is made up of six *ken* (prefectures): Ōsaka, Hyōgo, Kyōto, Nara, Wakayama, and Shiga. The Kantō district is comprised of Tōkyō, plus six surrounding prefectures. (Note that the names Kyōto and Ōsaka apply to both the city and its prefecture. Kyōto-fu refers to the urban prefecture, while Kyōto-shi refers to the city; likewise, Ōsaka-fu is the prefectural name, while Ōsaka-shi is the city.) The Kansai people are regarded by the rest of Japan as possessing some distinct characteristics, such as a love of new things, as well as being practical-minded and impulsive.

Kansai has a relatively high population of registered foreign residents—almost 460,00—meaning that more than one out of four foreigners in Japan lives in Kansai. Of these, half live in Ōsaka, and 93 percent of Ōsakans of foreign nationality are Korean (meaning third- and forth-generation descents of Koreans who came or were brought over during Japan's occupation of Korea). This may be why the city of Ōsaka and the region are quite active in promoting human rights, women's rights, and equality in housing, education, and jobs. This consciousness seems to operate at a higher level than what I've experienced in Tōkyō and other areas of Japan, which could be a plus for foreigners contemplating a move to this region of the country.

Kyōto

Kyōto, a city of 1.5 million, was the capital of Japan for 1,000 years, beginning with the Heian court in A.D. 794 and lasting until the end of the Tokugawa era in 1868, when the emperor and the capital shifted east to Tōkyō. Kyōto is a living museum of ancient culture, religion, arts, literature, and architecture. On broad and narrow streets between timeless temples and shrines, imposing palaces, and gardens, modern Kyōto goes about daily life. A mix of office workers, *maiko* (apprentice geisha), tourists, and uniformed students thread their way between banks, department stores, teahouses, and construction zones. Successive *shinkansen* slide in and out of multistory Kyōto station, minutes apart, while consumers fill the boutiques, restaurants, and coffee shops. Across from the station is the Kyōto Tower Hotel, a candle-shaped tower that almost looks out of place in a city of 1,000 temples.

> *Kyōto is a living museum of ancient culture, religion, arts, literature, and architecture.*

When Kyōto was first built, the streets were modeled after those of Chang-An in China of the T'ang dynasty, with wide main boulevards laid out like a grid. Those running east to west are *jō* (numbered avenues), starting with Ichi-jō (1st) in the north, followed by Ni-jō, San-jō, Shi-jō (2nd, 3rd, 4th Avenues), and so on. Hachi-jō (8th Avenue) is where Kyōto station and the *shinkansen* entrance are located today. Three of the important north–south streets are Kawaramachi-dōri, Karasuma-dōri, and Horikawa-dōri (*dōri* means road).

Kyōto-shi, the city, is the capital of larger Kyōto-fu, which is long and narrow, extending from the Sea of Japan in the north to Ōsaka and Nara in the south. Mie and Shiga prefectures are to the east, and Hyōgo-ken and the city of Kōbe lie to the west. About 2.6 million people live in Kyōto prefecture, many concentrated in the city of Kyōto, which borders Ōsaka.

The city of Kyōto is divided into 11 *ku* (city wards) with names that orient you: Kita-ku (north); Ukyō-ku (right Kyō, if you're facing south); Sakyō-ku (left Kyō, if you're facing south); Kamigyō-ku (upper Kyō); Nak-

Yasaka shrine in Kyōto

agyō-ku (central Kyō); Shimogyō-ku (lower Kyō); Higashiyama-ku (east mountain); Yamashina-ku (mountain); Nishigyō-ku (west Kyō); Minami-ku (south); and Fushimi-ku (Fushimi).

Kyōto prefecture's main products are computer and electronic equipment, transportation, beverages, food, tobacco, and general machinery. Some brand names originating in Kyōto are Kyōcera, Omron, and Wacoal. Traditional industries are also alive and well here, including *nishijin-ori* (a 1,200-year-old technique for weaving kimonos), *yūzen* (dyed silk), *tango chirimen* (silk crêpe), and *kiyomizu-yaki* (ceramics).

Kyōto has long fostered international gatherings, from actively welcoming Chinese and Korean people and cultures in the 7th and 8th century to stepping up to host critically important conventions today. In 1997, the Third Session of the Conference of the Parties to the United Nations Framework Convention on Climate Change, better known as the Kyōto Global Warming Conference, took place in the city. In addition, Kansai Science City and its world-class research institutions are international in focus.

If you're interested in teaching at a university, you might like to know that Kyōto prefecture has six national and public universities and 19 private universities. There are more universities here per person than in any other prefecture, with 140,000 students from Japan and other countries. Kyōto University, Kyōto Institute of Technology, Dōshisha, and Ritsumeikan are some of the better known schools. Kyōto University has a strong engineering program, and the Faculty of Sciences produced a Nobel Prize–winner. There are also several research-oriented technical and polytechnic colleges.

WEATHER AND CLIMATE

The Kyōto Basin Mountains and highlands cover 70 percent of the Kyōto prefecture, and the Tamba range divides it into two different climates. The Sea of Japan dumps moisture onto the northern half, while the southern inland area of Kyōto city has extreme temperatures in both summer and winter. The average temperature in the prefecture is 4°C (39°F) in January and 27°C (81°F) in August, with an average annual temperature of 15°C (59°F). Yearly precipitation averages 1,660 millimeters (65 inches), some of it in the form of snow.

HOUSING

I don't know why, but in Kyōto, the *reikin* (landlord's fee) when signing a lease is much higher than in Tōkyō and other areas—as high as six months' rent, nonrefundable! Thus, be prepared to hand over a great deal of money just to move into a unit. Prices rise as you move from the outskirts to the center of the city. For example, 1DK units (one room plus dining room-kitchen) range ¥48,000–70,000 ($436–636) per month and up; when signing the contract, a security deposit of ¥200,000 ($1,818) and a landlord fee of ¥150,000 ($1,364) or more are not unusual. Add also a monthly maintenance fee of up to ¥10,000 ($91) into your budget.

If you need more space, a 2DK in the Fushimi district south of the city may be available for a reasonable ¥60,000 ($545) per month, plus your deposit and ¥60,000 ($545) to the landlord, plus ¥5,000 ($45) in maintenance per month. At the opposite end of Kyōto, a 3LDK in a *manshon* (condominuim) built in 1993 with ample space rents for ¥74,000 ($673). The deposit is ¥350,000 ($3,181), and the landlord requires ¥250,000 ($2,273) as thanks. This apartment is located in Kita-ku in northern Kyōto, a six-minute walk to the nearest bus stop and then a 25-minute bus ride to Kita-Oji subway stop. The benefit is being close to the hills, surrounded by greenery.

It's also possible to live in the center of Kyōto. A 2DK *manshon* unit 12 minutes' walk from the subway station is yours for ¥100,000 ($909) per month. Add ¥300,000 ($2,727) for a security deposit and another ¥300,000

Traditional house in Gion quarter, Kyōto

for the landlord, plus an additional ¥13,000 ($118) every month for maintenance, and moving in will cost you a whopping ¥713,000 ($6,482). But you will be on the 8th floor, looking out over Kyōto, sharing the sameaddress as Nijo Castle (which once belonged to a shōgun)! In the same part of town, you can rent spacious 3LDKs for ¥130,000–190,000 ($1,182–1,727) per month, and the deposit also rises to ¥500,000 ($4,545; but you can get most of it back).

Most rentals require a two-year rental lease, but usually there's no penalty for moving out early, as long as you give 30 days' notice. When the two years are up, it's possible—and likely—that the landlord will raise the rent.

Public housing is another option, if you meet the conditions. For information, contact the Housing Division of the Department of Public Works and Construction.

On final tip: According to a Japanese professor friend in Kyōto, it's possible to rent old, traditional-style houses where the owners no longer live, but don't want to sell. They may cost as little as ¥50,000 ($455) per month to rent, but may require an equal amount per month to heat in winter. If you've always wanted to live in an authentic house, it's worth asking a real estate agent about such properties, or start with an inquiry or by posting on the bulletin board at a tourist information center.

Real Estate Agents: Kyōto

Able Co., Ltd. Fushimi-ten
184-3 Gokogu-monzen-chō
Fushimi-ku, Kyōto-shi
tel. 075/601-6251
fax 075/601-6252

ERA Daikyō Jūhan
72-9 Umekōji Higashi-machi
Shimogyō-ku, Kyōto-shi
tel. 075/315-1331
fax 075/313-7788
daikyo-j@realtor.ne.jp
www.realtor.ne.jp/era/daikyo-j
(in Japanese)

GETTING AROUND

The best ways to sightsee and shop in Kyōto are via public transportation and by foot. There is abundant information in English on how to get around, both on the Internet and in print (see the Resources section for details). The city of Kyōto has an extensive network of buses and two subway lines. The Karasuma subway line goes from Takeda, south of Kyōto station north to Kokusaikaikan (Kyōto International Conference Hall) in the northeastern part of the city. The Tōzai (east–west) line runs from Ni-jō (Second Avenue) in the west to Daigo in the east.

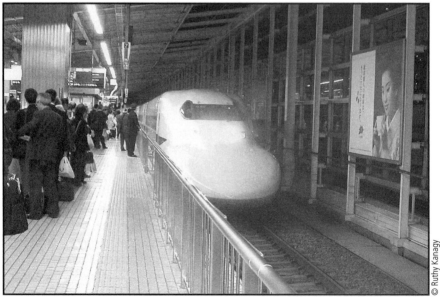

© Ruthy Kanagy

A *shinkansen* (high-speed train) pulls into Kyōto station.

Many local trains and streetcars crisscross the city and prefecture. Kintetsu Railway goes between Kyōto and Nara, while the Keihan Railway goes from northeast Kyōto to Ōsaka and other areas. Hankyū Railway goes from central Kyōto southwest to Umeda in Ōsaka, with a branch to Katsura and Arashiyama areas of Kyōto. Another way to go to the latter two areas is by *keifuku dentesu* (electric streetcar) from Shi-jō Ōmiya (intersection of Fourth and Ōmiya Streets). Confusing? Perhaps at the beginning, but take your time and have an adventure. You can pick up English maps at the station, or check out the Kyōto Municipal Transportation Bureau's Kyōto City Bus and Subway Guide online.

One handy tool is the Kansai Thru Pass, which enables you to ride subways, private railways, and buses in Kyōto, Nara, Ōsaka, Kōbe, and Wakayama for two or three days. Passes may be purchased at train stations in any of the cities.

The most efficient (albeit expensive) way to arrive in Kyōto is by *shinkansen*. Nozomi, the fastest type, whisks you from Tōkyō to Kyōto in 2.5 hours. The Hikari takes slightly longer, and Kodama takes about four hours from Tōkyō. The latter two trains travel almost as fast, but stop at more stations. If you're going from Ōsaka to Kyōto, the Hankyu or Keihan Railway is your best bet; trains operate every 15 minutes, take 40 minutes, and cost less than the *shinkansen*.

Two airports serve Ōsaka and Kyōto: Kansai International Airport (KIX) is on an island in Ōsaka Bay, an hour from Ōsaka. Itami (Ōsaka International Airport) is further north and a bit closer to Kyōto. JR "Haruka" has direct service from Kyōto station to KIX in just under 1.5 hours. Two expressways cross Kyōto-fu: the Meishin runs east–west through Kyōto city and southern Kyōto-fu; Kyōto expressway runs north to south through the prefecture. Maizuru Port is a major port on the Sea of Japan and handles domestic shipping and foreign trade. You can take a ferry from Maizuru to Otaru in Hokkaidō—an inexpensive and adventurous way to travel (and your bicycle can go with you).

Ōsaka

The city of Ōsaka has 2.6 million residents in an area covering 222 square kilometers (86 square miles), yielding a population density of 11,800 persons per square kilometer (in 2003). In the daytime, the population swells by an additional one million commuters. Ōsaka paints itself as a city of commerce, culture, international sports, and history—an environmentally advanced economic and industrial center.

Made in Ōsaka

In Ōsaka, Japan's city of commerce for 1,400 years, businesspeople greet each other on the street by saying, *"Mōkatte makka?"* ("Making any dough?") Ōsakans are known for their love of new things, their practical minds, and their impulsive nature, qualities that have shaped their enterprising spirit. The following creative and innovative products all came out of Ōsaka:

1958 Chicken Ramen (the world's first instant noodles, by Nissin Foods)
1959 Prefabricated housing

1967 Moving walkway (at Hankyū Umeda Station)
1968 Automatic ticket machines (at Hankyū line stations)
1970 Automatic Teller Machines (ATMs)
1970 Automated ticket gate machines at railway stations
1971 Cup o' Noodle (the world's first ramen in a cup, by Nissin Foods)
1972 Karaoke
1983 Home video game console (by Family Computer)
1986 Breadmaker

Ōsaka's comprehensive plan for the 21st century calls for it to become a "City of International Cultural Exchange." To this end, the city plans to create an environment where Japanese and non-Japanese residents can live together in harmony. Ōsaka has many minorities, the largest group being resident Koreans. There are 121,000 registered foreign residents, or almost 5 percent of the city's total population. This is the highest percentage among Japanese cities.

Ōsaka's GDP of $192 billion in the fiscal year ending March 2000 was greater than that of Hong Kong. The city is home to a World Trade Center, Ōsaka Business & Investment Center, and Ōsaka Business Partner City. Science industries are concentrated in northern Ōsaka.

In 2001, there were 123 foreign firms headquartered in Ōsaka. The city offers a number of investment incentives to foreign-affiliated firms, such as a business establishment promotion subsidy, office rent subsidy, and tax incentives (e.g., a reduction of Ōsaka's prefectural corporate business tax).

Ōsaka prefecture contains 33 cities, 10 towns, and one village covering 1,890 square kilometers (729 square miles) with a population of 8.8 million—the second highest in a prefecture after metropolitan Tōkyō. About 210,000 foreign residents live in this urban prefecture.

CLIMATE

Ōsaka prefecture borders Ōsaka Bay on the west and is surrounded by mountains on the other three sides. The bay makes winters a bit milder than in Kyōto, with an average January temperature of 5.8°C. Summers are

© Ruthy Kanagy

Lighting up the night at Dōtonbori

hot and humid, averaging 28.4°C in August. Humidity is high year-round, with an average of 1,300 millimeters (51 inches) of precipitation.

HOUSING

To begin your housing search, you can go through a real estate agent, look through housing information magazines (in Japanese) sold in bookstores or outside real estate agent's offices, and make inquiries of anyone you know in the city or in the neighborhood you are considering. The Ōsaka Municipal Housing Information Center provides housing information in English, Chinese, and Korean.

A recent housing listing priced a 1DK (one room plus dining room-kitchen) with 28 square meters (300 square feet) in a new *manshon* at ¥69,000 ($627) per month, plus an ¥8,000 ($73) monthly maintenance fee. A refundable security deposit of ¥50,000 ($455) and a landlord's fee of ¥250,000 ($2,273) were also required. The apartment was located in Nishi-ku in Ōsaka, a one-minute walk from the Chūō line subway. The same rental agency also advertised a 2DK with 35.5 square meters (382 square feet) in a *manshon* built in 1996 for ¥65,000 ($591), plus a ¥9,000 ($82) maintenance fee per month. A security deposit was not required, but the nonrefundable landlord's fee was ¥250,000 ($2,273). The unit was in Nishi-ku, and the nearest subway stop was six minutes away.

Japan Homes caters to foreigners and has listings for rentals starting from ¥150,000 ($1,364) per month and up. For example, a one-bedroom apartment near the Honmachi station in Nishi-ku, Ōsaka listed for ¥350,000 ($3,182) per month. For ¥400,000 ($3,636) per month, you can move into a three-bedroom apartment in Chūō-ku.

Public housing is also available in Ōsaka and it is assigned by lottery due to great demand. Contact the Ōsaka Municipal Housing Corporation (Application Department), tel. 06/6882-7024, fax 06/6882-7021; Municipal Housing Telephone Service (recorded message in Japanese), tel. 06/6945-0031.

Real Estate Agents: Ōsaka

Able Victory Housing
1F Park Heights Mikuni, 3-30-10
Mikuni Motomachi
Yodogawa-ku, Ōsaka-shi
tel. 06/6398-5055
fax 06/6398-5055
westsinosaka@realtor.ne.jp
www.v-able.jp (in Japanese)

H&R Consutants
4F Ōsaka Ekimae Dai 1 Bldg.,
3-1-400 1-chome Umeda
Kita-ku, Ōsaka-shi
tel. 06/6344-2223
fax 06/6344-2227
contactus@japanhomesearch.com
www.japanhomesearch.com

Century21 Will House
2F Yagyu Dai Bldg.,
10 Nagasone-chō
Sakai-shi, Ōsaka-fu
tel. 072/246-3123
fax 072/246-3128
www.century21willhouse.co.jp
(in Japanese)

GETTING AROUND

Ōsaka has city-operated subways and buses. The subway connects the city center and many outlying cities. Seven subway lines and one new tramline provide a fast, easy way to get around. Each line is color-coded and operates 5:00 A.M.–midnight. For details, see the Ōsaka Municipal Transportation Bureau's website (see the Resources section for more information).

In addition, there are private and public JR trains, airport transportation, and taxis. A JR loop line goes around the city, with access to major terminals. JR trains for Kyōto and Kōbe depart from Ōsaka station, while *shinkansen* depart from Shin-Ōsaka (New Ōsaka) station. If you're headed to KIX (Kansai International Airport) on JR, depart from Namba station.

Private Railways offer service to some of the same places as JR. Hankyū Railways has service to Kyōto and Kōbe, and Hanshin Railways goes to Kōbe and Himeji further west. You can also ride the Keihan line to Kyōto and the Nankai line to Kansai International Airport. Kintetsu goes to Nara and destinations further east. In short, public transportation is intense and thorough. Get a good transportation book or map.

RECREATION

Ōsaka Castle, the premier symbol of the city's heritage, and modern buildings in the Ōsaka Castle are located inside a park popular for playing sports, walking, and learning about history. The main tower of the castle contains a historical museum; in the vicinity are the Ōsaka City Museum, Nishinomaru Garden, and Ōsaka Business Park. There are many shopping areas and department stores around the JR Ōsaka, Hankyū, and Hanshin Umeda stations, including underground shopping.

Dōtonbori is the place to go in search of food. Ōsakans express their love of good food as *"kuidaore"* (eat until you drop). You'll find *okonomiyaki* (a sort of Japanese-style pizza), *takoyaki* (grilled dough balls with octopus), *kushiage* (skewered portions of meat, seafood, and vegetables ready to dip in batter and deep-fry at the table), and much more. The neighborhood surrounding Tennōji Temple in the northeast contains both old and new Ōsaka, with lots of greenery. Shitennōji temple was built in the 6th century. At the end of January, the Ōsaka International Women's Marathon is held at Nagai Park.

Ōsaka is also your chance to see a performance of *bunraku,* traditional puppet theater developed in the 17th century. Very realistic puppets, two-thirds life-size, are manipulated by three puppeteers in black, while the narrator and *shamisen* (three-stringed lute) tell the story. Most Japanese have never seen *bunraku* . . . but you can.

The city is also home to numerous museums, including the Municipal Museum of Art, Museums of Oriental Ceramics, History, Natural History, and Liberty, a Science Museum, and Ōsaka International Peace Center, among others.

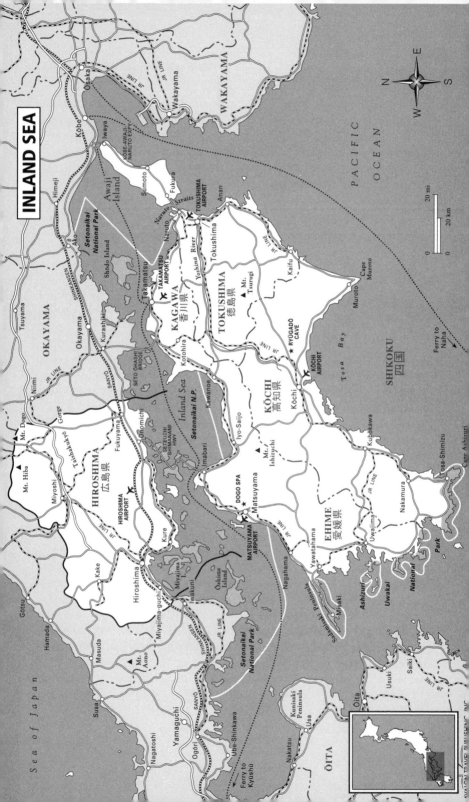

Inland Sea:
Hiroshima and Shikoku

Hiroshima

Hiroshima-ken (*ken* means prefecture) is located at the western end of Honshū, in the area of Japan known as Chūgoku (midcountry region). The prefecture is sandwiched between the mountains to the north and the inland sea to the south. About 2.9 million people live in an area of 8,477 square kilometers (3,273 square miles). The city of Hiroshima is set along Setonaikai (Inland Sea), which is dotted with myriad islands. Mountains surround the city on three sides and change their appearance with each season; six rivers flow through the city and into the sea.

As the hub of the Chūgoku region, Hiroshima-shi (*shi* means city), with a population of 1.1 million, is developing economically, culturally, and administratively. The city is divided into seven *ku* (wards). Today, the city promotes itself as an International City of Peace and Culture, with sister-city relationships with Honolulu and Montreal, among others.

Hiroshima Castle and urban housing

On August 6, 1945, Hiroshima was the first city in the world attacked by a nuclear weapon. Instantly, 92,000 buildings were destroyed, and by December of that year, 140,000 people had died as a result of the bombing. Mayor Awaya Senkichi died at his home, and many other officials were killed in their offices. Transportation, communication systems, and factories were also destroyed.

Almost 60 years later, to all appearances, Hiroshima has recovered from the tragedy of the atomic bombing, although the suffering of the survivors has not abated. Neither has the city's message of peace among nations. In November 2004, Hiroshima plans to host the first Japan–U.S. Cities Summit to appeal for the realization of lasting world peace. In part, the summit aims to discover ways in which cities can achieve sustainable development while addressing global environmental concerns.

In Hiroshima, the largest industries (beginning with the biggest employer) are wholesale, retail, eating and drinking establishments, manufacturing, construction, transportation and communication, government, finance and insurance, real estate, agriculture, utilities, fishery, and forestry. One of the biggest manufacturers is Mazda, which has a very large factory in Hiroshima.

In addition to its varied professional undertakings, Hiroshima prides itself on being an education prefecture. Fifty-two percent of high school students matriculate into university, as compared with the national average of 44 percent. There are 12 universities and nine junior colleges. Hiroshima City University is the newest, established in 1994.

Hiroshima citizens are inclined to remain in their home prefecture for employment. Many young people who go to other areas for higher education come home to find work, unlike the situation in other outlying regions of Japan. Locals are encouraged to stay local by such organizations as the Hiroshima Institute for the Study of Medium and Small Business Enterprises, which aims to nurture talent and provide information on small and midsize businesses.

> *To all appearances, Hiroshima has recovered from the tragedy of the atomic bombing, although the suffering of the survivors has not abated. Neither has the city's message of peace among nations.*

Everyone in Hiroshima knows standard Japanese from school and television, but when they want to convey warmth with family and neighbors, they speak Hiroshima-*ben* (dialect). My friend Yoshida-san says it's partly a matter of using different vocabulary, like saying *"dekin"* instead of the standard Japanese *"dekinai"* (meaning "can't do"). The accent and intonation are also different. Take the word for "thank you"—Tōkyōites say, *"a-RI-ga-tō"*; people from Kōbe say, *"a-ri-ga-TŌ"*; and Hiroshimans say, *"a-ri-GA-tō,"* with the capitalized syllable spoken at a higher pitch (not with greater emphasis or volume, as English-speakers tend to do).

CLIMATE

Residents of Hiroshima enjoy every season: smelling *sakura* (cherry tree blossoms and planting rice in the spring; swimming, sailing, and attending the Peace Memorial service in summer; admiring fall colors in the Taishakukyō Valley; and skiing in winter. In the northern part of the prefecture, the Chūgoku Highlands spread east and west. Two rivers, the Ōta and Ashida, flow south from the mountains into the Inland Sea, while Gono River flow flows north through Shimane prefecture into the Japan Sea. The Inland Sea provides a relatively mild climate, and the region is not badly affected by typhoons and earthquakes. Hiroshima prefecture has an annual average temperature of 15°C (59°F) and yearly average humidity of 73 percent. Annual precipitation is 1,555 millimeters (61 inches). In Hiroshima city, the average temperature is 6°C (43°F) during January and 27°C (81°F) in August.

HOUSING

The Hiroshima City International House, a five-minute walk from Hiroshima station, is a place where foreign students can live (up to 20 families and 80 singles) and interact with the community while studying at Hiroshima's universities and language schools. The rent is ¥26,000 ($236) per month for a single room and ¥36,000 ($327) per month for families, with utilities additional. There is no security deposit or landlord fee. Tenancy is limited to a year. Applications are taken starting in mid-November, and the move-in date is April 1.

Going through a realtor, you might find such rentals as a 1DK (one 8-mat room plus dining room-kitchen) in a three-year-old *manshon* (condominium) in the Minami-ku (*ku* means city ward) area of Hiroshima for ¥69,000 ($627) per month, plus a ¥3,000 ($27) monthly maintenance fee and an initial refundable deposit of ¥207,000 ($1,881). The streetcar is just two minutes away. A 2DK with one 6-mat and one 4.5-mat (i.e., very small) room plus dining room-kitchen in a brand-new *manshon* lists for ¥65,000 ($591) per month. There is no maintenance fee, and the security deposit is equivalent to four months' rent. A 3LDK unit in a newer *manshon* rents for between ¥81,000 ($736) and ¥100,000 ($909) per month, plus a ¥5,000 ($45) monthly maintenance fee and a security deposit worth three months' rent. All of these sample rentals are within three minutes of public transportation.

© Ruthy Kanagy

The Inland Sea has been a passageway for centuries.

Real Estate Agents: Hiroshima

Anesisu Corp.
Inagaki Bldg., 1-3-3 Ōtemachi
Naka-ku, Hiroshima-shi
tel. 082/544-0920
fax 082/242-2223
anesisu@ci.mbn.or.jp

Central Shōji Co., Ltd.
Oto Nakamachi Bldg.,
2-2 Nakamachi
Naka-ku, Hiroshima-shi
tel. 082/247-4630
fax 082/247-6889
central1@lime.ocn.ne.jp

I-House
1-1 Nishi-Kōjin-machi
Minami-ku, Hiroshima 732-0806
tel. 082/568-5931
fax 082/568-5600
i-house@hicat.ne.jp
www.hicat.ne.jp/home/ryugaku/
english.htm

GETTING AROUND

Hiroshima is a great walking city with a very efficient streetcar system (stops are announced in both English and Japanese). To set out in the right direction, obtain the number of the streetcar you need from the information booth. Recently, the "Green Mover" electric streetcars imported from Germany with low floors have made the process of getting on and off a breeze for baby strollers and wheelchairs.

To visit Miyajima Island, take the JR train from Hiroshima station to Miyajima-guchi station (30 minutes), then walk three minutes down to the pier. The ferry to Miyajima departs about every 15 minutes, and the ride is just 10 minutes. It's a leisurely stroll through the town and past restaurants to Itsukushima Shrine.

The New Hiroshima Airport is located 60 minutes from Hiroshima city and has international flights to Seoul (an hour and 20 minutes), Hong Kong (three hours), Singapore (seven hours), Shanghai (just under two hours), Xian (just over four hours), Honolulu (just under 10 hours), Dalian (an hour and 50 minutes), and Beijing (three hours and 50 minutes). Domestic routes connect to Tōkyō (Haneda) in an hour and 10 minutes; to Sapporo, Hakodate, Aomori, or Sendai in around two hours; to Miyazaki in Kyūshū in 45 minutes; and to Naha and Ishigaki in Okinawa in just under two hours. The Hiroshima Nishi (West Hiroshima) Airport has regular flights to five other regional cities in Japan.

Train travel is quite convenient here, with a JR regional line hugging the coast and a *shinkansen* line speeding through tunnels further inland. The *shinkansen* takes you from Hiroshima to Ōsaka in 1.25 hours and to Tōkyō in just under four hours. There are also intercity highway buses linking Hiroshima to Tōkyō (11 hours and 45 minutes), Ōsaka (7.5 hours), and Tokuyama in Shikoku (one hour and 45 minutes), among other cities. Though the travel time is longer by bus, you'll save a night's lodging if you travel at night, and the price is half or less that of *shinkansen*.

With direct access to the Inland Sea, Hiroshima prefecture has many ports, including Hiroshima, Kure, Fukuyama, and Onomichi Itozaki Ports. International container lines operate regularly from the Ports of Hiroshima and Fukuyama to Korea, Taiwan, and China and beyond.

The Chūgoku Expressway links the eastern and western ends of the prefecture, the Sanyo Expressway links the coastal cities, and the San'in–Sanyo Chūgoku Expressway goes north to south. A series of seven bridges connecting the islands of the Inland Sea takes you from Onomichi in Honshū to Imabari in Shikoku—this road is descriptively named Setouchi Shimanami Kaidō (Seto Inland Sea Highway).

RECREATION

Hiroshima Castle was built in 1589. Mostly destroyed during the atomic bombing of 1945, it was reconstructed in 1958, with a historical museum inside. From JR Hiroshima station, take the streetcar for 15 minutes, get off at Kamiya-chō Nishi (West Kamiya-chō), and walk for 10 minutes. You'll be rewarded with a memorable view of the castle's reflection in the moat and a bird's-eye perspective on the entire city from the top floor.

The Atomic Bomb Dome, formerly the Hiroshima Prefectural Industrial Promotion Hall, was built in 1915. The bombing left only the walls and steel skeleton of the dome standing. It was registered as a World Heritage Monument in 1996 by UNESCO and has been left standing as a message to the world of the importance of peace. The dome is inside the larger Peace Memorial Park, which houses statues, markers, and an eternal flame on its grounds, along with a Peace Memorial Museum displaying documents and artifacts from the nuclear tragedy. The park has an open, spacious feeling, with trees and greenery. To get to the park from Hiroshima station, ride the city streetcar for 15 minutes, exit at Genbaku Dōmu Mae (Atomic Bomb Stop), and walk for about minute.

Many of Hiroshima city's museums and gardens are worth a visit, including the Hiroshima Botanical Garden, the Transportation Museum, the Hiroshima City Museum of Contemporary Art, and the Health Sciences Museum. The Kamiyachō underground shopping center near the station is considered a fashionable spot, and it's a handy place to buy *momiji*

Hiroshima Castle moat

manjū (traditional Japanese sweets shaped like a maple leaf). Note that most of the museums and Peace Park building are closed December 29–January 2 for the New Year's holiday.

Miyajima is an island off the shore of Hiroshima, best known for its historic Itsukushima Shrine, with a *torii* (shrine gate) that appears to float on the waves at high tide. The shrine was originally built in A.D. 593, then rebuilt in 1168 in its present form. It represents the "Shinden Zukuri" style, with painted pillars carrying a massive roof thatched with cypress bark. In 1996, it was registered as a World Heritage Site.

The pleasurable tastes of Hiroshima include *okonomiyaki*. This dish is sometimes called Japanese pizza—but unlike the Ōsaka variety, which is based on a battered pancake, the local version in this part of the country consists of a thin crêpe topped with thin soba or thick udon noodles, chopped cabbage, and green onions, with an egg on top. Flip it over and pour on a special sweet sauce. Oysters grown in the Inland Sea are best in winter—batter-dipped and fried, steamed in sake, grilled in the shell, wrapped with bacon, dipped in vinaigrette, or added to *okonomiyaki*. Hiroshima prefecture grows 60 percent of the oysters raised in Japan.

Shikoku

Across the Inland Sea from western Honshū is Japan's fourth and smallest island, Shikoku. True to its name, Shikoku (literally, four districts) has four prefectures. Going clockwise from the northeast, they are Kagawa, Tokushima, Kōchi, and Ehime. The prefectural capitals are Takamatsu, Tokushima, Kōchi, and Matsuyama, respectively. Steep mountain ranges running east and west slice across Shikoku.

If you're looking for a slower pace of life than you'll find in the hectic cities on Honshū, you might fit well in Shikoku. Shikoku is rural and more traditional, and it has planted firm cultural and religious roots. You will likely see pilgrims in white garb carrying walking sticks as they visit the 88 famous temples of Shikoku. The people are described as rugged, independent, open-minded, and generous. A number of English-speaking foreigners have found a home in Shikoku and written about it in print or online.

> *If you're looking for a slower pace of life than you'll find in the hectic cities on Honshū, you might fit well in Shikoku. Shikoku is rural and more traditional, and it has planted firm cultural and religious roots.*

Kagawa introduces itself to visitors as "the smallest prefecture with the biggest heart." Located along the center of the Inland Sea, this land area of 1,875 square kilometers (724 square miles) means Kagawa ranks 47th and smallest among the prefectures of Japan. (By contrast, Hokkaidō, the largest prefecture, is 83,400 square kilometers/32,200 square miles). A population of just over one million works out to 545 people per square kilometer, giving Kagawa a ranking of 11th in population density in the county (Tōkyō has the highest density at 5,550 people per square kilometer, while Hokkaidō is lowest at 72 people per square kilometer).

Kagawa has five universities—two public, including Kagawa Medical University, and three private—as well as six junior colleges. Major industries include agriculture, forestry, fisheries, manufacturing (truck crane and current transformers), trade, commerce, and traditional industries (from lacquerware and bonsai trees to paper fans, gloves, and *sōmen* noodles). Formerly dominated by the basic trades of processing of petroleum, coal, and metal and the manufacturing of food and textiles, the prefecture is now promoting expansion into microelectronics and other technology. The capital city of Takamatsu has 333,000 residents.

Tokushima-ken, population 820,000, is located in eastern Shikoku and has a land area of 4,145 square kilometers (1,600 square miles). Eighty percent is mountains, with deeply carved gorges, rivers, and abundant water.

Sometimes called the Awa Kingdom, this small prefecture is just a jump southwest from Kōbe and Ōsaka across Awaji Island. The ferry journey was made obsolete by the construction of the Akashi and Ōnaruto Bridges that support the Kōbe-Awaji-Naruto Highway, resulting in a travel time of just 100 minutes. As of 2001, foreign residents of Tokushima numbered 3,300, 80 percent of whom have Asian heritage. Every August, the 270,000 citizens of Tokushima city and millions of visitors dance the Awa-odori (*odori* means dance) together for four days.

Kōchi, the largest prefecture, occupies the whole southern coast of Shikoku. It is far enough removed from Tōkyō and Ōsaka to provide a taste of the real *inaka* (country). The mountains, rivers, and sea are suited for outdoor sports, and the region's long history and local crafts of sword- and paper-making are of interest to many. Kōchi Castle, built in 1603, overlooks the city of Kōchi from a hill.

Ehime prefecture is situated at the northwest corner of Shikoku, facing the Inland Sea, with a population of 1.5 million. To the west is the Uwa Sea, and to the south are the Shikoku Mountains, in sum covering an area of 5,676 square kilometers (2,192 square miles). Matsuyama, the

© Ruthy Kanagy

View of Matsuyama city from the castle

prefectural capital, has 460,000 residents and is well known for Matsuyama Castle, which overlooks the city; and for Dōgo Hot Springs, a spa with the longest history in Japan. The main industries are shipbuilding and the production of heavy chemicals, paper, and textiles. In addition, agricultural machinery, pottery, and porcelain are made near Matsuyama. Ehime is famous for cultured pearls and abundant *mikan* (mandarin oranges), harvested in winter; fishery, forestry, and agriculture are the main industries outside the cities. Historically, Ehime was called Iyo-no-kuni (Iyo country) and divided into eight *han;* in 1873, they were combined to form present-day Ehime-ken.

To promote international economic expansion, the prefectural government has created an Ehime Foreign Access Zone (FAZ) to stimulate the import of foreign goods. These zones are in place at Matsuyama Airport and Port. An Ehime World Trade Center was also built, and it hosted a Pan-Pacific Business Fair in 2003 with the goal of helping local companies find business opportunities through direct trade, investment, and technological exchange with foreign companies.

CLIMATE

Kagawa is blessed with a moderate Inland Sea climate, with an average January temperature of 6°C (43°F) and an August average of 28°C (82°F). Average annual precipitation is about 1,100 millimeters (43 inches), less than neighboring Ehime (1,300 millimeters/51 inches), Tokushima (1,500 millimeters/59 inches), and Kōchi (at 2,600 millimeters/102 inches, the highest in Japan).

Tokushima's average temperature is 6°C (43°F) in January and 27°C (81°F) in August. The southeast coastal area enjoys the wet and warm Pacific climate, while Mount Tsurugi to the west is cool. In the winter, there is enough snow accumulation on the mountains for skiing, and in the summer, surfers head to the beach. The damp, warm, humid climate is also perfect for raising *awa* (millet), formerly the region's main crop.

Kōchi also has hot, humid summers, with an average temperature of 27°C (81°F) in August. Winters are mild along the coast and colder in the mountains, with an average of 6°C (43°F).

Ehime has a mild climate, with an average temperature of 27°C (81°F) in summer and 5°C (41°F) in January. Average annual precipitation is 1,300 millimeters (51 inches), most of which fall during the rainy season in June and July. Nearby are such sights as the Seto Inland Sea National Park and Mount Ishizuchi—the highest mountain in western Japan at almost 2,000 meters (6,562 feet).

HOUSING

A real estate agent in Takamatsu city (Kagawa prefecture) offers 1DK (one room plus dining room-kitchen) units in a brand-new *manshon* for ¥55,000 ($500) per month, including fees, about a 20-minute bus ride and a five-minute walk from downtown. If you want two rooms and a spacious kitchen-dining-living room, you can rent a 2LDK in a *manshon* built in 1992 for ¥63,000 ($572) per month; a security deposit worth three months' rent is required, and the building is a 13-minute walk from public transportation. 3LDK apartments in Matsuyama city (Ehime prefecture) range from ¥60,000 ($545) to ¥102,000 ($927) per month, depending on age and distance from public transportation.

Real Estate Agents: Shikoku

City Home Co., Ltd.
Kawaramachieki-mae Center
Kawaramachieki-mae Bldg. 4F
1-2-25 Tokiwa-chō
Takamatsu-shi, Kagawa-ken
tel. 087/862-6600
fax 087/862-6609

Ehime-ken Takuchi Tatemono
Torihikigyō Kyōkai
(Prefectural Housing
Authority)
6-5-1 Heiwa-dōri
Matsuyama-shi, Ehime-ken
tel. 089/943-2184

Nihon Housing Co., Ltd.
Matsuyama Branch
4-7-10 Samban-chō
Matsuyama-shi, Ehime-ken
tel. 089/934-9611
fax 089/934-9622

Oka Jūtaku
2-36 Okinohama-higashi
Tokushima-shi, Tokushima-ken
tel. 088/625-2112
fax 088/655-3556

Nomura Shōkai
1-6-13 Ōtesuji
Kōchi-shi, Kōchi-ken
tel. 088/822-6191

GETTING AROUND

You can fly to the capital cities of Takamatsu, Tokushima, Kōchi, or Matsuyama from Tōkyō in an hour and 10 minutes; or you can save money and take the express bus from Tōkyō (about nine hours) or Kyōto (about three hours). If you're headed to Tokushima in northeast Shikoku, another option is to travel by *shinkansen* to Ōsaka or Kōbe (three hours) and transfer to a highway express bus that crosses the bridges and through Awaji Island (total travel time is 2.5 hours). If you have time and love the sea, pack up some good books and take the ferry from Tōkyō to Tokushima (about

19 hours). Within each prefecture are trains, buses, and sometimes street-cars to take you where you want to go.

The JR railway line links the major cities of all four prefectures in Shikoku—Takamatsu, Tokushima, Matsuyama, and Kōchi—and also crosses the Seto Ōhashi Bridge to Okayama. Kagawa has a private Kotohira line, which is handy for travel within the prefecture.

All the coastal cities have ferry service to other prefectures and are busy with cargo ships and tankers bound for domestic and international ports.

RECREATION

Ritsurin Park in Takamatsu city, the capital of Kagawa prefecture, is well-known for its natural serenity. Nine-kilometer (5.6-mile) Seto Ōhashi Bridge links the prefecture to Okayama prefecture across the Inland Sea and has two levels—an expressway for cars on top, and a railway on the bottom.

Naruto Whirlpools, just off the coast of Naruto-shi, in Tokushima, are a very interesting natural phenomenon. Measuring up to 20 meters (66 feet) across at low tide in the spring, the whirlpools are caused by the clash of the Pacific Sea and the Inland Sea at different levels. The annual Awa-odori (*odori* means dance) in Tokushima city in August gives you a chance to join the fun. The dance is so famous that it has been transplanted to Kōenji in Tōkyō (a stop on the Chūō line), where crowds gather every August to participate or watch.

Fishing boats in Shikoku

© Ruthy Kanagy

Resources

Contacts

Embassies and Consulates

UNITED STATES

Embassy of Japan
2520 Massachusetts Avenue NW
Washington, D.C. 20008
tel. 202/238-6700
fax 202/328-2187

Consulate-General of Japan
3601 C Street, Suite 1300
Anchorage, AK 99503
tel. 907/562-8424
fax 907/562-8434
www.embjapan.org/
anchorage

Consulate-General of Japan
One Alliance Center, Suite 1600
3500 Lenox Road N.E.
Atlanta, GA 30326
tel. 404/240-4300
fax 404/240-4311
www.cgjapanatlanta.org

Consulate-General of Japan
Federal Reserve Plaza, 14th Floor
600 Atlantic Avenue
Boston, MA 02210
tel. 617/973-9772
fax 617/542-1329
www.embjapan.org/boston

Consulate-General of Japan
Olympia Centre, Suite 1100
737 North Michigan Avenue
Chicago, IL 60611

tel. 312/280-0400
fax 312/280-9568
www.jchicago.org

Consulate-General of Japan
1225 17th Street, Suite 3000
Denver, CO 80202
tel. 303/534-1151
fax 303/534-3393
www.embjapan.org/denver

Consulate-General of Japan
400 Renaissance Center, Suite 1600
Detroit, MI 48243
tel. 313/567-0120
fax 313/567-0274
www.embjapan.org/detroit

Consulate-General of Japan
1742 Nuuanu Avenue
Honolulu, HI 96817-3201
tel. 808/543-3111
fax 808/543-3170
www.embjapan.org/honolulu

Consulate-General of Japan
Wells Fargo Plaza, Suite 2300
1000 Louisiana Street
Houston, TX 77002
tel. 713/652-2977
fax 713/651-7822
www.cgjhouston.org

Consulate-General of Japan
1800 Commerce Tower
911 Main Street

Kansas City, MO 64105
tel. 816/471-0111 or 816/471-0118
fax 816/472-4248
www.embjapan.org/kansascity

Consulate-General of Japan
350 South Grand Avenue,
Suite 1700
Los Angeles, CA 90071
tel. 213/617-6700
fax 213/617-6727
www.embjapan.org/la

Consulate-General of Japan
Brickell Bay View Centre,
Suite 3200
80 S.W. 8th Street
Miami, FL 33130
tel. 305/530-9090
fax 305/530-0950
www.cgjapanmia.org

Consulate-General of Japan
One Poydras Plaza, Suite 2050
639 Loyola Avenue
New Orleans, LA 70113
tel. 504/529-2101, 504/529-2102,
or 504/529-2641
fax 504/568-9847
www.embjapan.org/neworleans

Consulate-General of Japan
299 Park Avenue
New York, NY 10171
tel. 212/371-8222
fax 212/319-6357
www.ny.cgj.org

Consulate-General of Japan
2700 Wells Fargo Center

1300 S.W. 5th Avenue
Portland, OR 97201
tel. 503/221-1811
fax 503/224-8936
www.embjapan.org/portland

Consulate-General of Japan
50 Fremont Street, Suite 2300
San Francisco, CA 94105
tel. 415/777-3533
fax 415/974-3660
www.cgjsf.org

Consulate-General of Japan
601 Union Street, Suite 500
Seattle, WA 98101
tel. 206/682-9107
fax 206/624-9097
www.cgjapansea.org

JAPAN

U.S. Embassy
1-10-5 Akasaka
Minato-ku, Tōkyō 107-8420
tel. 03/3224-5000
fax 03/3505-1862
www.tokyoacs.com

American Consulate Fukuoka
American Citizen Services
5-26, Ohori 2-chome
Chuo-ku, Fukuoka 810-0052
tel. 092/751-9331
fax 092/713-9222
http://fukuoka.usconsulate.gov
(For Fukuoka, Kagoshima, Kumamoto, Miyazaki, Nagasaki, Oita, Saga, and Yamaguchi)

American Consulate Nagoya
American Citizen Services
Nishiki SIS Building 6F 10-33,
Nishiki 3-chome
Naka-ku, Nagoya 460-0003
tel. 052/203-4011
fax 052/201-4612
http://nagoya.usconsulate.gov

American Consulate-General Naha
American Citizen Services
No. 2564 Nishihara
Urasoe-shi, Okinawa 901-2101
tel. 098/876-4211
fax 098/876-4243
http://naha.usconsulate.gov
(For Okinawa, Amami Oshima Islands, and parts of Kagoshima prefecture)

American Consulate-General Ōsaka-Kōbe
American Citizen Services
11-5, Nishitenma 2-chome
Kita-ku, Ōsaka 530-8543
tel. 06/6315-5912
fax 06/6315-5914
www.senri-i.or.jp/amcon
(For Ōsaka, Aichi, Ehime, Fukui, Gifu, Hiroshima, Hyogo, Ishikawa, Kagawa, Kochi, Kyōto, Mie, Nara, Okayama, Shimane, Shiga, Tokushima, Tottori, Toyama, and Wakayama)

American Consulate General Sapporo
American Citizen Services
Kita 1-jō, Nishi 28-chome
Chuo-ku, Sapporo 064-0821
tel. 011/641-1115
fax 011/643-1283
http://sapporo.usconsulate.gov

Immigration and Residency

Immigration Bureau, Ministry of Justice
www.immi-moj.go.jp
(in Japanese)

Kōbe Information Center
tel. 052/973-0441 or 052/973-0442

Ōsaka Information Center
tel. 06/774-3409 or 06/774-3410

Tōkyō Information Center
tel. 03/3213-8523, 03/3213-8524,
03/3213-8525, 03/3213-8526, or
03/3213-8527

Tōkyō Regional Immigration Bureau
5-5-30, Konan
Minato-ku, Tōkyō
tel. 03/5796-7111
www.immi-moj.go.jp/soshiki/
iten.html (in Japanese)

Yokohama Information Center
tel. 045/651-2851 or 045/651-2852

People and Culture

THEATERS

You can see the *kabuki, bunraku,* and *noh* styles of traditional theater at the following locations:

Kabuki Theater (Kabuki-za)
4-2-15 Ginza
Chuo-ku, Tōkyō
tel. 03/3541-3131

Kongō Noh Theatre
Shijō-agaru, Muromachi-dōri
Nakagyō-ku, Kyōto
tel. 075/221-3049

**National Bunraku Theater
(Kokuritsu Bunraku Gekijō)**
1-12-10 Nipponbashi
Chuō-ku, Ōsaka
tel. 06/212-2531

**National Noh Theatre
(Kokuritsu Nōgakudō)**
4-18-1 Sendagaya
Shibuya-ku, Tōkyō
tel. 03/3423-1331

**National Theater of Japan
(Kokuritsu Gekijō)**
4-1 Hayabusa-chō
Chiyoda-ku, Tōkyō
tel. 03/3265-7411
www.ntj.jac.go.jp/english

South Theater (Minami-za)
Higashizume, Shijō-Ōhashi
Higashiyama-ku, Kyōto
tel. 075/561/1155

Language and Education

JLPT Communication Square
http://momo.jpf.go.jp/hiroba
/home.html
Site maintained by the Japan Foundation for learners and teachers of Japanese living outside Japan.

Study in Japan: A Comprehensive Guide
http://www.studyjapan.go.jp/en
/index.html

To take the Japanese Language Proficiency Test in the U.S., contact:

Japan Foundation Los Angeles Language Center
tel. 213/621-2267
fax 213/621-2590
noryoku@jflalc.org

To take the Japanese Language Proficiency Test in Japan, contact:
Association of International Education Japan
JLPT Section, Testing Division
tel. 03/5454-5577
www.aiej.or.jp/examination/jlpt_
guide_e.html.

Health and Emergency Services

Animal Quarantine
www.maff-aqs.go.jp/english/
index.htm

**Emergency Translation
Services**
tel. 03/5285-8185
An on-the-spot telephone translation service for foreign patients
who need help communicating
with a doctor.

Fire, Rescue, or Ambulance
emergency tel. 119

**International Mental Health
Professionals Japan**
www.imhpj.org
A database of professional
therapists.

Japan Helpline
tel. 0120/46-1997
http://jhelp.com
A 24-hour multilingual service with
practical and emergency information.

Medical Resources in Tōkyō
http://japan.usembassy.gov/e/acs
/tacs-tokyodoctors.html

Police
tel. 110

**TELL (Tōkyō English
Life Line)**
tel. 03/3968-4099
www.weekender.co.jp/tell
Offers problem-solving assistance,
counseling, referrals, and other
information.

**Tōkyō Metropolitan
Health and Medical
Information Center**
tel. 03/5285-8181
www.himawari.metro.tokyo.jp/q
q/qq13enmnlt.asp

U.S. Department of State
http://travel.state.gov
Travel and security information.

Employment

**American Chamber of
Commerce in Japan**
www.accj.or.jp/accj.or.jp
/content/01_home

Aquent, Inc.
www.aquent.co.jp/jobmagazine
/steven.html
A recruiting firm for marketing,

communications, and other creative fields.

Career Forum
www.careerforum.net/bizpro/us/
index.asp
For mid-career bilingual people.

Dave's ESL Cafe
www.eslcafe.com

DigitalEve Japan
www.digitalevejapan.org
Global nonprofit community that
works to empower women in new
media and digital technology,
with monthly meetings and
workshops to enhance IT skills.

Gaijinpot
www.gaijinpot.com
A job site with listings in English.

Ganbatte: A Webliography
www.thingsasian.com/goto_
article/article.1590.html
Information on how to become
an English teacher in Japan.

Interac
Fujibo Building 2F, Fujimi 2-10-28
Chiyoda-ku, Tōkyō 102-0071
tel. 03/3234-7857
fax 03/3234-6055
www.interac.co.jp (in Japanese)
Recruits assistant teachers for
schools.

**Japan Association of
Language Teachers**
http://jalt.org

**Japan Exchange Teaching
Program (JET)**
Contact the JET Office at the Embassy of Japan in Washington, D.C.
(tel. 202/238-6773)

J@pan Inc.
www.japaninc.net
Includes job listings and a recruitment directory.

Jobs in Japan
www.jobsinjapan.com

Kimi Information Center
tel. 03/3986-1604
www.kimiwillbe.com
A job-search and answering service in Tōkyō.

Ohayō Sensei
www.ohayosensei.com
An online newsletter about teaching jobs in Japan.

Teaching in Japan
www.teachinginjapan.com/japan
siteguide.html

TEFL Professional Network
www.tefl.com
English-teaching jobs and a daily
job bulletin.

Tōkyō Art Index
www.artindex.metro.tokyo.jp
(in Japanese)
The Tōkyō Metropolitan Government's website to support artists
and promote art and culture. Includes information on grants and
contests.

Tōkyō PC Users Group
www.tokyopc.org/jobs/index.html
Job listings for individuals working in IT.

KYŌTO WORK CENTERS

Ayabe Branch, Fukuchiyama
23 Miya-no-shita, Miyashiro-chō
Ayabe-shi 623
tel. 0773/42-8609

Fukuchiyama
10-11 Aza-naiki
Fukuchiyama-shi 620
tel. 0773/23-8609

Fushimi
232 Furoya-chō
Fushimi-ku, Kyōto-shi 612
tel. 075/602-8609
Kizu Branch, Kyōto Tanabe
50-1 Oaza-kizu-koaza-
minamigaito, Kizu-chō
Soraku-gun 619-02
tel. 0774/72-0202

Kyōto Nishijin
439-1 Wasui-chō, Omiya-dōri
Nakadachiuri Sagaru
Kamigyo-ku, Kyōto-shi 602
tel. 075/451-8609

Kyōto Shichijo
590-19 Higashi-shiokoji-chō,
Shinmachi-dōri Shichijo Sagaru
Shimogyo-ku, Kyōto-shi 600
tel. 075/341-8609

Kyōto Tanabe
33-1 Oaza-kawara-koaza-uketa,
Tanabe-chō
Tsuzuki-gun 610-03
tel. 07746/2-4646

Maizuru
107-4 Aza-nishi-koaza-
nishi-machi
Maizuru-shi 624
tel. 0773/75-8609

Mineyama
147-13 Aza-sugitani-koaza-
ibara-yama, Mineyama-chō
Naka-gun 627
tel. 0772/62-0143

Miyazu Branch, Mineyama
2534 Aza-nakano-chō
Miyazu-shi 626
tel. 0772/22-8609

Senbon Branch,
Kyōto Shichijo
1 Sujaku-shokai-chō
Shimogyo-ku, Kyōto-shi 600
tel. 075/371-5910

Sonobe Branch,
Kyōto Nishijin
71 Miya-machi, Sonobe-chō
Funai-gun 622
tel. 0771/62-0246

Uji
16-4 Uji-ikemori
Uji-shi 611
tel. 0774/20-8609

Finance

Japan External Trade Organization
www.jetro.org

Tōkyō Stock Exchange, Inc.
Information Services Department
tel. 03/3666-0141
mains@tse.or.jp
www.tse.or.jp/english

BANKS

Mizuho Bank
www.mizuhobank.co.jp/english/index.html

Sumitomo Mitsui Banking Corporation
www.smbc.co.jp/global/index.html

UFJ Bank
www.ufj.co.jp/english/index.html

BONDS

Bank of Tōkyō-Mitsubishi, Ltd.
www.btm.co.jp/english/ir/index.htm
Issues a variety of bonds, including domestic publicly-offered senior bonds, capital securities, and the Euro MTN program.

The Mitsubishi Tōkyō Financial Group
2-4-1 Marunouchi
Chiyoda-ku, Tōkyō 100-6326
tel. 03/3240-8111

www.mtfg.co.jp/english

SECURITIES

JAFCO Co., Ltd.
8-2 Marunouchi 1-chome
Tekko Building
Chiyoda-ku, Tōkyō 100-0005
tel. 03/5223-7536
fax 03/5223-7561
www.jafco.co.jp/eng/e_index.htm

Japan Securities Agents, Ltd.
2-4 Nihonbashi Kayabacho
1-Chome
Chuo-ku, Tōkyō 103-8202
tel. 03/3668-9211
fax 03/3661-7484

Wakō Securities Co., Ltd.
4-1 Yaesu 2-chome
Chuo-ku, Tōkyō 104-8481
tel. 03/5203-6000
fax 03/5203-6415

THE COMPANIES

Ashigin Financial Group
4-1-25 Sakura
Utsunomiya-shi 320-8610
tel. 028/626-0008
www.ashiginfg.co.jp (in Japanese)

Nihon Denshin Denwa (NTT)
2-3-1 Ōtemachi
Chiyoda-ku, Tōkyō 100-8116
tel. 03/5205-5111
www.ntt.co.jp/index_e.html

Nippon Steel
2-6-3 Otemachi
Chiyoda-ku, Tōkyō 100-8071
www.nsc.co.jp (click on "English")

Nissan Motors
6-17-1 Ginza
Chūō-ku, Tōkyō 104-8023
tel. 03/3543-5523
www.nissan.co.jp/en

NTT DoCoMo
Sannō Park Tower, 2-11-1
Nagata-chō
Chiyoda-ku, Tōkyō 100-6150
tel. 03/5156-1111
www.nttdocomo.co.jp/english

Prime Systems Corporation
2-8-1 Sakurai Building, 2-8-1
Fukagawa

Kōtō-ku, Tōkyō 135-0033
tel. 03/5245-1885
www.psd.co.jp (in Japanese)

Resona Holdings
2-2-1 Bingo-machi
Chūō-ku, Ōsaka 540-8608
tel. 06/6268-7400
www.resona-hd.co.jp (in Japanese)

Toshiba
1-1-1 Shibaura
Minato-ku, Tōkyō 105-8001
tel. 03/3457-4511
www.toshiba.co.jp/index.htm

Toyota
1 Toyota-chō
Toyota-shi, Aichi-ken 471-8571
tel. 0506/28-2121
www.toyota.co.jp/en

Communications

INTERNET SERVICE PROVIDERS

Asahi Net
tel. 03/3569-3522
www.asahi-net.or.jp/en

AT&T WorldNet Service
tel. 03/5561-5768
www.att.ne.jp/indexe.html

Global Online Japan
tel. 03/5341-8000
http://home.gol.com/start/kto

IIJ
tel. 03/5276-6240
www.iij.ad.jp/index-e.html

Kitakyushu Internet Exchange
tel. 093/873-1241
www.kix.or.jp

PSINet
tel. 03/5574-7172
www.jp.psi.net/english

Sanynet
tel. 078/325-5777
www.sanynet.ad.jp/english

Threeweb
tel. 03/3476-8555
www.threeweb.ad.jp/index
.en.html

TWICS
tel. 03/5740-1155
www.twics.com

LAND LINES

Cable & Wireless IDC
tel. 0066-11
www.cw.com/jp/en

KDDI
tel. 0057
www.kddi.com/english/tele-
phone

Japan Telecom
tel. 0088-41
www.japan-telecom.co.jp/english

Mobile Phones
www.broadbandreports.com

NTT Communications
tel. 0120/532-839
www.ntt.com/index-e.html

Yellow Pages (in English)
http://english.townpage.isp
.ntt.co.jp

CELL PHONES

AU (KDD)
www.au.kddi.com/english
/index.html

NTT DoCoMo
www.nttdocomo.com/index.html

TangoTown
www.tangotown.jp/tangotown
A mobile phone site that supports
Japanese communication and
learning for native English-
speakers.

Vodaphone (J-Phone)
www.vodafone.jp/scripts
/english/top.jsp

POSTAL SERVICES

**International Mail
Information**
tel. 03/3241-4891

**International Telegrams
(KDDI)**
tel. 0053-519

Postal Information Service
tel. 03/5472-5851 or 03/5472-
5852 (in English)

**Tōkyō International
Post Office**
2-3-3 Otemachi
Chiyoda-ku, Tōkyō

SHIPPING COMPANIES

DHL Japan
tel. 03/5479-2580

Federal Express
tel. 0120/003-300 (toll-free in
Japan)

**Nippon Express
Moving Services**
tel. 0120/1504-22 or 0120/22-
0202 (toll-free in Japan)
moving-tokyo@nittsu.co.jp
www.nittsu.co.jp/moving/index.htm

OPAS Ship to Japan
tel. 877/905-2726
www.shiptojapan.com
(in Japanese)
Affiliated with DHL, this company will pick up packages anywhere in the U.S. and deliver
them to Japan in about a week.

Overseas Courier Service
tel. 03/5476-8311

MEDIA

Newspapers
The Asahi Shimbun
www.asahi.com/english/

The Daily Yomiuri
www.yomiuri.co.jp/index-e.htm

Japan Times
www.japantimes.co.jp

Mainichi Daily News
http://mdn.mainichi.co.jp

Television
Fuji TV
www.fujitv.co.jp (in Japanese)

NHK
www.nhk.or.jp/englishtop

Nippon Television
www.ntv.co.jp/english/index.html

TBS
www.tbs.co.jp/eng/top.html

Radio
Beach FM
78.9 FM (Jazz)
www.beachfm.co.jp/index_e.html

InterFM
76.1 FM (Bilingual programming)
www.interfm.co.jp

J-WAVE
81.3 FM (Pop)
www.j-wave.co.jp

NHK World Radio Japan
(Short wave)
ww.nhk.or.jp/rj/index_e.html

Tōkyō FM
80.0 FM (Pop)
www.tfm.co.jp/index.html (in
Japanese)

Travel and Transportation

All Nippon Airways (ANA)
tel. 0120/029-222
www.fly-ana.com

Air Do
www.airdo21.com/index.shtml
(in Japanese)

East Japan Ferry
tel. 03/3578-11270

Eidan Subway
tel. 03/3834-5577

Hakodate City Transportation Bureau
4-19 Suehiro-chō
Hakodate
tel. 26-0131

Hakodate Service Office
10-1 Takamori-chō
tel. 51-3137

Haneda Airport
tel. 03/5757-8107

Hiroshima Airport
www.hij.airport.jp/english

Intercity Highway Buses
www.jrbuskanto.co.jp/mn/aetop.cfm

Japan Airlines (JAL)
tel. 0120/25-5971
www.jal.co.jp/en

Japanese Traffic Guide
www.jorudan.co.jp/english
/norikae/e-norikeyin.html

Enter your departure station and your destination, and this site tells you how to get there.

JR (Japan Rail) Hakodate Station
tel. 23/3085 (information)
tel. 23/4436 (reservations)

JR Shinjuku Station
tel. 03/3354-4019

JR *Shinkansen*
tel. 03/3423-0111
www.jreast.co.jp/e_charge/index.asp
Routes and fares for Japan's fleet of high-speed trains.

JR Tōkyō Station
tel. 03/3231-1880

JR Ueno Station
tel. 03/3841-8069

Keisei Skyliner
tel. 03/3831-0131

MetroPlanet
http://us.metropla.net/index2.htm
Information on subways in Japan.

Toei Subway (Tōkyō)
tel. 03/3812-2011
www.kotsu.metro.tokyo.jp/util
/english/index.html

Tōkyō Narita Airport
tel. 03/5757-8111 (flight information)
tel. 0476/32-2105 (Terminal 1)

tel. 0476/34-5220 (Terminal 2)
www.narita-airport.or.jp/air-
port_e/index.html

Tōkyō Taxi Kindaika Center
tel. 03/3648-0300

Driver's Licenses
**Fuchū Driver's License
Testing and Issuing Center**
3-1-1 Tama-machi
Fuchū-shi, Tōkyō
tel. 042/362-3591 or
042/334-6000 (English)

**Kōtō Driver's License Testing
and Issuing Center**
1-7-24 Shinsuna
Kōtō-ku, Tōkyō
tel. 03/3699-1151

**Samezu Driver's License
Testing and Issuing Center**
1-12-5 Higashi-Ōi
Shinagawa-ku, Tōkyō
tel. 03/3474-1374 or
03/5463-6000 (English)

Housing Considerations

The Building Center of Japan
www.bcj.or.jp/src/soug-e02.html
A nonprofit incubator that helps
evaluate and foster the growth of
new building technologies.

Century 21 Home Net Co., Ltd.
Mr. Tomoyuki Sato
2-16-10 Saseda
Misato-shi, Saitama-ken 341
tel. 0489/59-1881
fax 0489/59-1884
century21homenet.sato@nifty.ne.jp
English-speaking real estate agent
for renting, buying, and building.
Located 12 miles north of Tōkyō.

CLAIR
www.clair.or.jp/tagengo/general
/en-top.html
Information on housing, status of
residence, alien registration, and
medical services in nine languages.

**Nomura Real Estate Develop-
ment Company, Ltd.**
www.nomura-reim.com
A real estate organization with $2.5
billion in equity invested in commercial projects internationally.

ONLINE RENTAL RESOURCES

Able
www.able.co.jp (in Japanese)

Chintai
www.chintai.co.jp/index.html

Home Adpark
http://adpark.co.jp (in Japanese)

ISIZE
www.isize.com/house (in Japanese)

Tōkyō Classifieds
http://classifieds.japantoday.com

Prime Living Locations

GENERAL RESOURCES

Japan National Tourist Organization (JNTO)
www.jnto.go.jp/eng

Japan Today
www.japantoday.com
Includes news, information, a business directory, classifieds, a discussion forum, and a friend-finder service.

Kintetsu International
tel. 03/5998-1612
fax 03/5998-5399
www.knt.co.jp/kokusai/pack-jht/2003/coverpage.html
Offers half- to six-day organized tours of cities and sights throughout Japan.

OregonJapanLink
http://oregonjapanlink.com
Photos of cycle touring and daily life in Hokkaidō and Honshū.
Japan Travel and Living Guide
www.japan-guide.com

Japan Visitor
www.japanvisitor.com
Includes tourist and resident information.

TŌKYŌ
Information for foreign residents on Tōkyō's core *ku* (city wards):

Arakawa-ku:
www.city.arakawa.tokyo.jp/2/aramasi/index.htm

Bunkyō-ku:
www.city.bunkyo.tokyo.jp/english/guide2001/index.html

Chiyoda-ku: www.city.chiyoda.tokyo.jp/english/enjoy.html

Itabashi-ku:
www.city.itabashi.tokyo.jp/index-e.htm

Meguro-ku:
www.city.meguro.tokyo.jp/english/index.htm

Minato-ku:
www.city.minato.tokyo.jp/e/index.html

Mitaka City:
www.city.mitaka.tokyo.jp/english/

Nakano-ku:
www.city.tokyo-nakano.lg.jp/toppage-e.html

Nishi Tōkyō City:
www.city.nishitokyo.tokyo.jp/english/index.html

Setagaya-ku:
www.city.setgaya.tokyo.jp/english/index.html

Toshima-ku:
www.city.toshima.tokyo.jp
/english/index.html

Tōko Metro Website
www.chijihonbu.metro.tokyo.jp/
english
Includes a *Guide for Foreign Residents,* issued by the Metropolitan Government.

Tōkyō Tourism Info
www.tourism.metro.tokyo.jp
/english/index.html

Tōkyō Tourist Information Centers
www.kotsu.metro.tokyo.jp/util/
english/link/4_1.html

Tōkyō Weekender
www.weekender.co.jp
An online publication for foreigners living in the city.

HOKKAIDŌ

Future University-Hakodate (FUN)
http://www.fun.ac.jp/en/index.html
Established in April 2000, with an emphasis on communication technology.

Hokkaidō Insider
www.ne.jp/asahi/hokkaido
/kenhartmann
News and information services, primarily for English teachers living in Japan.

Hokkaidō International School
tel. 816-5000
fax 816-2500
his@his.ac.jp
www.his.ac.jp

Hokkaidō International Women's Association (HIWA)
Sapporo International Communication Plaza Foundation
Kita 1, Nishi 3
Chuo-ku, Sapporo-shi 060-0001
tel./fax 221-3501
hiwa@k7.dion.ne.jp
Association meetings, Japanese language lessons, city news and events, exhibits, bilingual TV programs, concerts, and movies.

JALT Hokkaidō
http://jalthokkaido.org
The local chapter of the national association of language teachers.

Japanese Language Institute of Sapporo
tel. 011/562-7001

Joy English Academy
11-69 Nishi-17 Minami-5
Obihiro, Hokkaidō 080-0027
tel. 0155/33-019
fax 0155/36-7930
joy@joyworld.com
www.joyworld.com/pages/home/
englishindex.html
A valuable source of information on living in Obihiro.

Resident's Advisory Service Desk, City Affairs Section
tel. 21-3136 or 21-3197

Sapporo Traffic Net
www.city.sapporo.jp/kensetsu/st
n/eng/map.html
A guide to roads, parking, cycling, and walking in Sapporo.

SIL Sapporo Nihon-go Gakkou
tel. 011/614-1101
www.silnihongo.com/homeeng
.html
A Japanese language school in Sapporo.

Xene
tel. 011/272-0757
info@xene.net
www.xene.net
A free, bilingual monthly magazine with Hokkaidō information.

CENTRAL MOUNTAINS: GUNMA AND NAGANO

Gunma
Gunma International Association (GIA)
3F Gunma Kaikan, 2-1-1 Ote-machi
Maebashi-shi, Gunma-ken
371-0026
tel. 027/243-7271
fax 027/243-7275
gia@mail.wind.ne.jp
ttp://gia.sugoe.com/english/inde
x2.htm.
GIA assists foreign residents with

daily life, work, and education; offers professional assistance with legal and medical matters; and provides translation and interpreting services, a newsletter, and a bimonthly magazine.

Gunma Prefecture Office
1-1-1 Otemachi
Maebashi-shi, Gunma-ken
371-8570
tel. 027/223-1111
kokusaika@pref.gunma.jp
www.pref.gunma.jp/english

This Week in Kamimoku
www.kamimoku.com/index_kam
imoku.html
Tips on what to do and see in Northern Gunma.

Nagano
Karuizawa Town Hall
2381-1 Oaza Nagakura,
Karuizawa-chō
Saku-gun, Nagano-ken 389-0192
tel. 0267/45-8111
fax 0267/46-3165
kto@town.karuizawa.nagano.jp
www.town.karuizawa.nagano.jp/
html/english/index.html

Matsumoto City Hall
3-7 Marunouchi
Matsumoto-shi 390-8620
tel. 0263/34-3000
fax 0263/36-6839
pi_int@city.matsumoto.nagano.jp

Nagano Prefectural Government
International Relations Division
692-2 Habashita Minami-Nagano
Nagano-shi 380-8570
tel. 026/235-7173
fax 026/232-1644
kokusai@pref.nagano.jp
www.pref.nagano.jp/english/indexe.htm

Nagano Prefecture Housing Management Public Corporation
tel. 026/227-1211
tel. 0263/47-0240 (Matsumoto Branch)

Nagano Women's Consultation Center (Nagano Fujin Sōdanjo)
tel. 026/235-5710
A support center for women experiencing domestic violence, marriage, divorce, and other challenges.

The Shinano Mainichi Shimbun
www.shinmai.co.jp/shinmai/shim1e.html
An award-winning local newspaper based in Nagano City.

Tōkyō Regional Immigration Bureau, Nagano Branch Office
tel. 026/232-3317

THE WEST: KYŌTO AND ŌSAKA

Kyōto
Kyōto City Clinic for Emergency Illness
tel. 075/811-5072

Kyōto City Tourism and Culture Information System
http://raku.city.kyoto.jp/sight_e.phtml

Kyōto Prefectural Office
Shimodachiuri-dōri, Shinmachi Nishi-iru
Kamigyo-ku, Kyōto-shi 602-70
tel. 075/451-8111
www.pref.kyoto.jp/index_e.html

The Kyōto Shimbun News
www.kyoto-np.co.jp/kp/index_e.html

Ōsaka
Ōsaka City Hall
1-3-20 Nakanoshima
Kita-ku, Ōsaka 530-8201
www.city.osaka.jp/english

Ōsaka Employment Service Center for Foreigners
Umeda Center Building 9F 2-4-12 Nakazakinishi
Kita-ku, Ōsaka City
tel. 06/6485-6142
fax 06/485-6144
Job consultation, placement, and information for foreign students and workers of Japanese descent.

Ōsaka Labor Standards Office
Ōsaka-godo-chōsha-dai 2, 4-1-67
Otemae
Chuo-ku, Ōsaka City
tel. 06/6949-6490
fax 06/6049-6034

**Ōsaka Municipal Housing
Information Center**
6-4-20 Tenjinbashi
Kita-ku, Ōsaka
tel. 06/6242-1177
fax 06/6354-8601

Ōsaka Prefecture Government
Department of Commerce, Industry and Labor, Commerce and Industry Promotion Office, Industry Location Division
tel. 06/6944-8160
fax 06/6944-6733
shokoshinkog02@sbox.pref.osaka.jp
Offers information on business subsidies for foreign firms.

**Ōsaka Women's
Counseling Center**
1-7-4 Eiwa
Higa-shi, Ōsaka
tel. 06/6728-8858

INLAND SEA:
HIROSHIMA AND SHIKOKU

Hiroshima
**Hiroshima City Tourist
Information Center**
tel. 082/263-6822

**Hiroshima Convention
& Visitors Bureau**
International Conference Center,
3rd Floor
1-5 Nakajima-chō
Naka-ku, Hiroshima
tel. 082/244-6156
fax 082/244-6138
hcvb@hiroshima-navi.or.jp
www.hiroshima-navi.or.jp
(click on "English")

**Hiroshima International
Information Network**
http://hiint.hiroshimaic.or.jp
/hiint_eng

**Hiroshima Peace Memorial
Museum Virtual Museum**
www.pcf.city.hiroshima.jp
/virtual/index.html

Shikoku
Awa Life
www1.pref.tokushima.jp/kankyou
/seikatsubunka/awalife/index.html
A monthly newsletter for international residents of Tokushima.

Ehime Prefectural International Center (EPIC)
tel. 089/917-5678
fax 089/917-5670
haiku575@lib.e-catv.ne.jp
www.epic.or.jp/english/index.html
Offers foreign-language newspapers and magazines, books and videos about living abroad, Japanese language classes, and bicycle loans for foreign students.

Foreign Wives Club
http://foreignwivesclub.com
Jennifer Brown, who lives with her Japanese husband and daughter in Kōchi prefecture, runs this international online community for women in intercultural marriages.

Glossary

awa: millet
bungaku: literature
chintai: rental
conbini: convenience store
denwa: phone line
dōri: road
doyōbi: Saturday
en: yen (Japanese currency)
gaijin: outsider, foreigner
gaman: bearing it
ganbaru: effort
geijutsu: art
ginkō kōza: bank account
hashi: chopsticks
heijitsu: weekdays
hibakusha: atomic bomb victims
hōgen: regional dialects
inkan: name stamp or seal
joya no kane: temple bell
jūminzei: residential tax
kabuki: traditional theater
kami: divine
kana: Japanese linguistic characters
kanji: Chinese linguistic characters
katakana: phonetic letters
keijidōsha-zei: light motor vehicle tax
keitai: cell phone
ken: rural prefectures
kōban: police box
koseki: family register system
kotatsu: family hearth
koteishisan-zei: municipal property tax
ku: city ward
manshon: condominium
matcha: powdered green tea
mikan: mandarin oranges

mikoshi: portable Shintó shrine
minshuku: family-run inns
minyō: folk music
nashi: Asian pears
nichiyōbi: Sunday
odori: dance
onsen: hot springs
Oshōgatsu: New Year's Day
rakuyaki: Raku firing
risaikuru shoppu: recycle shop, secondhand store
rotenburo: outdoor spa
ryokan: Japanese-style inns
sabi: elegance
sakura: cherry trees
sashō: visa
shika: deer
shiori: beauty
shodō: calligraphy
shohōsen: prescriptions (pharmaceutical)
shotokuzei: income tax
shukujitsu: holidays
sumi: ink
taifū: typhoons
takushii: taxis
tanchō-tsuru: red-crested crane
tanka: short poems
tatami: woven rush mats
teiki-ken: commuter pass
tomodachi: friend
tsuyu: rainy season
ukiyo-e: wood-block prints
undōkai: sports day
yakkyoku: pharmacies
yukata: cotton kimono
yukiguni: snow country
zeikin: taxes

Phrasebook

PRONUNCIATION

Japanese has only five vowel sounds. Each vowel is distinct and, unlike in English, always has the same sound: *a* as in papa, *i* as in pizza, *u* as in put, *e* as in pet, and *o* as in port.

Most Japanese words contain consonant-vowel, consonant-vowel syllables. Japanese syllables—*ra, ri, ru, re,* and *ro*—are different from the American "r" and "l." Instead, they sound more like the Spanish "r" (or British "very"), almost like a soft "d." Americans produce this same flapping sound regularly in words like par*t*y, lit*t*le, bet*t*er, and but*t*er.

And finally, note that while English words have strong and weak beats, Japanese syllables fall on low and high pitches instead.

NUMBERS

1	*ichi*
2	*ni*
3	*san*
4	*shi/yon**
5	*go*
6	*roku*
7	*shichi/nana**
8	*hachi*
9	*ku/kyū**
10	*jū*
100	*hyaku*
1,000	*sen*
10,000	*ichi-man*

(*Form depends on context.)

DAYS OF THE WEEK

Monday	*getsu-yōbi*
Tuesday	*ka-yōbi*
Wednesday	*sui-yōbi*
Thursday	*moku-yōbi*
Friday	*ki-n*-yōbi*
Saturday	*do-yōbi*
Sunday	*nichi-yōbi*

(*The Japanese "n" is a nasal sound; your tongue does not touch any part of your mouth.)

Is today Tuesday?	*Kyō wa kayōbi desu ka?*
Yes, that's right.	*Hai, sō desu.*
What day of the week is it?	*Nan-yōbi desu ka?*
It's Friday.	*Kinyōbi desu.*

TIME

1 o'clock	*ichi-ji*
2 o'clock	*ni-ji*
3 o'clock	*san-ji*
4 o'clock	*yo-ji*
5 o'clock	*go-ji*
6 o'clock	*roku-ji*
7 o'clock	*shichi-ji*
8 o'clock	*hachi-ji*
9 o'clock	*ku-ji*
10 o'clock	*jū-ji*
11 o'clock	*jūichi-ji*
12 o'clock	*jūni-ji*
What time is it?	*Nan-ji desu ka?*
It's 7 o'clock.	*Shichi-ji desu.*

GREETINGS

I'm Kanagy. [Japanese use family names]	*Kanegi desu.*
Pleased to meet you.	*Dōzo yoroshiku.*
Good morning, Dr. Tajima. [formal]	*Tajima-sensei, ohayō gozaimasu.*
Good morning. [informal]	*Ohayō.*
Thank you very much. [formal]	*Dōmo arigatō gozaimasu.*
Good day.	*Konnichiwa.*
See you later.	*Ja, mata.*
See you tomorrow.	*Mata ashita.*

TRAVEL AND TRANSPORTATION

train station	*eki*
subway	*chikatetsu*
bus	*basu*
Where is the post office?	*Yūbinkyoku wa doko desu ka?*
It's over there.	*Asoko desu.*
Is this Shinjuku?	*Shinjuku desu ka?*
No, Shinjuku is next.	*Iie, Shinjuku wa tsugi desu.*
Excuse me, where is the (train) station?	*Sumimasen, eki wa doko desu ka?*

ACCOMMODATIONS

Single, one-night reservation, please.	*Shinguru ippaku yoyaku onegai shimasu.*
How much is it?	*Ikura desu ka?*

FOOD

Here you go. [offering something]	*Dōzo.*
Thanks.	*Dōmo.*
No, thanks.	*Kekkō desu.*
I'll have American coffee.	*Amerikan kudasai.*
I'd like another cup.	*Mō ippai kudasai.*

SHOPPING

What's this?	*Kore wa nan desu ka?*
It's an MP3.	*MP surii desu.*
How much is it?	*Ikura desu ka?*
It's ¥20,000.	*Ni-man en desu.*
Give me this. [I'll take this.]	*Kore kudasai.*
What size are your shoes?	*Kutsu wa nan-senchi desu ka?*
25 centimeters.	*Nijū-go senchi desu.*

HEALTH

medicine	*kusuri*
doctor	*isha*
hospital	*byōin*
(My) head hurts.	*Atama ga itai.*
(My) stomach hurts.	*Onaka ga itai.*
(My) leg/foot hurts.	*Ashi ga itai.*
(I) have a fever.	*Netsu ga arimasu.*

Suggested Reading

HISTORY

Booth, Alan. *The Roads to Sata: A 2,000-Mile Walk Through Japan.* Tōkyō, Japan: Kodansha International, 1997 (reprint).

Chang, Iris and William C. Kirby. *The Rape of Nanking: The Forgotten Holocaust of World War II.* New York, NY: Basic Books, 1997.

Hicks, George L. *The Comfort Women: Japan's Brutal Regime of Enforced Prostitution in the Second World War.* New South Wales, Australia: Allen & Unwin, 1996.

Elwood, Robert S. and Richard Pilgrim. *Japanese Religion: A Cultural Perspective.* Essex, UK: Pearson Education, 1984.

Kerr, Alex. *Lost Japan.* Victoria, Australia: Lonely Planet Publications, 1996.

Molasky, Michael S. *The American Occupation of Japan and Okinawa: Literature and Memory.* New York, NY: Routledge, 1999.

FICTION

Kamata, Suzanne (Ed.). *The Broken Bridge: Fiction from Expatriates in Literary Japan.* Albany, CA: Stone Bridge Press, 1997.

Molasky, Michael S. and Steve Rabson. *Southern Exposure: Modern Japanese Literature from Okinawa.*

Honolulu, HI: University of Hawai'i Press, 2000.

Shikibu, Murasaki. Translated by Richard Bowring. *The Tale of Genji.* New York, NY: Cambridge University Press, 1988.

Yasunari, Kawabata. Translated by Howard Hibbett. *Beauty and Sadness.* New York, NY: Vintage Books, 1996.

Yoshimoto, Banana. Translated by Megan Backus. *Kitchen.* New York, NY: Washington Square Press, 1993.

TRAVEL AND MAPS

American Chamber of Commerce in Japan, The. *Living in Japan.* Tōkyō, Japan: The Japan Times, 2002.

De Mente, Boye Lafayette and Atsushi Umeda. *Tōkyō Subway Guide: Including 40 Bilingual Station Maps.* Tōkyō, Japan: Kodansha International, 2002.

Globetrotter Japan Travel Map. Tōkyō, Japan: Kodansha International, 2001.

Kinoshita, June and Nicholas Palevsky. *Gateway to Japan,* 3rd edition. Tōkyō, Japan: Kodansha International, 1998.

Kyōto-Ōsaka: A Bilingual Atlas. Tōkyō, Japan: Kodansha International, 1993.

Maruyama, M. Enman, L. Picon Shimizu, and N. Smith Tsurumaki. *Japan Health Handbook,* revised edition. Tōkyō, Japan: Kodansha International, 1998.

Norton, Joy and Tazuko Shibusawa. *Living in Japan: A Guide to Living, Working, and Traveling in Japan.* Boston, MA: Tuttle Publishing, 2001.

Pover, Carolyn. *Being a Broad in Japan: Everything a Western Woman Needs to Survive and Thrive.* Tōkyō, Japan: Alexandra Press, 2001.

Rowthorne, Chris et al. *Lonely Planet Japan,* 8th edition. Victoria, Australia: Lonely Planet Publications, 2003.

Tōkyō Metropolitan Area Road and Rail Atlas. Tōkyō, Japan: Kodansha International, 2002.

Zarifeh, Ramsey. *Japan by Rail: Includes Rail Route Guide and 29 City Guides.* Guilford, CT: The Globe Pequot Press, 2002.

Suggested Films

Kinkakuji (Temple of the Golden Pavillion), dir. Yoichi Takabayashi, 1976. Based on the story by Yukio Mishima.

Ran (Chaos), dir. Akira Kurosawa, 1985.

Sasameyuki (The Makioka Sisters), dir. Kon Ichikawa, 1983. Based on the novel by Junichiro Tanizaki.

Senbazuru (Thousand Cranes), dir. Yasuzo Masumura 1969. Based on the novel by Yasunari Kawabata.

Sen to Chihiro no Kamikakushi (Spirited Away), dir. Miyazaki Hayao, 2002.

Sugata Sanshiro (Sanshiro Sugata) (also part II), dir. Akira Kurosawa, 1943. Based on the novel by Tsuneo Tomita.

Suna no Onna (Woman in the Dunes), dir. Hiroshi Teshigahara, 1964. Based on the novel by Kobo Abe.

Shoe and Clothing Sizes

Women's Clothing

Japan	7	9	11	13	15
U.S.	8	10	12	14	16

Women's Shoes

Japan	23	23.5	24	24.5	25
U.S.	5.5	6	6.5	7	7.5

Men's Shirts

Japan	36	37	38	39	40	41	42
U.S.	14	14.5	15	15.5	16	16.5	16

Men's Shoes

Japan	24.5	25	25.5	26	26.5	27	27.5
U.S.	6	7	7.5	8.5	9	10	11

Index

U.S.~Metric Conversion

1 inch	=	2.54 centimeters (cm)
1 foot	=	.304 meters (m)
1 yard	=	0.914 meters
1 mile	=	1.6093 kilometers (km)
1 km	=	.6214 miles
1 fathom	=	1.8288 m
1 chain	=	20.1168 m
1 furlong	=	201.168 m
1 acre	=	.4047 hectares
1 sq km	=	100 hectares
1 sq mile	=	2.59 square km
1 ounce	=	28.35 grams
1 pound	=	.4536 kilograms
1 short ton	=	.90718 metric ton
1 short ton	=	2000 pounds
1 long ton	=	1.016 metric tons
1 long ton	=	2240 pounds
1 metric ton	=	1000 kilograms
1 quart	=	.94635 liters
1 US gallon	=	3.7854 liters
1 Imperial gallon	=	4.5459 liters
1 nautical mile	=	1.852 km

To compute Celsius temperatures, subtract 32 from Fahrenheit and divide by 1.8. To go the other way, multiply Celsius by 1.8 and add 32.

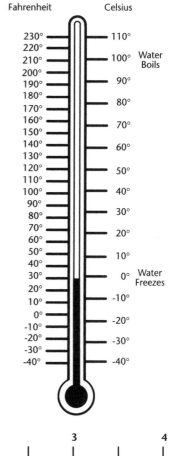

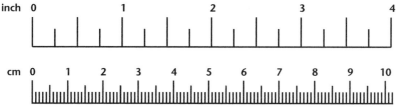

www.moon.com

For helpful advice on planning a trip, visit www.moon.com
for the **TRAVEL PLANNER** and get access to useful travel
strategies and valuable information about great places to
visit. When you travel with Moon, expect an experience that is
uncommon and truly unique.

Living Abroad in Japan
Avalon Travel Publishing
A member of the Perseus Book Group
1400 65th Street, Suite 250
Emeryville, CA 94608, USA
www.moon.com

Editors: Mia Lipman, Amy Scott
Series Managers: Mia Lipman, Erin Raber
Copy Editor: Helen Sillett
Designers: Amber Pirker, Justin Marler
Graphics Coordinator: Susan Snyder
Production Coordinators: Amber Pirker, Tabitha Lahr
Map Editors: Olivia Solís, Naomi Adler Dancis
Cartographers: Kat Kalamaras, Mike Morgenfeld
Indexer: Rachel Kuhn
Translation Assistant: Sarah Juckniess

ISBN-10: 1-56691-672-0
ISBN-13: 978-1-56691-672-1
ISSN: 1548-6478

Printing History
1st edition—October 2004
5 4 3

Some photos and illustrations are used by permission and are the property of the original copyright owners.

Front cover photo: © John Elk III

Printed in the United States by Malloy

Some photos and illustrations are used by permission and are the property of the original copyright owners.

KEEPING CURRENT

Although we strive to produce the most up-to-date book that we possibly can, change is unavoidable. Between the time this book goes to print and the time you read it, the cost of goods and services may have increased, and a handful of the businesses noted in these pages will undoubtedly move, alter their prices, or close their doors forever. Exchange rates fluctuate—sometimes dramatically—on a daily basis. Federal and local legal requirements and restrictions are also subject to change, so be sure to check with the appropriate authorities before making the move. If you see anything in this book that needs updating, clarification, or correction, please drop us a line. Send your comments via email to atpfeedback@avalonpub.com, or write to the address above.